T0355209

Pioneers in the Attic

Pioneers in the Attic

Place and Memory along the Mormon Trail

SARA M. PATTERSON

OXFORD

UNIVERSITY PRESS

OXFORD
UNIVERSITY PRESS

Oxford University Press is a department of the University of Oxford. It furthers
the University's objective of excellence in research, scholarship, and education
by publishing worldwide. Oxford is a registered trade mark of Oxford University
Press in the UK and certain other countries.

Published in the United States of America by Oxford University Press
198 Madison Avenue, New York, NY 10016, United States of America.

Library of Congress Cataloging-in-Publication Data
Names: Patterson, Sara M., 1974– author.
Title: Pioneers in the attic : place and memory along the Mormon Trail / Sara M. Patterson.
Description: New York, NY, United States of America : Oxford University Press, [2020] |
Includes bibliographical references and index.
Identifiers: LCCN 2019048948 (print) | LCCN 2019048949 (ebook) |
ISBN 9780190933869 (hardback) | ISBN 9780190933883 (epub) | ISBN 9780190933890 (online)
Subjects: LCSH: Church of Jesus Christ of Latter-day Saints—Doctrines. |
Zion (Mormon Church) | Mormon Church—Doctrines. |
Mormon Pioneer National Historic Trail.
Classification: LCC BX8643.Z55 P38 2020 (print) | LCC BX8643.Z55 (ebook) |
DDC 289.309—dc23
LC record available at https://lccn.loc.gov/2019048948
LC ebook record available at https://lccn.loc.gov/2019048949

1 3 5 7 9 8 6 4 2

Printed by Integrated Books International, United States of America

For my parents

Contents

Illustrations

Acknowledgments

When I first moved from the American West to the territory situated between the Midwest and the South, a friend recommended a book to help me understand the culture I was entering. Tony Horwitz's *Confederates in the Attic* explores the ways southern history and white supremacy continue to shape the region today. It helped me to understand the symbolic landscapes I inhabit. The book gave me some of the tools I needed to "read" my new community and the Confederate flags that dot its landscape. Years later, my book group decided to read Julie Otsuka's *The Buddha in the Attic*. The book follows the lives of women who journeyed from Japan to San Francisco as "picture brides." In it, readers find an interesting discussion of the ways Japanese and Buddhist culture continue to affect the lives of women put in very new contexts where they must adapt to survive in a new cultural landscape. The two books could not be more different, yet they share a similar concept. In all of our "attics," we have histories that continue to shape our experiences whether we acknowledge those influences or not. They are the stories that contribute to who we are. They form us every time we hear them, and they influence us in their absence. They are our stories. This book has a similar assumption—that Mormon culture today is profoundly shaped by the stories of the nineteenth-century pioneers in obvious and not-so-obvious ways. These are some of the stories that populate the Mormon imagination. I am reminded of Elizabeth Smart's autobiography, *My Story*, in which she recalls the time she was kidnapped by Brian Mitchell, a man who believed himself to be a prophet and believed that Smart was called to be his second wife. For that reason, he kidnapped, raped, and shackled her. During her time in captivity, Smart called on the stories of the nineteenth-century pioneers in order to maintain hope and faith. The stories fed her when she was disoriented by the landscapes of her captivity.

I, too, have an attic; people and stories that have shaped who I am. We all do. We do not always see or acknowledge those influences, but they shape us nonetheless. Our attics are not just storied but are stuffed with material objects; those material objects carry cultural and spiritual significance. They carry the weight of our stories. They hang over us as we move through our lives. We carry them with us.

Over the course of this project, my attic has been populated by many special people who have influenced me in many seen and unseen ways. I would like to thank all of the archivists at the LDS Church Archives, the University of Utah Archives, and the Brigham Young University Archives, who helped me find the sources I needed. I would also like to thank the librarians at Hanover College, particularly Patricia Lawrence, for helping me to gather all of the necessary books, articles, and sources for my research. I was a grateful recipient of a Project Grant for Researchers from the Louisville Institute, which helped me travel to archives and visit sites along the Mormon Trail. The Faculty Development Committee at Hanover College also helped fund archival and research trips. The Wabash Center for Teaching and Learning in Religious and Theological Studies helped fund my research for chapter 1, the research that inspired my interest in this project. I am so thankful for the financial support of those institutions. A version of chapter 1 was previously published as "The Plymouth Rock of the American West: Remembering, Forgetting, and Becoming American in Utah" in *Material Religion* v. 11, no. 3 (2015): 329-353. As well, a version of chapter 6 was previously published as "Everyone Can Be a Pioneer: The Sesquicentennial Celebration of Mormon Arrival in the Salt Lake Valley" in Patrick Q. Mason and John W. Turner, eds., *Out of Obscurity: Mormonism since 1945*. Oxford University Press, 2016.

At Hanover College, I have benefited greatly from regularly meeting with my scholarship group to discuss research. Thank you to Dominique Battles, Paul Battles, James Buckwalter, Saul Lemerond, Mandy Wu, Xialong Wu, Mi Yung Yoon, and Fernanda Zullo. I also appreciate the support of my departmental colleagues: David Cassel, Michael Duffy, Lake Lambert, Beatrice Marovich, and Dhawn Martin.

Over the course of the research and writing of this book I received support in relationships that have sustained me, especially my family. Evan Patterson always reminds me of the importance of place and spends much time with me moving through landscapes. Veronica Patterson has taught me a love for words and for objects, she appreciates the beauty of the everyday and shares her passion for it in everything she does. Carrie Lee Patterson has always asked me the irreverent questions that help me consider new ideas and possibilities. My network of friends has also supported me through relationship and care. Thank you, Sharon Benton, Fay Botham, Dave Cassel, Eli Chandler, Guillermo Cortez, Mike Duffy, Tahlia Fisher, Joyce Flanagan, Katy Hadley, Amy Hoyt, Natalia Hubbs, Krista Hughes, Amir Hussain, Steve Jobe, Terry Jobe, Kate Johnson, Tina Jones, Jamie Kepros, Sara Moslener,

Jennifer Naccarelli, Quincy Newell, Maureen O'Connell, Zephirin Ryan, Robyn Ryle, David Sanchez, Kerri Schnulle, Nasrin Shahinpoor, Jan Shipps, Steve Steiner, Kay Stokes, Ruth Turner, and Karla Van Zee. Several people read pieces and versions of this manuscript. Thank you especially to Richard Bushman, Patrick Mason, Veronica Patterson, and John Turner. I would also like to thank the anonymous reviewers for and editors at Oxford University Press. Karla Van Zee has been a wonderful and willing travel companion during many of my visits to sites along the Mormon Trail. She brings levity and curiosity to everything she does, including pushing handcarts and engaging guides in conversation—whether the path is narrow or wide, I do not know, but I am glad to have you with me on it. Soji, Grimke, and Pru were constant reminders that there are always more fun things to do than writing on a computer. And finally, Kayla, you burst into my life during the writing of this book and changed my world in so many ways. May your future journeys be smooth. I will always be pulling for you on the trail.

Prologue

Just like so many other religious believers in early nineteenth-century New York, Joseph Smith Jr. wished that he knew which of the many Christian denominations was the correct one. He felt like the future of his own soul and his family's salvation depended on getting it right. The fact that so many religious revivals swirled around him only made the question seem ever more pressing. Each church claimed to be *the* church, but none seemed to have the evidence to convince him and everyone else in his family. And so fourteen-year-old Joseph went out into a grove in the woods to pray. It was that prayer, a plea for surety in a confusing world, that finally gave Joseph the beginnings of what he believed the answer was: not one of the churches currently on earth was the true church. All of the contradictions that seemed to abound in their disagreements with one another only served as evidence of this.[1]

For a few years, that was what Joseph knew. He still had spiritual questions. He still wanted to better know God and what God wanted for him and his family. On September 21, 1823, Joseph prayed before going to sleep, seeking God's forgiveness. He later recalled that as he was praying, he noticed that the room became illuminated with daylight, and an angel, who identified himself as Moroni, appeared to him clothed in white. Moroni let Joseph know that his sins had been forgiven and that he had a much higher calling in life.

As Smith told it, Moroni began to spell out that calling for Joseph. He told him of a book that was written on gold plates that included a history of the peoples of the Americas. He also explained that along with the gold plates, there were two stones, the Urim and Thummim, which would allow Joseph to translate the plates. Moroni appeared three times with a similar message, once warning Joseph that if he used the plates for wealth rather than for their true purpose, Satan would have won. If he succeeded in the translation, though, the true church would be restored on earth.

Moroni told Joseph that the gold plates were buried in a hill about three miles from the Smith farm. Joseph, who had seen the hill in a vision, knew exactly where the plates were located. After the visitations he went to the hill he had seen in the vision and attempted to procure the plates but could not. Moroni explained that he could not yet have them because he was not spiritually ready: he was too caught up in the personal and financial gains that having the plates might bring. Excited and anxious about what this all might mean, Joseph shared the story with his family. Even though his family members were enthusiastic in their support, the activities that were required to get the plates did not happen immediately. Shocked by the rather sudden death of his older brother Alvin on November 19, 1823, and busy with ensuring that the family could afford to pay the money owed on their farm, Smith's family continued on with their lives, hoping that Joseph could access the plates as soon as possible. Despite all of their efforts in the meantime, the Smiths lost the family farm.

Over the coming years, Smith never forgot the plates or Moroni's command to dig them up, to lead a righteous life, and to move away from money-seeking endeavors. Every year he tried to get the plates and was thwarted because he was not yet ready. During those years, his family struggled to survive, and he turned to many opportunities to increase the family income, including treasure seeking. Those activities later led others to file charges of fraud against him. In the midst of all of these struggles, Smith met and married Emma Hale in 1827, despite her protective father's concern about Smith's reputation.

In September 1827 the call to dig up the plates grew even stronger. On September 22, Smith again went to the hill. He did not initially bring the plates home, saying that he had left them in an old log, squirreling them away for protection. Once he decided to bring them home, he was challenged on many fronts by people trying to see them. They either wanted a part of the golden treasure or wanted to expose him as a fraud. These obstacles did not deter him for long. Eventually, he began the work of translating the plates, using the stones as a guide. Amid many trials, obstacles, and time delays, he translated the work that was published in 1830 as the Book of Mormon.

When Joseph recounted his visit from the angel Moroni, who told him of gold plates and stones buried in a hill, he confirmed for believers that God continued to speak. It was because of that visit that Joseph came to understand himself as a prophet, seer, and revelator. It was because of that visit that he founded a church and a movement that continues to this day. When he recounted Moroni's visit, he set up a pattern that has echoed throughout Mormon theology up through the present day—place, material objects, and theological claims became inextricably tied to one another. This work explores these intersections.

Figure I.1 The two stones marking the site of the temple in Independence, Missouri.

Introduction

Map, Marker, Memory

It seems that Joseph Smith Jr. understood that places and objects mattered; he knew the importance of *feeling* religion. The community that followed Smith believed that the Book of Mormon was a revelation of God and that Smith was a prophet, seer, and revelator. Their beliefs were confirmed by the continuing revelations that came through him. Thus, it was no surprise that when there was pressure from outsiders to move elsewhere, believers sold their belongings and followed Smith westward to Kirtland, Ohio, where missionaries had preceded them. Then in 1831, some church leaders went to Jackson County, Missouri, and encouraged others to follow. One of those visitors who came to Missouri after hearing enthusiastic reports was the prophet himself.

In 1831, Smith visited Independence, Missouri, and saw in it the promise of a place that would allow his community to flourish. In an August 3, 1831, revelation, Smith declared Independence to be Zion, the place recognized by the ancient biblical prophets as the promised land. Smith's revelation stated: "hearken, O ye elders of my church, saith the Lord your God, who have assembled yourselves together, according to my commandments, in this land, which is the land of Missouri, which is the land which I have appointed and consecrated for the gathering of the saints. Wherefore, this is the land of promise, and the place for the city of Zion. . . . Behold, the place which is now called Independence is the center place." The revelation went on to encourage believers to build a temple and to buy up as much of the surrounding land as possible. Finally, the revelation declared: "and thus let those of whom I have spoken be planted in the land of Zion, as speedily as can be. . . . And now concerning the gathering—Let the bishop and the agent make preparations for those families which have been commanded to come to this land."[1] When Joseph Smith identified Zion as a place on the American map, not in some imagined biblical land, when he said it was a spot one could point to, could move to, he again made concrete for believers the theological

Pioneers in the Attic. Sara M. Patterson, Oxford University Press (2020). © Oxford University Press.
DOI: 10.1093/oso/9780190933869.001.0001

concepts they had imagined and dreamed about. He called for not just a re-ligious community, but a place, an ever-expanding place, that would live under God's rule.[2]

Believers coupled the revelations that promised Zion with a revelation Smith had given in 1830. The expectation created by that 1830 revelation was that believers would gather themselves together as young chicks under a hen's wing.[3] Together, these revelations reinforced the idea that believers were a people, a gathered community, with an anticipated place, Zion, that was meant just for them. Gathering together, both spiritually and physically, in a special place they believed God had designated and set aside, encour-aged many to uproot their lives and follow their leader and their community.

Church members quickly moved to buy up the land Smith had identi-fied as the center place. On the sixty-three and a half acres purchased for the church by Edward Partridge, Smith located and laid stones to mark the site where the temple should be built; from it, he and the Saints imagined Zionic principles moving outward into the world. Since the very beginning of the church, the two concepts, gathering (the idea that believers should gather together) and Zion (that there was a sacred, central place) were intertwined. As Smith came to identify *a particular place* as Zion, movement toward that place and the work to build it up became a religious imperative. It was on that spot that Smith located Zion and created for the Saints an imagined and uni-fied map of the world. In addition to designating Independence, Missouri, as Zion, Smith declared other sites in Jackson County, Missouri, as sacred and significant. Most notable was that he identified a site he called Adam-Ondi-Ahman as the original Garden of Eden where Adam and Eve had dwelt be-fore their expulsion.

Smith's envisioned map was only ever realized in fragmented ways, and there were eventually many practical and spiritual reasons that the shared, unified vision fractured. Even though believers had tried to follow Smith's instructions, the practical concerns of their non-Mormon neighbors meant that no temple was built on the site Smith identified. In fact, Smith and his followers created maps of their Zion with little to no regard for what was already built and owned in Independence.[4] Other Missourians felt that the Saints were encroaching on what was rightfully theirs. They had their own imagined maps, which were well developed and already in process, and they were willing to fight out of a belief that the two maps could not coexist. In fact, by 1833, about 1,200 Mormons driven by the principle of gathering to Zion made up about one-third of the county's total population, a cause for much concern in their non-Mormon neighbors who were frightened that Mormons would attempt to take over politics, welcome free blacks into the county, and shape the economies of the county around their own interests.[5]

After tensions boiled over with their neighbors and his followers were violently forced to leave Jackson County, Smith laid out an explanation for why they had to depart so quickly after they had arrived. That explanation was theological in nature: the people were being disobedient and God was angry. In the words of geographer Craig Campbell, "the common view, accepted by factions of Saints to the present, was that the church, as a whole had been self-centered, disobedient, and in need of rebuke."[6] Thus, Smith fashioned a narrative that placed the blame on believers and God's wrath rather than the very angry neighbors who were nervous about the new arrivals in Independence.

Angry neighbors forced Mormons out of the state of Missouri, and an extermination order issued by Governor Lilburn W. Boggs on October 27, 1838, declared that Mormons "must be treated as enemies, and must be exterminated or driven from the State if necessary for the public peace." The gathering that had begun in Missouri dissipated, and many believers moved on to Commerce, Illinois (later Nauvoo), where again they met with disgruntled and overwhelmed neighbors. Not only were Mormons pushed out of their Zion, but what happened in Missouri planted the seeds for future discord within the Mormon community. As Craig Campbell has noted, "Nauvoo was a city that was not easily inserted into the existing view of a Missouri-centered Zion."[7] Believers raised questions about the meaning of gathering and Zion when they had been so quickly expelled and *de*centered: why were they in Nauvoo, Illinois, when their Zion was in Missouri? Why would God show them Zion, let them live there, and then allow others to seemingly snatch it away? What did it mean for Mormons to gather together? Was Zion a place or a principle? As the unified map and vision fragmented, multiple interpretations of these key principles arose.

Twenty-first-century Spatial Politics in Zion

The Church of Jesus Christ of Latter-day Saints (LDS Church) began as the group who followed Brigham Young westward to Utah after the death of Joseph Smith Jr. and is one of several movements in the Mormon tradition. When a friend and I entered the LDS visitors' center in Independence,

Missouri, in the summer of 2014, a retired missionary greeted us and asked us if we were on a "history tour." We said we were. "Where have you been so far?" she asked. It was our first day in the area, but we had already been to the Community of Christ (COC) temple across the street. The COC, now numbering somewhere around 250,000 members worldwide, began as the group who chose to follow Joseph Smith III in the decades after the death of Joseph Smith Jr. and stayed in the Midwest, first calling themselves the Reorganized Latter Day Saints and later the Community of Christ.[8] "We've been to the Community of Christ temple across the street," I replied. That first missionary waited with us for our guide. A few minutes later, when our guide came up and asked if we were on a history tour, the missionary responded in the affirmative. When the guide asked where we had been so far, the missionary, just minutes after our initial exchange, answered: "they haven't been anywhere; they are just starting their history tour."

I started to correct her but realized that indeed she believed that we had yet to go anywhere on our history tour. Her understanding of a history tour did not include the claims of rival churches; it accounted only for the sites that were officially a part of the LDS historical narrative. From her perspective, we had, in fact, been nowhere. And this sense of conflicting narratives, of groups who define themselves over and against one another through their understandings of place, the material world, and history, echoed throughout our visits in Independence. The presence of rival groups in a shared sacred space clearly serves as a reminder that the truth from *our* view is not the only truth, and that others just across the street would give visitors a different interpretation of shared spaces and shared histories.[9]

Today, the sixty-three and a half acres Edward Partridge purchased in response to the 1831 revelation are divided and owned by three separate groups, all claiming in some way to be the heirs of Joseph Smith's legacy. Each group understands part of its inheritance to be the charge to build Zion and to gather together. Despite these rival claims and interpretations, the groups on the sixty-three and a half acres maintain a peaceful coexistence. Even so, there is a battle going on: who gets to tell the historical narrative and how that narrative gets tied to place demonstrates the complex identity politics at work. The seeds planted in the nineteenth century have come to full fruition. Each church believes it best understands Smith's call to gather and build up Zion. Each church believes it has the correct map of the world.

* * *

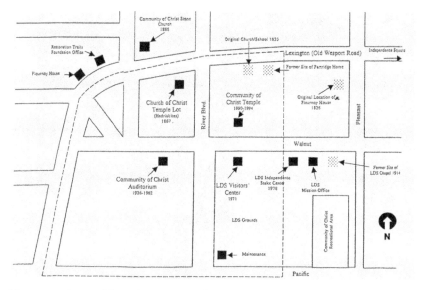

Figure I.2 Map of shared spaces in Independence, Missouri.

The borders between the churches run along streets. Jutting up into the sky on the corner of River Boulevard and Walnut Street is the COC temple, sitting on forty acres (of the sixty-three-and-a-half-acre original lot) that the COC owns. (See Figure I.2) The COC began in the 1860s as members of the church who had stayed in the Midwest after Smith's death came together around two central issues: they believed, first, that the next and future leader of the church would come from the family of Joseph Smith Jr., and second, that Smith had opposed the practice of plural marriage that the Utah Mormons (LDS) were so publicly embracing in the 1860s. From the beginning, the COC group's own identity was defined over and against the Utah Mormons, and vice versa. The COC formed around Joseph Smith III, the oldest son of the original prophet.

Though sarcastic visitors have often suggested that the COC temple resembles a metallic upside-down ice cream cone (the temple is covered in satin-finished stainless steel), the principal architect, Gyo Obata, intended the temple to be modeled on the nautilus, the swirl found in conch shells, the swirl of Fibonacci's golden ratio. (See Figures I.3 and I.4) As described in a COC promotional film, a divine nudging began the building process: "in 1968 divine counsel to the church through President William Wallace Smith, a grandson to Joseph Smith, Jr., called for a start to be made on the

Figure I.3 Community of Christ Temple, Independence, Missouri.

long-awaited temple in Independence. In 1984 inspired direction through his successor and son Wallace Bunell Smith, great grandson of Joseph Smith, Jr., further revealed the temple's purposes."[10] That 1984 instruction told church members to build the temple and to dedicate it to world peace. In addition, the 1984 document offered women the priesthood in the church.

A conservative faction protested both the temple and the ordination of women, causing schism.[11] Interestingly, historians played a role in the debate when conservatives brought up that the new temple's location was

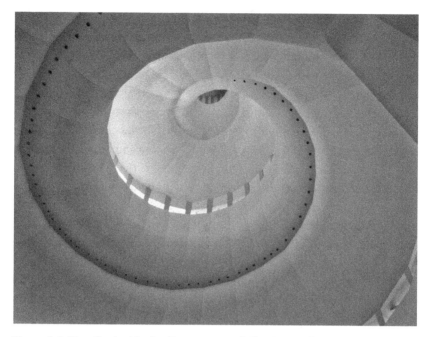

Figure I.4 Nautilus inside the Community of Christ Temple

not the exact place Joseph Smith had identified as the temple lot but was a connected site, which was then a parking lot. Church historians "argued that the parking lot site was in fact part of the temple parcel of land dedicated by Smith in 1831 as the site for the temple in the City of Zion," also pointing out that Smith's plans for Zion evolved over time.[12] In the end, the majority of the COC membership confirmed the revelation, and the groundbreaking ceremony occurred on April 6, 1990.

The main route of entry into the temple's sanctuary requires visitors to circle around, walking upward as they move inward toward the sanctuary. A pamphlet for the temple explains that the path "offers time for reflection and preparation for worship." As people move inward, "light increases. . . . symbolizing the spiritual light that is available to all through the grace of God."[13] Entry into the pathway requires people to move through a carved-glass arch that represents the sacred grove to which the teenage Joseph Smith Jr. retreated when he had spiritual questions and where he encountered God and the answers to his questions. As visitors move up the pathway, they see artwork that depicts scriptural scenes important to the COC.

Standing in the second aisle of the main sanctuary, one can look up at the ceiling and see the spiral continuing to move inward toward a center point. The ceiling is designed to draw people's attention "infinitely upward" so that they can meditate on the "glorious metaphor of peace, hope, and oneness."[14] Just outside the west entrance to the temple lies World Plaza, which contains a map of the world made of different colored bricks. The spirit of the nautilus continues in this process of growth outward from the center. Tour guides suggest to visitors that the map represents how Zion and the faith will move outward into the world from the temple, the center. They imagine the world in much the same way Smith did: Zion radiating outward until the whole Earth is overspread. Their vision of what that will look like rests primarily in their late twentieth- and early twenty-first-century emphasis on peace.[15] Zion will be realized in large part when there is peace in the world, a peace they pray for daily during an open-door prayer meeting in the temple. For the COC, the vision of a temple in Zion, the center place, has been realized. They believe that they have constructed the temple on the site Joseph Smith identified as the center of Zion. They are praying for the fulfillment of that peaceful zionic vision in the world.

As the COC membership has developed over time, and as the community has had to reckon with aspects of history that members did not or chose not to know (an issue discussed further in chapter 3), the COC has distanced itself from some of the teachings and rituals of Joseph Smith Jr. While still claiming Smith as a significant figure in their history, the COC embraces some aspects of what he taught and rejects others.

Throughout the COC temple, signs remind people that "everyone is welcome" and that the temple is "open to all people." These signs serve two functions: first, to indicate to visitors precisely what the signs say—that they are welcome to come inside, to tour, and to explore. Second, the signs can serve as an assertion of identity over and against the LDS Church. Whereas the COC has an open temple, where all are welcome to participate in gathering and rituals, the Latter-day Saints keep their temples closed to outsiders, welcoming only worthy believers inside to participate in rituals that are meant only for believers. Though it may seem like a small assertion, those small assertions become meaningful in the identity politics of the shared sixty-three and a half acres. From the temple, the center place, COC members imagine Zion radiating outward. Though Zion is still imagined in a spatial way, COC members have added a spiritualized notion of Zion to their theology. Zion is a cause, a way of living, one that will spread when they choose to live righteous lives and help foster peace in the world.

* * *

At the intersection of Lexington Street and River Boulevard, across the street from the COC temple, is another church that claims to have the correct interpretation of Zion and ties much of its identity to the two and a half acres of the original sixty-three and a half that it owns: the Church of Christ-Temple Lot (CCTL). This group uses "Church of Christ" as its name because that was the name of the church as revealed to Joseph Smith Jr. in 1830. The "Temple Lot" portion of its name helps to distinguish this group from others using the "Church of Christ" nomenclature.[16] The CCTL, also referred to as the Hedrickites (so named after Granville Hedrick, who was chosen as the group's leader after the death of Joseph Smith Jr.), holds a prominent place in Independence, a place that might seem out of proportion to its small congregational size or its worldwide membership of fewer than 10,000. For the members of the CCTL, Smith meant what he said when he declared that Zion was to be built *in that place*. And they don't just mean that Independence is the place or even that the sixty-three and a half acres constitute the place. The members of the CCTL root their claim in the idea that they own the exact spot where Smith wanted the temple built, and they are waiting there until they receive a revelation instructing them to move forward with the construction of the temple.

While waiting, the CCTL maintains a small building adjacent to the actual temple lot that houses a sanctuary for group gatherings and the church's visitors' center. Most prominent inside the visitors' center is a display case that contains two stones, both found on the site during a ground-breaking ceremony in 1929. One is the stone Smith used to mark the site of the temple; the other is a cornerstone they believe marked the outline of the temple site. Both were found on their two and a half acres (see Figure I.1).

In 1852, eight years after the death of Joseph Smith Jr. in 1844, the CCTL formed when three Illinois branches of the church merged and began to worship together at the home of Granville Hedrick, an elder in the early church. In 1863, he was ordained an apostle by John E. Page, a longtime church member and part of Joseph Smith's Quorum of the Twelve. Later that same year, Page also ordained Hedrick as a "Prophet, Seer, Revelator and Translator" for the church. In that capacity, Hedrick received a revelation on April 24, 1864. He explained that he had been visited by an angel who "instructed him and his followers to 'gather together upon the consecrated land which I have appointed and dedicated by My servant Joseph Smith.'" And so again the concepts of gathering in the center place echoed for these believers very quickly after Smith's death. They had to head back to Zion.

Instructions in the revelation also said that members should return to the center place by 1867. After that 1864 revelation, members of Hedrick's group began to slowly move back to Independence in 1865 and 1866. In 1867, Granville's brother John H. Hedrick purchased three lots of the original acreage and signed them over to Granville as the "Trustee in Trust" for the church. In 1873 and 1874, another church member, William Eaton, purchased five more adjoining lots, including Lot Number 15, now considered the dedication site of the temple.[17] These believers spent many years, from 1867 to 1874, selling their property in Illinois and buying up the two and a half acres that had been designated as the center place.[18]

In the coming decades, other Mormon groups reinvigorated their interest in the land that Smith had deemed Zion. The original sixty-three and a half acres, that center space, became a part of complicated identity negotiations. The COC developed an interest in returning to the site and building a temple there. That interest led COC leaders to go to the local court and file a Notice to Quit Possession against the CCTL on July 11, 1887. The claim asserted that the land should be granted to the rightful successor of Edward Partridge's original trust and that the COC was that rightful successor. Four years later, the COC filed a Bill of Equity against the CCTL in the U.S. District Court in Kansas City, Missouri. Known as the Temple Lot Case, the legal action embroiled two churches in a battle to be declared the rightful heir to the land Smith called Zion and the site where he laid the stones to mark where the temple should be built. In January 1896, the U.S. Supreme Court refused to hear a COC appeal, thus ending the legal battles and declaring the CCTL the rightful legal owners of the land.[19]

And so, for a very long time, the CCTL has defined itself spatially, over and against the other groups sharing the original acreage. Ownership of the land itself served a symbolic function for both the COC and the CCTL. In participating in the legal disputes, they accepted that ownership of the land indicated orthodoxy and served as evidence of who was the rightful heir to Joseph Smith Jr. Although the COC ultimately lost its claim to the land and shifted its understanding of its relationship to Joseph Smith, the incident can tell us a lot about how space can play a role in battles over orthodoxy and doctrine. That Smith had tied the concept of Zion to an actual place, one that church members could point to on a map, meant that he concretized and literalized a spiritual concept. In so doing, he made ownership of the land evidence of right belief.

Members of the CCTL take those ideas very seriously. Their *History of the Church of Christ*, the official account of the CCTL, makes the argument that from the beginning, for the church Smith founded in 1830, "the idea of a material Zion has been regarded as a fundamental feature" and that this Zion is to be "a literal city" and should "contain a holy sanctuary of the Lord; or in other words, a temple."[20] That same history discusses the branch of Mormons who followed Brigham Young westward and declares that they found a "new Zion in the West" and that it was there that church leaders became ruthless, setting up "a despotism of the most tyrannical type."[21] In CCTL history-telling, the LDS shift of Zion from place to place was accompanied by a shift away from righteous living and alignment with God's vision. Thus, place and governance, setting and legitimacy, are tied together in the CCTL's understanding of orthodoxy.

One of the most popular pamphlets in the CCTL visitors' center is a slim text called the "Temple Lot Deed." This document goes to great lengths to offer the historical evidence that the CCTL has always owned the land and that the church is the rightful heir to it. Merging the church's name with their claim to the landscape, the pamphlet asserts: "because the question as to the real ownership of the property known as the TEMPLE LOT, in Independence Missouri, seems to be of so much importance to all believers in what is known as the . . . Mormon [Church] this tract has been written."[22] The pamphlet argues that the CCTL alone has remained unchanged from the church Smith restored in 1830 and the land he identified as Zion.

In fact, most of the literature offered in the CCTL visitors' center explains why the other branches of Mormonism are incorrect. When we entered the building during the summer of 2014, our greeter explained that he would not ask us what our religious affiliation was but promised that he would soon say something that would make us "jump out of our seats and run out the door." Assuming that we were LDS, an assumption that makes sense based on the religious breakdown of tourists to that area of Independence, the greeter proceeded to explain many of the reasons that the LDS Church had incorrectly interpreted the revelations of Joseph Smith Jr. Standing out in our greeter's historical interpretation were two things: the CCTL's identity is tied to its *name* (claiming the original name Joseph Smith used for his church and thus its status as the "true church") and to its ownership of the *place* where

Smith stood and outlined the temple. The central feature of this group's identity is two and a half acres, acres from which they imagine the whole Earth being overspread.

The CCTL has a distinct relationship with its Joseph Smith heritage. It asserts that Smith "gave many revelations, but not all were divine." Thus, each revelation must be measured to see if it is "in harmony with the Bible and Book of Mormon, the only safe standards." Members of the CCTL explain that they are members of the only church that can trace its heritage back to Joseph Smith in an unbroken lineage, because of the line from Smith through Hedrick. Even so, they argue that Smith went astray in his later revelations and thus moved away from the fullness of the gospel that he inaugurated.[23] One of the key ways they believe Smith went astray was in establishing the office of the presidency. Instead, the CCTL is led by a quorum of twelve members, who are understood as equal to one another. Members agree that within a few short years of the church's founding, Joseph Smith Jr. had failed in his role as prophet, and they assert that his *authentic* revelations had acknowledged that Zion would be bought with money rather than won by force.[24]

In the main display area at the CCTL visitors' center, and surrounding the two stone markers, a large photograph shows an aerial view of the two and a half acres that includes the church's current building alongside an outlined area that is the future temple site. Another CCTL pamphlet explains the church's view that "it has been erroneously assumed that this total 63 acres was dedicated in 1831 as the 'spot for the temple'"; and that between 1867 and 1877 the COC purchased deeds to multiple lots that contain "the exact 'spot for the temple.'"[25] Though written in passive voice, the pamphlets nonetheless target the other two Mormon groups who have ownership of portions of the sixty-three and a half acres as the source of these wrongheaded claims. Included in the pamphlet is a letter signed by church members James Richard Lawson, Harry Taylor, M. M. Case, and Thomas B. Nerrin that describes finding the "Marker Stone" on May 31, 1929. The letter explains the excavation process and the finding of the stone that had "1831" carved into it.

In 1929, the CCTL started the process of laying the groundwork for their temple. The digging began with hopes that they could finally build the temple that Joseph Smith had foreseen. Yet a number of events slowed and eventually halted their progress. First, Otto Fetting, a church apostle who had prompted the ground-breaking, left the church. He left after having received various revelations that some members of the church believed and others dismissed. He took about half the membership with him. At the same time, the economy collapsed, stalling the process at its very beginning. Eventually, once Independence became known as the home of Harry S. Truman, the city encouraged the church to fill in and landscape the area in order to beautify it.

In addition to the stones displayed in the center of the visitors' center, the stones the CCTL offers as material evidence of inheritance and orthodoxy, several markers concretizing the CCTL's spatial and material claims are placed around the building. One marker declares that it sits on the "Spot for temple dedicated by Joseph Smith on August 3, 1831." Two others mark the "Spot where stone was found" and the "N.E. Corner of temple." Together, these markers function to create a spatial imagination, working to encourage visitors to visualize a temple rising up from the initial stones held in the prophet's hands. On the west side of River Boulevard, near those markers, is a sign that proclaims that this space is the "Temple Site . . . [that] Joseph Smith, Jr. dedicated . . . for the Temple in the city of Zion, where this Church believes the Lord will come to His people in The Last Days."

On both of our visits to the CCTL visitors' center, in 2014 and 2018, our guides said that the majority of visitors to their space were members of the LDS Church. Interestingly, it is members of that group who most want to see the stones. Our second guide noted, though, that LDS visitors often will

Figure I.5 Markers outside the Church of Christ-Temple Lot visitors' center.

not stay to chat and hear the Temple Lot version of history, space, and the material world. Rather, he said, "they rush in and say 'We only have a few moments to stay and then we have to be on our way.' They don't want to hear what I have to say." They see the stones, they may even purchase postcard photographs of the stones, but they do not want to hear a different version of the truth. That may well be expected at many of the sites where different religious factions share the same space and history.

The prominence of the stones, the markers, and the outline of the temple site at the CCTL visitors' center points to the way the material world serves as evidence of immaterial realities for members of the CCTL. Each day, they can return to what they imagine as the center of the world; they can reach out and touch the stones their prophet used to mark that place as the center. Their ownership of the land and the stones allows them to *feel* in a kinesthetic way that they are the rightful heirs to the promise of Joseph Smith's restoration. It doesn't matter that the other churches claiming Smith as their prophet have more members, more money, and a louder voice. The CCTL has the stones and the spot that is the center on their map. And they have their history to prove that everyone else should see that spot as the center of Zion.

* * *

Just kitty-corner from the CCTL acreage, on the southern side of the intersection of Walnut Street and River Boulevard, is the LDS visitors' center, built in 1971. The LDS Church is the branch of the Mormon tradition that was founded by those who, after Smith's death, followed Brigham Young westward to Salt Lake City, where they imagined and set up a new Zion, or promised land. Nonetheless, the LDS Church claims Independence as part of its heritage and contemporary identity. This claim is represented in the Walnut Street block between River and Pleasant, where there are three LDS sites: the visitors' center, the Stake Center, and the Mission Office. At the far corner of the property is the former site of an LDS chapel. All of these are part of the twenty acres owned by the Utah church.

The upper floor of the LDS visitors' center in Independence mirrors the visitors' centers found around the United States and in Salt Lake City, where the LDS Church completed its central temple in 1893. In that regard, the Independence visitors' center promotes a sense of familiarity for those members who might be visiting their historic sites and concerned or anxious about the presence of other churches claiming to be the rightful heirs to Joseph Smith Jr. As visitors enter, they see a twenty-foot-tall Christus, an all-white sculpture of the resurrected Jesus with pierced hands and sides. He stands with his palms out in a welcoming fashion. Behind him, the wall is painted as the universe, covered in clouds, stars, planets, and a daytime sky. In addition to the central room where the Christus stands are two other rooms. The room off to the right is filled with multimedia activities meant to engage children in LDS beliefs and practices. This room also houses a display, fairly common in LDS visitors' centers, that features the Book of Mormon and several translations of the text into other languages. Around the periphery of the room runs an historical timeline. Notably absent is Joseph Smith's designation of Independence as Zion.[26] Instead, the timeline only states that in 1831 he identified the spot where the temple should be built. Off to the left of the center room is a series of small scenes, decorated like the rooms of a home, where visitors are reminded of the LDS concept of the eternal family and are taught about the power of familial bonds.

The lower floor of the visitors' center offers the LDS displays and activities that are most unique to Independence. Here are provided the historical perspective and the analysis of the space. Not a part of the main tour, one room presents a photographic narrative of the church's history. For the main tours, visitors enter a reconstructed log cabin and hear the story of Latter-day Saints flooding into Missouri after Smith identified it as Zion. Citing the sixty-third section of the Doctrine and Covenants, a book of revelations collected and canonized by the LDS Church, missionaries explain that Smith was cautious in his call for believers to gather to Zion and wanted them to proceed slowly: "this is the will of the Lord your God concerning his saints, that they should assemble themselves together unto the land of Zion, not in haste, lest there should be confusion, which bringeth pestilence." Even though instructed by the prophet to move slowly, the missionaries explain, believers were so excited that Zion had been identified and that they could physically touch and dwell in that sacred land that they quickly flocked there, causing the pestilence Smith had foreseen. That "pestilence" surfaced primarily in the form of hatred from their non-Mormon neighbors, coming out of a feeling of being rapidly outnumbered. In these exhibits, the history is turned into a theological lesson that believers are to listen to the prophet no matter what.

The second station in the historical section houses a printing press; there, missionaries tell the story of W. W. Phelps, the man who was instructed to publish the Book of Commandments, the first compilation of Smith's revelations, and who also participated in the creation of a newspaper. Finally, visitors are told about the press being destroyed by angry Missourians who felt overwhelmed by the Mormons entering their Zion and wanted them to leave town.

During my first visit to Independence in 2014, the final station downstairs included a film that connected the historical to the modern-day church in Utah. One might expect that the film would explain how the LDS Church moved from *this place* (Independence), which its prophet and founder had identified as Zion, to *that place*, Utah, the place many Latter-day Saints now call Zion. What kind of historical narrative might be offered to explain the shifting Zions? The film never mentioned that shift, though; it did not need to because it embraced a different kind of shift. The film began by explaining that Zion had been identified as Independence, Missouri, and then asserted that the concept of Zion had shifted from the literal to the metaphorical. In modern times, the film explained, "Zion is more about a people than a place." The film ended by talking about how today's Mormons do not need to gather but need to create Zion wherever they are.[27] Thus, the film did not need to make mention of Utah but could move directly to a message that speaks to a globalized community—Zion is wherever you are; it is metaphor.

Here we see another interpretation of the LDS Church that offers the metaphorization of the concepts of gathering and Zion in response to the historical narrative it has come to embrace. The Utah church can thus explain how its central temple is more than one thousand miles away from the site Smith identified as Zion and the spot on which he said the temple must be built and yet still believe itself to be the rightful heir to his restoration. Yet to say that Latter-day Saints who followed Brigham Young westward simply shifted from map to metaphor in their understanding of Zion simplifies something much more complex. Rather, because of circumstances I will explore in more detail, the LDS Church map shifted the concept of Zion and the center elsewhere. Nevertheless, the LDS Church continues to hold its concept of Zion in tension with Smith's historical identification of Independence as Zion. Deploying Zion as a metaphorical concept in certain circumstances allows the lens through which contemporary Mormons view the map to move in and out of clear focus. When map and metaphor blur, the theological concept of Zion can remain salient and meaningful in the lives of Mormons today while also still carrying the weight of historical groundedness *and* timelessness. It is this group and the complexity of these relationships that this book will explore.

Map

When Joseph Smith set the stones on the ground to mark the site of the temple, when he put his finger on the map and declared Independence to be Zion, he began to fashion a meaningful world that oriented believers to place and to the material realm. In doing so, he told them what was important and what was on the periphery of their beliefs and their orientations. He laid out on the landscape a series of claims about what mattered.[28] For believers this meant that the world was being ordered in a new way. Zion became the center place, the place where they should gather. And from that center place, which located the individual in relationship to others, to God, and to all else, all other symbols and theological concepts could derive their meaning.[29] Ideas, people, and religious claims could be measured by their relationship to a Zion that could be felt and touched, walked on, and pointed to on a map. For them, salvation and a millennial future were intimately tied to the concept of sacred space.[30]

How do sacred spaces become sacred spaces? Are they, as some scholars theorize, simply irruptions of the divine or the numinous into the material world? Are they the production of humans, the designation of *this place* as separate from and more special than *that place*? Are they the spots where the divine encountered humans in events and people, thereby making the spot sacred because something important happened there? Or is the space sacred in and of itself? Does the landscape participate in its creation and designation as a sacred space?

According to religion scholar Mircea Eliade, who set the framework for so many conversations about sacred spaces, sacred space is important in human life because it sets spaces apart as the opposite of the profane, making them a center and a point of reference. "Every sacred space implies a hierophany," Eliade wrote, "an irruption of the sacred that results in detaching a territory from the surrounding cosmic milieu and making it qualitatively different."[31] The place is transformed. From Eliade's perspective, humans do not choose sacred spaces, they simply discover them. They are sacred because of the hierophany that happened in them, and humans then recognize them as sacred in return, treating them as such in their ritual practices.[32]

Critics of Eliade often argue that in his insistence on the hierophanic nature of sacred space, he downplayed the human role in a problematic way. They argue, as Yi-Fu Tuan does, that we need to understand humans as parts of groups, cultures, and societies and that, as such, they make differentiations between *us* and *them* and between "home ground and alien territory." As a pattern, cultures claim that *we* occupy the center and *they* occupy spaces that are on the periphery. To have a place is to designate that there is something here and not there.[33]

David Chidester and Edward T. Linenthal have emphasized human labor in the production of sacred space, shifting the discussion away from the idea that the divine marks the space as sacred, with humans simply acknowledging it, and noting that people play an active role. Chidester and Linenthal argue that there are three features of that human production. First, they argue, sacred space is ritual space where humans repeat activities that designate it as different. Second, sacred space "is significant space, a site, orientation, or set of relations subject to interpretation because it focuses crucial questions about what it means to be a human being in a meaningful world." Thus, humans fashion meaningful worlds for themselves by using symbol systems to explain who they are in relationship to the spaces they occupy. Finally, these two scholars recognize sacred space as contested space, noting that individuals and groups use space to define themselves against one another and deploy symbol systems to claim spaces as theirs. Sacred spaces are never "merely 'given' in the world, [their] ownership will always be at stake."[34] Because sacred space is a symbolic system, it is the beginning of "an endless multiplication of meaning" that can "become almost infinitely extended through the work of interpretation."[35] Space and the interpretation of it are often, if not always, sites of contest and disagreement, struggles over ownership, and analysis. The physical landscape becomes the ground on which identity and meaning are defined and defended. Chidester and Linenthal emphasize that sacred space intersects with all aspects of human society and is intimately tied to politics and power.

As an individual or group comes to understand a space as sacred, they begin to "story" that space, which can often become a ritual in and of itself. Storying space allows people to share the emphasis on meaning-making that takes place as part of the construction of sacred spaces. Yet, as religion scholar Belden C. Lane reminds us, the world is not simply a blank canvas on which humans construct their meaning systems. Instead, the world is full of landscapes, and one must take the landscape into account in one's understanding of sacred spaces. The place, Lane argues, "demands its own integrity, its own participation in what it 'becomes,' its own voice. A sacred place is necessarily more than a construction of the human imagination alone."[36] Lane offers an important check on other scholars, like Eliade, who emphasize the "magical" qualities of place, forgetting the social and political, and on those who emphasize the cultural construction of place. Place is culturally constructed, imagined and storied, by human actors working in particular contexts, yet one must also re-member the "web of interconnectedness that extends deeply into the natural world" in order to fully consider the complicated dimensions of sacred space. Lane reminds us that identity, both individual and communal, "is fixed for us by the feel of our own bodies, the naming of the places we occupy, and the environmental objects that beset our landscape."[37]

And so it is the connection between space, bodies, and material objects that enables humans to create meaningful worlds for themselves. It is the material that allows people "to delineate in spatial parameters the site or point at which the holy is manifested and made to communicate to believers the crucial signifiers of their identity as believers. The sacred is therefore experienced as invested in a place."[38] Place and stuff, people and the landscape they interpret through complex symbolic systems, create the sacred and set certain places apart.

Marker

It is important in many branches of the Mormon tradition that Smith pointed to the ground on which he and others stood and declared it Zion, a Zion they could map, build, and dwell in. It is equally important that he placed markers there, designating the spot where the temple, the center of the center, would be built. Once again, he connected place and the material world to religious and spiritual claims. Spaces are, in fact, not empty of things. Rather, the objects and the material realm contribute to human interpretations of space. Joseph Smith placed that marker, and in doing so he said that that place was *the place*. In the process, he also claimed that this place was "our place," over and against others and their spaces. He set in motion a process that was already germinating in Missouri, the politics of space and the material realm.

And so we must examine the role of objects in the lives of Smith's followers. If we can know, how did the objects feel? What did they symbolize? What was their placement in relation to humans and to other objects? How were they used, seen, felt, and revered? What were the intentions of those who placed the objects and first used them? Does that intersect with the way they have been used or understood by others?

Religion scholars have often accepted a dualistic framework for thinking about religion, separating belief and action, spirit and matter, sacred and profane. In taking on this framework for thinking about religion, they have relegated the material, the profane, and action to a lesser realm.[39] However, religious believers do not often make these distinctions in their daily lives, even if they do so in their theological conversations. Instead, in their daily lives the sacred and profane, the spiritual and the material, the unseen and the seen often intersect in interesting ways. It is those intersections that I will explore here. When believers hold an object, feel its heft, place their hands around its size, act with it and understand it as significant, that object takes on much more than its thing-ness. David Morgan, a scholar of material religion, has emphasized that objects are always in relation to our bodies; that when considering an object, we must think about "what it offers us physically— pleasure, pain, or threat of harm . . . a thing is more than a thing, more than itself. A thing is a thing-for-us."[40] When Smith placed that marker on the spot where he imagined the temple, the heft and weight of it carried the belief systems he envisioned going into creating his map of the world. The weight of the marker was much more than the weight he felt in his hands. It held his imagined map of the world in its being.[41]

When Smith placed the marker, it was an embodied activity representing a larger religious truth that he had come to teach: that God had selected his community to restore the true church and to model for the world what living in line with that message would be. Smith physically interacted with the space he knew was Zion and placed a stone marking the center place. For Smith and his followers, the human body was important and sacred. He had already made claims about the human body, claims that he would later build on and expand. He posited a corporeal God who, in the words of Terryl Givens, had once had "a glorified body of flesh and bones, which is immortal and divine."[42] Smith moved away from a dualistic framework when he imagined the difference between divine and human, spirit and matter, as a difference of degree rather than kind. The human body was the home of the spirit and would play a role in the individual's movement toward salvation.[43]

Smith also taught that before existence in this life, humans were spirit bodies. Men and women in this world, through the act of sexual intercourse, provide the physical bodies for other spirit bodies to enter so that they may take on a physical existence. That physical existence, according to Smith was an "ascent in relative power." That physical body then goes through a refinement as it progresses and is the vehicle through which humans can experience joy.[44] Because of this, becoming parents is a spiritual calling of sorts; believers have the responsibility of providing physical bodies for waiting spirit bodies. And so the human body houses an individual spirit that needs to progress into physicality. For that reason, God expects believers to follow certain bodily restrictions and to mark their bodies as sacred by donning temple garments.

This understanding of the body shapes the way Mormons understand their relationship to the physical world; it plays an important role in how they move through space, interact with objects, and experience their senses. Many forms of Christianity have relegated the body to the earthly, sinful realm and have seen it as the "suit" that is holding the soul back, providing temptations and desire that could lead humans to hell. Protestantism especially claimed that it focused primarily on *the Word*, pushing aside all of the lesser-than, bodily senses and focusing the mind on words and emphasizing belief over any sensory activity. Scholars of religion have often followed suit, assuming that religion is primarily about belief rather than bodies and the senses. A movement made up of scholars who study material religion has sought to highlight the fact that religion can only happen within a body and that it happens in communities whose beliefs shape bodily practices, rituals, and lived experiences.[45] We must not just think about what humans believe but explore what they do. As David Morgan reminds us, "most believers live their religion in the grit and strain of a felt-life that embodies their relation to the divine. . . . The transcendent does not come to them as pure light or sublime sensations . . . but in the odor of musty shrines or moldering robes or the pantry where they pray." Beliefs shape expectations about how the world works, but it is in the actions and interactions that it gets played out in the world: "belief shows itself to be a corporeal assumption or expectation . . . belief is what I know with my body."[46]

Sensory experiences have been an integral aspect of Mormon claims from the beginning: Smith dug up and carried the tablets, he saw and heard the angels, and he inspired others to trust their sensory experiences.[47] This is evident in "The Testimony of the Three Witnesses" and "The Testimony of the Eight Witnesses," which appear at the beginning of the Book of Mormon. The eight witnesses testified that Joseph Smith Jr. had "shown unto us the plates of which hath been spoke, which have the appearance of gold; and as many of the leaves as the said Smith has translated we did handle with our hands; and we also saw the engravings thereon. . . . And this we bear record with words of soberness . . . for we have seen and hefted, and known of a surety." Seen. Hefted. Known with surety. Here, the eight witnesses demonstrated the importance of sensory evidence for belief in early Mormonism. The three witnesses testified that they had "seen the plates," that they knew that they had been translated by the gifts of God, "for his voice hath declared it unto us." Later, their testimony emphasized sight, explaining that "an angel of God came down from heaven, and he brought and laid before our eyes, that we beheld and saw the plates, and the engravings thereon; and we know that it is by the grace of God . . . that we beheld and bear record that these things are true. And it is marvelous in our eyes." Following what they heard from God, they bore witness to the text. Thus, we see that sight, hearing, and touch mattered not only to Joseph Smith Jr. but also to his immediate and earliest followers, who themselves also had sensory spiritual confirmation of the claims he was making.

When scholars do explore the senses and their relationship to religious experiences and beliefs, they tend to privilege sight in their discourse.[48] This privileging is tied to the dualistic frameworks discussed earlier. Sight tends to reinforce a dualistic framework because it suggests that there is a dualism: there is me, and there is the thing that I am looking at. There is self, and there is other. At the same time, sight allows us to anticipate our interactions in the world: we see and we imagine what the object we see will weigh, feel like, smell, and sound like. Sight anticipates. It is the sense that mediates much of human relations with the physical world.[49]

We often imagine sight as a highly individualized experience and as separate from other sensory experiences. Yet vision happens within communities, and our communities teach us both what and what not to see. They tell us what is significant, where to focus our attention. In religion, community often shapes the ways people see and the significance they ascribe to what they see. In discussing the role of vision and images, David Morgan argues that "the truth, trust, or reliability of an image depends on the operation of a compact, an agreement that sets out the conditions under which an image may deliver what the viewer expects from or seeks in it."[50] And so sight must be taken into consideration in our discussions of religious believers' interactions with the material world and with the communities that shape those interactions.

Although sight has been privileged by religious believers and scholars alike, the sense of touch has often been denigrated. Yet touch is one of the most important senses for religious believers.[51] Touch often collapses the dualism of self and other; when I place my hand on an object, my hand is transformed in the process, taking on the shape of what I am touching. While sight can reinforce distance, touch cannot. In stores we are often told to look but not touch, the old "you see with your eyes, not with your hands." Why

is this statement repeated so often? Precisely because the relationship between sight and touch is an important one; sight leads to touch, and touch
allows us to engage an object from multiple angles, allowing for a more complete understanding. We want to hold what we behold. It is often touch that
transforms an assertion of belief into a *felt religion,* an embodied knowledge
that believers describe as a confidence about what they know to be true.[52]

An example of how simple objects can inspire sensory experiences and
how those experiences are shaped by communal expectations jumped out at
me as I visited several sites along the Mormon Trail. Those sites had Kleenex
boxes scattered around particular rooms: the room where Smith was murdered in Carthage Jail, the movie theaters where films recounted the history
of his death and the subsequent movement of Utah Mormons westward.
Then I noticed that many of the people who watched these films left crying
and needing the Kleenex that had been offered. The Kleenex box indicates
a material aspect of Mormon religion; the boxes communicate to believing
visitors that what they are about to see or hear will overwhelm their spiritual selves and will move them to tears. Anthropologist Hildi Mitchell has
described the process that can take place: "while individual Mormons may
construct their own paths through Mormon heritage, and feel personal
feelings whilst on them, they are highly likely to experience these places,
events and objects in a hegemonic, culturally standardized way."[53] Thus,
believers who experience certain emotions have been taught to interpret
those emotions as "signs of the spirit," and so when they see such movies,
"which contain memories of previous experiences" and emotions, they find
the films to be "testimony-building and spiritual."[54]

It is as feeling and sensing bodies that humans experience the ritual life
of their communities, and Mormons take part in many rituals both inside
and outside the temple. I argue that there are several more recently developed rituals that participate in the making of sacred space within the LDS
tradition. These include the ritual of pilgrimage to historic sites, pushing
handcarts over rough terrain, and walking in the steps of great leaders.
Popular key chains sold in Far West, Missouri, communicate the importance of these feelings: "I walked where Joseph walked" and "I walked where
Adam walked" offer believers reminders of these powerful physical activities. Ritual activities allow Mormons to "participate actively in their theology
and cosmology" and to engage the material objects of their faith and history.
Being able to touch historical objects or to walk in the steps of Joseph Smith
and of Brigham Young concretizes the history and theology for Mormons.

In addition, the church has constructed these sites so that the theological meaning of the history is not left open to interpretation but is fed to visitors in small, easy-to-remember sound bites.

Memory

As Joseph Smith Jr. placed the marker as a cornerstone for what he imagined would be the future temple, he transformed the two-dimensional map of Zion into a three-dimensional world, creating sacred space in the process. That marker was to serve as a reminder to the people. This spot was to be the center from which Zion would unfold. The stone served as a material reminder of what believers were supposed to remember: that Zion was real, that it could be seen, touched, and built—that it was part of what made them a people. And so the space and the objects helped to shape the memory of who the people were, where they had been, and where they were supposed to go. The stones situated them not just in space but in history.

Scholars of religion have long pondered what the definition of religion is, how it functions for humans, and why it persists when so many other frameworks for viewing the world have arisen and fallen away. Danielle Hervieu-Leger argues that religion addresses "the human need for *assurance* which is at the source of the search to make the experience of life intelligible and which constantly evokes the question of why."[55] Hervieu-Leger provides a helpful framework for thinking about religion when she asserts: "there is no religion without the authority of a tradition being invoked . . . in support of the act of believing." Tradition is important because humans are swayed by the idea that they are part of a chain of memory, one that has continuity with the past. Hervieu-Leger describes the persuasive power of a sense of tradition this way: "as our fathers believed, and because they believed, we too believe."[56] It is worth noting here that Joseph Smith claimed that he and his followers were *restoring* the ancient church, thus drawing on an authority that was rooted in the aura of ancientness.[57] Hervieu-Leger argues that there are three parts of the concept of religion: "the expression of believing, the memory of continuity, and the legitimizing reference to an authorized version of such memory, that is to say tradition." Religious groups, then, rely on discussions of the past and the sense that memories are shared and passed down intergenerationally.[58] Believers, as they engage the chain of memory, sense that the chain connects them to both past and present. Yet it would be a mistake to imagine this chain as two-dimensional. Rather, memory is very much bound to map and marker; thus the chain of memory ought to be imagined as three-dimensional: the sense of past and future comes to believers through encounters with the material realm.

Eric Hobsbawm notes that religions must invent and reinvent the sense of tradition in order to "inculcate certain values and norms of behavior" that are inspired by a sense of continuity with the past. Memory serves as something to bind community members together and to legitimize their current behavior by calling on the past.[59] Binding the community through memory is often accomplished through repetition and ritualization.[60] Thus, it is not primarily through reading history books written by scholars that believers maintain their connection to the past. Rather, the group tells its own history, often through ritualized action. Davis Bitton, a scholar of Mormonism, has noted this process in the Latter-day Saints, pointing out that the ritualization of Mormon history "is not primarily the communication of knowledge but rather the simplification of the past into forms that can be memorialized, celebrated and emotionally appropriated."[61]

Many Mormon studies scholars have noted the importance of history in the Mormon tradition. Some have even suggested that the concern with history is so great in the LDS Church tradition that it often serves to replace theology. This emphasis on history may in part be tied to the LDS embrace of the idea of continuing revelation, but history seems to be functioning in several important ways. It is central to an understanding of identity as part of a chosen community; it allows believers to link themselves to a chain of memory. It is also through history-telling that Latter-day Saints often communicate their theological claims. At the same time, other Mormon studies scholars, such as Mark Leone, have suggested that there is a striking "memorylessness" in the tradition, an inability on the part of Mormons to recall the past they have lived through. While Mormons have been assiduous collectors of genealogies and memories, Leone argues that the tendency within the tradition is to read those historical "facts" as data points relating to the individual living in the present rather than viewing the data within larger economic, political, and cultural frameworks.[62] Yet this does not necessarily suggest a contradiction or that the Mormon community is especially distinct in this regard. Our memories operate as sieves; we embrace the aspects of history that are important to identity and forget those aspects that do not matter to the sense of who we are. This selectivity is tied to the primary function of history-telling in the community. The ritual act of history-telling communicates to believers' larger values and frames that, because they are rooted in an historical narrative, provide a sense of timelessness *and* rootedness. And so, as Douglas Davies has put it, "Mormon interest in history is soteriological not historiographic."[63]

Because history is ritualized and theologized, the simplification of the narrative that Bitton pointed to is an important aspect of Mormonism to examine. Scholars of collective memory have long noted that collective memory—what the group remembers as a part of its past, thus reinforcing for group members a sense of their identity as a "we"—is as much, if not more, about forgetting. Various aspects of the narrative that do not easily fit, or that no longer function for the group as useful to the process of identity formation, get pushed aside. Mostly this happens naturally. Because narrative cannot recall every detail of past events, the details must serve the larger purpose of the story. The linearity of western history-telling often demands this. Yet sometimes aspects of history are left out for reasons, a kind of willful group amnesia. One such example in the LDS Church tradition is the twentieth-century emphasis on the story of Smith's First Vision in the sacred grove and of Brigham Young's hegira westward. These stories were emphasized and ritualized while the narratives about polygamy were actively downplayed.[64] This was an attempt by the church as an institution, and by its individual members, to portray a history that would make the group palatable to their fellow non-Mormon Americans. As historian Jared Farmer has noted, polygamy and the missionization of the Lamanites (a group in the Book of Mormon who many Mormons believed and believe to be the ancestors of Native Americans) that did not proceed as Smith had imagined are "forgettable because they didn't live up to prophecy"; "by contrast, pioneering is a supremely usable past." It is therefore highly celebrated and ritualized. The stories continue to build on the stories, and "authenticity is as elusive as it is desirable, as problematic as it is powerful."[65] The stories are amassed, and the "real" events of history are transformed in the service of identity formation, of linking current members of the group to the chain of memory that fosters community and a sense of we-ness.

Map, Marker, Memory—and Metaphor

Two days after the first Mormon party arrived in the Salt Lake Valley in 1847, Brigham Young and eight other leaders climbed into the foothills on the north side of the valley. When they reached the top of one of the foothills, a foothill that Young declared Joseph Smith had shown him in a vision, they named the hill Ensign Peak. Young recalled that in the vision he had seen an angel "standing on a 'conical hill' [who pointed] to where the new temple and city should be built." He believed that the angel was "the resurrected Joseph Smith, and Ensign Peak was the hill of his dream." As they stood on the summit, the leaders surveyed the valley below them and pronounced "that all who were oppressed would find refuge in this place." Understandings of prophecy defined the moment. What Young had seen with "spiritual eyes" now shaped the way the church leaders read the landscape. They understood the landscape as visual confirmation of the role of prophecy and as the site of the new Zion, where their community would find "peace and prosperity."[66] They immediately set about planning the new city that they believed would be a beacon to the world.

After they gazed at and planned for their new Zion, the leaders descended from the peak and began the work of building Zion with their hands. Clearly, for them, Zion was a literal place, and they were called to physically gather and build it with one another; they sought to make their theological beliefs tangible through building and organizing the city.[67] "Zion" and "gathering" shaped the ways nineteenth-century Utah Mormons understood their relationship to one another and to the land they inhabited.[68] And as the Latter-day Saints were forced westward, they came to view the Salt Lake Valley through the lens of the concept of Zion that had been instilled in them in Independence. Religion scholar Claudia Bushman has said of Salt Lake City that it "is the most durable of the Church's Zions. . . . After the exodus from Nauvoo, Illinois, in 1846, Salt Lake became the place for the Saints to gather."[69] And historian Phil Barlow has noted that even as the concept of gathering was deemphasized, "the Mormon psyche still places Zion (Utah) at the world's center."[70]

With the globalization of the church over the course of the twentieth century, the concepts of Zion and gathering could no longer be understood literally in the way nineteenth-century believers had understood them.[71] It was impractical to expect every Mormon convert to move to Utah, and doing so would go against the church's goal of spreading its beliefs to all nations. And so a process of downplaying the emphasis on literally gathering to Zion began as early as 1891 with an editorial in the church periodical the *Millennial Star*. It took firmer root in 1921 when the First Presidency urged missionaries to stop calling converts to immigrate and then gained strength as leaders repeated theological comments that believers should gather out of Babylon, staying where they were and building Zion there.[72]

Over the course of the twentieth century, the Latter-day Saints shifted from a literal to a metaphorical understanding of the theological concepts of "gathering" and "Zion." As a late twentieth-century Sunday school guide put it, "the first members [of the church] could realize their spiritual dreams only by moving closer to the places where the ordinances were available—by literally gathering out of Babylon to find Zion. . . . Later generations, in stakes with access to temples around the world, would find a heightened spiritual meaning in gathering. Without leaving their homelands, they could express the same determination to abandon the evils of Babylon for the holiness of Zion."[73] Thus, gathering and Zion were no longer specifically tied to place; instead, Mormons scattered around the world could participate in spiritual versions of gathering and Zion by living righteous lives, rejecting evil, and visiting the temples that were proliferating around the globe.

As these two concepts were spiritualized, so too was the understanding of the church's pioneer identity. In the mid-twentieth century, church members who could trace their lineages back to the 1847 pioneers held places of privilege in the LDS community. In some LDS communities, this is still the case. More recently, and in an increasingly global church, church leaders have made the claim that the pioneers are the *spiritual ancestors* of all Mormons. Mormon studies scholar Eric Eliason has called this process the "pioneerification" of the LDS community.[74] Because the story of the nineteenth-century movement to Utah contained a usable past for the construction of a twentieth- and twenty-first-century "we," the stories of the Utah pioneers became central to the LDS chain of memory. That chain had to grow in flexibility, becoming spiritualized and metaphorized as the church expanded globally. Thus, as the concepts of Zion and gathering were spiritualized, so too was the understanding of ancestral ties to the pioneers, allowing more people to access the claims to the sacred narratives and spaces of the church.

Yet to say that what happened as the church globalized was a shift from the literal to the metaphorical is to understand only one piece of the puzzle. It is my contention that in the late twentieth and early twenty-first centuries, we can see creative slippages taking place within Mormonism between the literal and metaphorical, text and object, and history and space. Rather than simply moving to more metaphorical understandings, the Mormon community has spiritualized and metaphorized and then reconcretized concepts such as gathering and Zion in the material and physical realm so that believers can continue to touch and physically engage these central theological principles. Slipping between the literal and metaphorical, between the historical and the spatial, and between the textual and the material, late twentieth- and early twenty-first-century Mormons redeployed the theological concepts that were central to nineteenth-century believers. In so doing, they created a historical narrative that remembered their past and all of its potential contradictions as part of a seamless narrative of divine work in the world. Theological, historical, and spatial slippages enable contemporary Mormons to create a new theological and communal space for their global membership.

Such theological concepts as "gathering" and "Zion" continue to be significant concepts precisely because they have been embodied and spatialized in new ways. Latter-day Saints use new embodied activities, and they construct and then perform pilgrimages to historic sites to mitigate the loss of a common place and set of experiences. These activities help to bond a globalized, place-less religious community together. In order to bond that increasingly diverse group of believers to one another *and* to develop a historical narrative that appears seamless and linear, Mormons have had to creatively engage their central theological concepts. Slipping between metaphorical and literal interpretations of key theological concepts such as Zion and gathering, Latter-day Saints have rooted their theological and historical beliefs in the material realm, thus concretizing concepts (as beliefs that they can touch and feel) in particular places and making these places sacred by the rituals performed in them.

One place where we can observe this type of activity closely is at This Is The Place Park (TITP Park) in Salt Lake City. The construction of the park itself began in the 1940s as church members and state leaders sought to honor *the spot* where Brigham Young supposedly stood, looked out at the Salt Lake Valley, and knew that "this is the place." Since the 1940s this state-owned park has undergone many changes, adding new sculptures to commemorate various aspects of LDS and western history and offering "living history" activities through which visitors can engage the West "as it was." Because the development of TITP Park spans so much of the period this book explores, and because it represents many of the themes discussed herein, each chapter except the final one begins with a discussion of a monument, sculpture, or activity found at TITP Park and uses it as a lens through which to view this book's investigation of the intersections of history, space, matter, and memory in the lives of late twentieth- and early twenty-first-century Latter-day Saints.

Figure 1.1 This Is The Place Monument (1947).

1

This Is The Place!

Creating a Center Place in the Salt Lake Valley

A bronze Brigham Young stands twelve feet, four inches high as he confidently counsels his almost-as-tall friends and leaders of the LDS Church that this, indeed, is the place the Mormon pioneers sought when fleeing westward from their persecutors. The surety is written on his face—this is their Zion. (See Figure 1.1) This 1947 monument to the 1847 Utah pioneers sits in Emigration Canyon in the hills above Salt Lake City. Young and his friends, Heber C. Kimball and Wilford Woodruff, dominate the monument. Their pylon rises sixty feet above the rest. The scenes below them depict the Mormons' movement into the Salt Lake Valley and other early visitors and settlers to what became the state of Utah. A few feet below the three central figures, etched in granite, are the words of Young's famous declaration "this is the place."[1]

The negotiations that took place in order to create the monument and secure the land on which it stands demonstrate church *and* state authorities' attempts to construct place and memory in Utah. Latter-day Saints had to negotiate the retelling of their mythic entry into sacred space with their fellow Utahans. The desires to be historically accurate and to promote the mythic exodus story of the Mormon people clashed at times with the desire to claim that Mormons were part and parcel of the American nation. While portions of the monument confirm the narrative of the Latter-day Saints being part of God's chosen people, other portions affirm Mormons as leaders in the civic life of Utah and the larger United States. The monument itself represents the tension and ultimate compromise between these two often competing narratives at a pivotal moment in Mormon history.

It was during the 1940s and 1950s that LDS Church leaders and members put increased effort into memorializing this sacred space with a distinctive monument and emphasizing its centrality to the spatial aspects of Mormon faith. In this way, wherever they lived, believers could step into the mythic stories of their people; the journey that had begun with Abraham and Moses

Pioneers in the Attic. Sara M. Patterson, Oxford University Press (2020). © Oxford University Press.
DOI: 10.1093/oso/9780190933869.001.0001

and had been reconfirmed in the trek of the 1847 pioneers could become a personal story. They could return to their center, their Zion, and gaze out at the fruits of the labor of the generations who had gone before.[2] In standing where their Moses stood, Mormons could reaffirm that the values of the pioneers, their hard work and industry, continued to be the values of the group.

These efforts to maintain the site and encourage practitioners to return to this important center in the group's history ramped up at precisely the same time that the group was changing its spatial practices on a global level. Up until the first decades of the twentieth century, the focus in Mormonism had been on the notion of gathering—the idea that believers would gather at the center of Zion if circumstances allowed. The emphasis on gathering can account for the Mormons' emigration to Utah and their sense of being chosen members of God's new Israel. Yet as the church continued to grow exponentially and it became less practical to expect members to literally gather in Utah's Great Basin region, more emphasis was placed on staying where one was and helping to build part of Zion there, spiritualizing the notion of gathering.

Even though the monument served an important function in the LDS community at a time when the community was beginning to reimagine its relationship to space, the site also allowed Mormons to claim their status as leaders of a multireligious state. The monument told the story of a religious group's exodus from persecution alongside the story of its role in creating empire. There were distinct advantages to preserving and embracing both narratives, despite the tension. The monument suggested that the Latter-day Saints' claim to American identity was rooted in their participation in the activity of "civilizing" the American West. It encouraged both non-Mormon and Mormon Utahans to celebrate the Mormon pioneers as their state ancestors, suggesting that the character the pioneers developed in their westward journey—their determination to mold a civilization out of the wilderness—was everyone's inheritance. At the same time, the monument confirmed Mormons' identity as a chosen people. That the spot on which their Moses stood to look out over their promised land was being celebrated and sacralized in such a dramatic way, and by Mormons and non-Mormons alike, confirmed that chosen status. Both the monument and the peoples' memory could tolerate the tension of the two narratives because of a basic agreement about what would be forgotten at the same time. The narrative forgot just as much of the journey as it remembered, if not more. The persecution of Mormons by their fellow Americans, their subsequent persecution of Native Americans in the act of "civilizing" the West, and what were viewed as Mormons' religious peculiarities by their Protestant contemporaries were all forgotten in the push to herald Latter-day Saints as true Americans and the site where their prophet stood as the Plymouth Rock of the American West.

It took effort to make the space sacred, to make it *a center place*. Sacred spaces require the work of communities to story and ritualize their importance. The community proclaims that *something important happened here* and then continues to tell and retell those stories, setting the space apart. The stories then get reinforced through ritual activities that continue to proclaim that the place is special.[3] And the Mormon community and the people of Utah did just that at TITP Park. They proclaimed it a sacred space, each community in its own way. The overlapping but not identical stories that these communities told layered the monument with symbolic significance and prioritized its centrality to the identity of each group. Thus, during the mid-twentieth century and continuing on to this day, efforts have been made to make TITP Park a sacred space where believers and Utahans alike could return to the center of their origins and visit a physical location tied to their spiritual and civic roots.

The Pioneers of 1847

What were the events that inspired the 1947 memorial? What were the processes that made *that place* a site of both remembering and forgetting? Who were those pioneers and how did they make the space *a place*?

On April 18, 1847, 143 men, three women, two children, "72 wagons, 93 horses, 52 mules, 66 oxen, 19 cows, and 17 dogs, and chickens" left Winter Quarters on the banks of the Missouri River and headed westward. It was a trip for which the Latter-day Saints had prepared, yet it was also a journey into the unknown. The Mormons were fleeing persecution from fellow Americans who had murdered their prophet, destroyed their property, and deemed Mormons intolerable neighbors. Their church leadership, still somewhat in flux since the death of Joseph Smith Jr. and his brother Hyrum, attempted to plan for the trip. This group had chosen Brigham Young as Smith's successor. He and other leaders of the church preached that the future prosperity of the group relied on each member's behavior in the present. They were told that their entry into a new land was going to require a new way of living. As a leader, Young was not one to leave their destination completely to chance. Prior to their departure from Winter Quarters, he did extensive research on possible places in the west where Mormons could go and practice their faith unhindered. Too many struggles and too much persecution by neighbors had taught him that the ideal spot for Mormons would be one with *no* neighbors. Young researched options in California, the Rocky Mountains, and the Great Basin region. From fairly early on it seemed that the Great Basin region, currently part of the state of Utah, at that time in Mexico's territory, would be a good choice.[4] Though his records seem to evidence a relative surety about their destination, Young never claimed that he knew for sure where the pioneers were headed.

For a number of reasons, the Great Basin was an ideal spot. First, it had enough fresh water that the pioneers could grow many crops with a good irrigation system.[5] Though it had little timber available for buildings, the pioneers knew of other regional building processes, including the making of adobe bricks. Second, the area lacked one thing the Mormons knew they did not want: neighbors, at least of the European American sort. As for Native Americans, the Mormon pioneers settled in a territory that overlapped the areas disputed between the Utes and Shoshone.[6]

After the pioneers traveled for three and a half months and more than 1,000 miles, their arrival in the Great Basin was an important time. Even when they drew close to the Great Basin, there was some anxiety because a large number of the party, including Brigham Young, contracted mountain fever and fell quite ill. Recognizing this anxiety, Young sent out an advance party, led by Orson Pratt and Erastus Snow, which was the first to reach a view of the entire valley on July 22, 1847. The accounts of these men show that they immediately assessed and claimed the landscape around them. William Clayton wrote: "there is but little timber in sight anywhere, and that is mostly on the banks of creeks and streams of water which is about the only objection which could be raised in my estimation to this being one of the most beautiful valleys and pleasant places for a home for the Saints which could be found."[7] Thomas Bullock could not help but exclaim: "hurra, hurra, hurra, there's my home at last."[8] Erastus Snow remembered that they involuntarily "uttered a shout of joy at finding it to be the very place of our destination and the broad bosom of the Salt Lake spreading itself before us."[9]

Pioneers who came into the valley in the next days deemed it stunning: "my heart felt truly glad," wrote Howard Egan, "and I rejoiced at having the privilege of beholding this extensive and beautiful valley, that may yet become a home for the Saints."[10] Though most of the accounts of the valley were positive, not everyone found it sublime. In fact, some found it down-right uncomfortable. Harriet Page Wheeler Decker Young, wife of Lorenzo Dow Young, the brother of Brigham Young, kept her husband's journal for much of their journey. Though in ill health along the entire route, she recalled of July 24, 1847: "this day we arrived in the valley of the great Salt Lake my feelings were such as I cannot describe everything looked gloomy and I felt heart sick."[11] Samuel Brannan, a later arrival to the valley and one who believed that the pioneers' destiny lay in California, found the terri-tory equally depressing.[12] Though there were some disappointed gazes, the narratives the majority of Mormon pioneers told at the time about the land and its promise quickly confirmed that this was the site of their new Zion.

It was not until July 24 that Brigham Young reached the same location—on a sickbed set up for him in the wagon of Wilford Woodruff. The image of Young boldly standing with his friends and gazing out over their prom-ised land was the stuff of the 1947 memorial, not Young's actual state in 1847. Because he was ill, he did not write much about his experience that day. Woodruff's journal from that time recounts, and this account changed greatly over time, that July 24 was "an important day in the History of my life and the History of the Church of JESUS CHRIST of Latter Day Saints. On this important day after traveling from our encampment . . . we came in full view of the great valley or Bason [sic] [of] the Salt Lake and land of promise held in reserve by the hand of GOD for a resting place for the Saints upon which A portion of the Zion of GOD will be built."[13] Woodruff called it "the grandest & most sublime scenery Probably that could be obtained on the globe."[14]

Over the coming months Brigham Young instructed the pioneers to tie the success and fertility of the landscape to their own morality. Their errand to the wilderness would succeed only if they remained faithful to God. As the Nephites and Lamanites had learned in the Book of Mormon, the landscapes of the Americas were only fruitful and the people prosperous if God was on their side.

As they looked out over the valley, their Zion, they saw a moral expecta-tion written on the landscape. They had traveled far to get there, and they believed that the future, in this world and the next, lay in their ability to prove their worthiness for Zion.[15] That vision of Zion built their expectations of what the future might hold if they chose to live correctly. Thus the Zion they built—their irrigation systems, their crops, the temple—all confirmed their worthiness. In the future, the landscape could be read for signs of their status. A prosperous landscape equaled a godly people.

The theological interpretation of the landscape by the majority of pioneers motivated them to quickly set to work planting crops for the future and building structures that would house their families and their worship services. Over the course of the next decade, Latter-day Saints constructed the center of Zion, from which they, as Smith had instructed, imagined many spokes radiating outward until the whole Earth was overspread. Through their labor with the land they believed that they proved themselves worthy of Zion. Their toil and its outcomes served as evidence of their worthiness and subsequently reaffirmed one another.

Though the pioneers had armed themselves with what knowledge they could gather about the West—surveying maps of the West, speaking with explorers and traders, and reading accounts of earlier pioneers—the most important preparatory texts they read were their scriptures. Brigham Young read the pioneers' journey as typifying the same search Abraham had undertaken: "like Father Abraham, journeying we knew not wither; our only object being to find a resting place, a place of peace & safety for ourselves, for our families, & our friends." That sense of faithful journeying to a land they did not know was central to the pioneer identity; "they went, as did Abram, when he left his father's house—knowing not whither he went—only God had said, Go out from your father's house unto a land which I will show you."[16]

Envisioning the place where they chose to settle as their promised land did not make Mormons unique in the United States. In fact, by 1847 there was already a long tradition of reading scriptural accounts onto American events and landscapes. In reading their millennial expectations onto the landscape, the Latter-day Saints resembled some of their fellow Americans. The idea that the Salt Lake Valley could be the center of a Zion that overspread the Earth was what made the Mormons' interpretation of their journey so distinct. In their accounts they left the land of the Gentiles (non-Mormons), where they had met hostility, and journeyed to a new and foreign (literally foreign, as Utah was a Mexican territory at the time) place of rest. Yet in that transition they were able to take comfort in their interpretation that they were, despite what their senses and experiences might indicate, moving from the periphery to the center.

Part of their sense that they were fulfilling Hebraic history lay in their understanding of themselves as Israel, journeying to a promised land that was divinely set aside for them. In this narrative, the people and the land across and to which they were journeying were key.[17] As religious studies scholar Jan Shipps has noted, the pioneers underwent an "experiential 'living through' of sacred events in a new age."[18] For the Latter-day Saints, the scriptural promise that a land could be found for the chosen, faithful people took on a literal meaning. The pioneers' entry into the Salt Lake Valley, as Shipps has so aptly pointed out, was their entry into the meeting place of both sacred space and sacred time.

As they journeyed westward, the pioneers' concept of time and scriptural fulfillment changed. They were at one and the same time fulfilling the Hebraic prophecies, preparing the way for the Second Coming anticipated within Christianity, and living out the visions and prophecies of Joseph Smith. In this way, past and future merged with the people as they journeyed into the unknown. Zion was promised in the Hebrew and Christian scriptures, in the Book of Mormon and other Mormon scriptures, and by Joseph Smith himself.[19] The Mormons continued to believe that it would be a literal place they would build up. Thus numerous texts—every one that was sacred to the pioneers—reinforced the sacrality of their journey's resting point.

They understood their journey's events as inevitable. The sense that their story was part of divine history helped them to read it back into scriptural accounts. Within a week of their entry into the valley, Orson Pratt surmised that "the Book of Mormon never would have been fulfilled if the Saints had not left the gentiles as a people, for when the gentiles rejected the Gospel it was to be taken among the Lamanites. . . . This movement is one of the greatest that has taken place among this people."[20] Even though their movement to a place where they could live freely and set up Zion had an aura of inevitability to it, the pioneers believed that their behavior and their faith held the outcome in the balance. The notions of gathering and Zion were so powerful that believers were willing to give up their past identities, place ties, and inheritances for it.[21]

As the Saints built up their portion of Zion in the Salt Lake Valley, they continued to encourage their brethren in the East and in other countries to gather with them. Their work, and the orderly crops and city blocks they produced, their buildings, and their temple, all served as evidence to them that they had been called to this place. They believed that they were fulfilling the vision Brigham Young had seen of the future when he stood above the valley and declared that it was the right place. Their work to build up Zion was viewed as religious practice, marking their membership in the chosen people.[22] One of the interesting aspects of the faith was that the call to gather and the call to build Zion were calls to action, not merely beliefs.[23] This understanding of gathering enabled the Saints to assimilate converts of many different ethnic and national backgrounds into their understanding of peoplehood.[24] The boundary between religious insiders and outsiders became *the* key social identifier in Utah, profoundly shaping Mormons' interactions with non-Mormon Americans.

Because the Latter-day Saints believed in ongoing revelation and miracles, their sene that the story of the pioneer movement west was shrouded in the supernatural manifested itself not only in the way they read scripture but also in the miraculous accounts of their own journeys. The narratives of Brigham Young and the pioneers took on their own supernatural character, providing evidence of the divine errand. Perhaps the most frequently told miraculous story of the pioneers' experience occurred not long after their arrival. The seagull story recounts the disastrous effect that crop-devouring crickets had on the first full spring crop the pioneers planted in the valley. Many fields of crops were ruined. But just in the nick of time, according to the story, gulls appeared and began to feed on the crickets. That the seagulls ate more than their weight in crickets allowed the pioneers to survive. Fairly quickly the story of the seagulls became evidence of divine favor. Only a divine type of protection would ensure success against the whims of nature. This story, still lovingly repeated in the LDS community today, is also memorialized at TITP Park with a seagull sculpture crafted by Jonathan Bronson. The base of the sculpture reads: "God who was ever ready to bless his faithful children, sent the gulls who were truly saviors in our behalf, and saved our crops from total ruin" (see Figure 1.2).

The stories of miracles such as these in the lives of nineteenth-century Latter-day Saints indicated to them that their errand was part of the divinely ordained progression of God's peoples to their promised lands.

Where Was the Place?

Since 1847, one impulse within the LDS Church has been to document these events as precisely as possible. The pioneers themselves believed that the steps they were taking and the crops they were planting had implications for the future of the group. Efforts to be historically accurate have always been a central component of LDS identity. The imperative to be a record-keeping people was part of a commandment Joseph Smith Jr. offered to church members on April 6, 1830, at the first meeting that organized the church. That revelation, now canonized as *Doctrine and Covenants* 21:1, instructed: "there shall be a record kept among you."[25]

Figure 1.2 Seagull sculpture, This Is The Place Park.

Being historically fastidious was and is so central to the Latter-day Saints' identity that it has become a ritualized activity in its own right. This is especially true in relation to sacred space. Remembering—remembering as accurately as possible—serves as a significant ritual performance, especially during anniversary years. Therefore, figuring out precisely where Brigham Young was and precisely what he said as he looked out over the valley, or at least the ritual enactment of these activities, symbolically reinforced the identification of Emigration Canyon as a sacred spot and the participants as faithful people. In turn, the performative and ritual approach to the space then confirmed the Saints' errand as a divine one.

From their arrival, Mormons began to read the landscape as their Zion. Yet it was not until the twentieth century that efforts began to sacralize the spot on which Brigham Young stood when he first looked out over the valley. It was as the church began to downplay the concept of a literal gathering that the rituals of record-keeping and storytelling merged with one another in Emigration Canyon. Thus the process began of viewing not only the valley but the viewpoint from which their prophet had a vision of the future of the valley as sacred spaces.

One manifestation of the ritual of record-keeping arose in the discussions over precisely where Brigham Young was when he looked out over the Salt Lake Valley and exclaimed: "this is the place!" These efforts to literally ground the story in the landscape, to memorialize it and *to mark it*, began in the first decades of the twentieth century just as the church began to emphasize a spiritual interpretation of the gathering. The first such attempt was made in 1915, when church leader and historian B. H. Roberts guided a Boy Scout troop into Emigration Canyon and set up a wooden marker on what the troop figured was precisely the point where Young had declared: "this is the place!" Roberts had taken along five of the 1847 pioneers' journals, and the group spent a day covering the last steps of the pioneer journey into the canyon. After spending much time synchronizing the journals with the footsteps, "the group was unanimously of the opinion that we had reached the right place."[26]

Not many years later, at a 1921 dedication of a small monument to commemorate the site, an act that will be further discussed in chapter 2, ritual endeavors to sacralize the spot and to prove that it was the precise spot continued.[27] W. W. Riter, who had been nine years old when his family joined the Mormon emigration to the West, participated in the unveiling of the monument. At the dedication Riter "was present and was made the authority . . . for the correct placing of the monument marking the spot." In Riter's short speech, he sought to explain to the audience "how I know this to be the place where Wilford Woodruff swung his wagon around, and President Brigham Young, leaning on his elbow, looked from under the wagon curtain, over the valley, and said, 'This is the place.'" At a certain point, however, his reasoning became vague. "The reason I say that this is the place," Riter explained, "is because no other place could be the place . . . I was a little boy . . . I crossed this same spot ten weeks later, and my memory has always been, from the beginning, that this is the place." So Riter had no memory of the exact moment, but he remained certain of the spot. He continued by using measurements taken by the pioneer William Clayton to prove that the spot was not, as some had claimed, Big Mountain (a mountain not far from Emigration Canyon). In Riter's account, the sacred status of the place trumped any human understanding of it. "I doubt if Brigham Young himself, when he was on this spot . . . realized just what the power was that was with him. He said, 'This is the place.' "[28]

Other speakers at the event also confirmed that it was the exact spot where Young had said his famous words, even though none had been witnesses. Finally, church historian B. H. Roberts expressed ambivalence about the historicity of the story, especially in terms of what Young said. Roberts's discussion used Woodruff's 1880 account of the events rather than his 1847 account. Note how much and in what ways Woodruff's account had changed:

> and now for the only account of what happened on this spot 74 years ago. This is given in a discourse by Wilford Woodruff, delivered by him in Salt Lake City on the thirty-third anniversary of Pioneer day, 1880: "On the twenty-fourth I drove my carriage, with President Young lying on a bed in it, into the open valley, the rest of the company following. When we came out of the canyon into full view of the valley, I turned the side of my carriage around, open to the west, and President Young arose from his bed and took survey of the country. While gazing on the scene before us, he was enwrapped in vision for several minutes. He had seen the valley before in vision, and upon the occasion he saw the future glory of Zion and Israel, as they would be, planted in the valleys of the mountains. When the vision had passed, he said: "It is enough. This is the right place. Drive on.[29]

Roberts's desire to be historically accurate surfaces throughout the speech. Yet his desire to be certain about the record and the spot contradicts his participation in the mythic account of the story itself. His comments reflect another important disagreement about sacralizing space. What precisely *did* Brigham Young say when he observed the valley? As Roberts pointed out, Woodruff's account in 1880, not his journal account written at the time and quoted earlier, recalled that Young said: "it is enough. This is the right place. Drive on." So, more than thirty years after the actual event, Woodruff recalled Young saying words similar to "this is the place." Roberts chose to read

Woodruff's later and more symbolically laden accounts. And Woodruff's later account recalled that Young had a supernatural confirmation of the site's sacred status; the vision confirmed not only that they were in the right place but that the Saints had lived rightly enough to build up "the future glory of Zion." At the same time, Roberts felt compelled to point out that Young's own account of his entrance into the valley was "very simple" and lacked any heavenly visions or statements about this being any particular place.

Roberts's speech then shifted: "And now this memorable saying, 'This Is The Place,' historically established, what about it? Is it the place?" Roberts's answer was that this place was a beginning point for a "world-wide mission" and a "resting place" for Mormons from a world of persecution. For Roberts, the present served as evidence of the site's sacred status. " 'Is this the place?' To that there is but one answer. Look about you and behold what God hath wrought! Behold the miracle wrought under the blessing of Almighty God, but the toil and suffering and sacrifice of the pioneers of our state." He asked his audience to imagine when Brigham Young had viewed the valley. "There is no city in view; no smiling country marked with the careful lines of industry. No fields, no orchards. No paved or other kinds of roads." As audience members imagined an undeveloped land, Roberts then painted a picture of a leader who "calmly says to his friends—'This is the place, drive on.' " In his pictorial recollection of a past, Roberts elided the various different recollections, confirming at the same time the historical and symbolic versions of the place's history and its historicity.

It is important to note here that the marker placed at "the spot" in 1921 was part of a larger series of markers set up along the Mormon trail westward, a series that claimed western space as Mormon space. This small monument now stands about 100 yards behind the 1947 TITP monument. That the 1921 marker's appearance did not stand out from the other markers along the trail is significant. The 1921 ceremony dedicated the final stop for the pioneers, and the speeches acknowledged it as the spot where an American prophet looked out over his peoples' promised land. Nonetheless, the journey was marked in the same way as the destination.

As Latter-day Saints retold the story over the decades, it took on even more supernatural qualities and became less moored in the accounts of the pioneers themselves. At the same time, the destination began to loom even larger in their accounts. In fact, Mahonri M. Young, the sculptor of the 1947 monument, seems to have understood his role in myth-making when he named the monument and had "This Is The Place" carved into the granite.

Referring to "the words my grandfather said as he looked over the Valley on July 24, 1847," the sculptor said: "Wilford Woodruff is responsible for the version of [Brigham Young's] words on looking over the valley, but they were given years after the occasion. . . . They came down orally as 'This is the Place.' And, I believe they are the actual words. They are much the best."[30] The sculptor saw the symbolic power of the words. In fact, he acknowledged that even if his grandfather Brigham Young had not *actually* said the words "this is the place" they were, perhaps more importantly, "symbolically true."[31]

The merging of past revelations and supernatural events came to a culmination at the presentation of the 1947 TITP monument. Interestingly enough, it was an account that Mahonri Young, a "jack Mormon," later gave of its unveiling that memorialized an association between it and the supernatural aspects of the arrival story. The symbolic importance of seagulls in Utah was not new to him, as the sculptor who had created the Seagull Monument in Temple Square, which had been unveiled in 1913. The seagull merges sacred moments in Latter-day Saint history—Brigham Young *knew* the spot where the Saints should rest, and the seagulls were divine messengers who showed that no natural cause could ruin their errand. This symbolism echoes in the sculptor's recollection of the unveiling of the TITP monument: "when the fateful day did arrive and the crowds were gathering, seagulls appeared on the scene, a few and then more and more until the time, when all but [the] last belated ones with the crowd had arrived, there was a large flock of gulls flying around the canvas encased monument," Young recalled. Once the drapes had fallen and the monument was revealed, "the gulls continued to circle in intricate swinging circles around the monument. . . . It was a sublime spectical [*sic*]." At the end of the ceremony, Young concludes, the gulls flew away.[32]

As they were preparing for the unveiling of the monument, the 1947 government commission in charge of the centennial memorial once again demonstrated an interest in being as historically accurate as possible. That the commission sought to be historically accurate about the precise spot shows their desire to participate in the rituals of this record-keeping people. By that time, however, the space had already taken on its mythological status. The monument and the words written on it were as much about meaning-making in the present as they were about the past. Notice the merging of past and present in a July 1947 *Deseret News* editorial discussing the phrase: "to us of 1947 those same words also have great significance. To us they mean: This is the place chosen of God for His people. This is the place where the prophets of God abide. This is the place to learn the way of the lord.... This is the place to be clean, this is the place to be pure.... this is the kingdom."[33]

This type of memory play was by no means the first example of a symbolic narration of the Mormons' entry into Salt Lake Valley. From the very beginning, the pioneers engaged in describing their new space supernaturally. They read their entry into the Salt Lake Valley as a fulfillment of scripture while at the same time reading it as typifying scriptural history. Over time the corporate character of the narrative became subsumed under the story of Brigham Young, an "American Moses" entering into a new promised land. Thus the valley *and the viewpoint from which the valley was first seen* became sacred sites for the Latter-day Saints. Certainly, the pioneers were still a chosen people and were memorialized en masse, but corporate memory began to focus on *his* entry into the Salt Lake Valley, what he said, and how he subsequently led the people.

Remembering and Forgetting, Becoming American

That the Salt Lake Valley had not just been populated by Mormons—they entered indigenous lands and later acquired European American neighbors, after all—created an interesting tension in 1947 in the state's attempts to memorialize the space. For Mormons, the monument marked a sacred space where their Moses stood and viewed the land that had been promised to them by God. For this reason, pilgrims marched and continue to march through Emigration Canyon; they return to the place where they believe historic and godly events happened. In this way, they take a cyclical view of history; they follow the footsteps of the pioneers in order to call forth the historic significance of the place and the pioneer people.

At the same time that the monument sacralized the point of the Mormons' entry into sacred space, the monument and its unveiling were also acts of civic memory making. Here Latter-day Saints were claiming the myths, symbols, and rituals of being American for themselves.[34] The monument and its unveiling served to sanctify the ground where it stood as the point of origin of a regional culture and identity. Thus a second process of storying the site and declaring its status as sacred took place. At the unveiling ceremony, Utahans of all sorts were told that the site was sacred and central to their identity as western Americans. Layers of storytelling, of prophetic visions and pioneer fortitude, came together to cement the site as a sacred space for Mormon believers and for their fellow citizens of the state of Utah.

It was at the unveiling ceremony that viewers were told how to interpret the monument and the space.[35] And the message for Mormons and non-Mormons was shockingly similar.[36] They were taught that that ground had been doubly sanctified: first, as the point where an American Moses saw the promised land of his people, and second, as the point where American pioneers had looked out over a wilderness valley and imagined the American civilization of the future. The men atop the monument were jointly celebrated as religious visionaries and the embodiment of the western values of thrift, sobriety, dedication, and rugged individualism.

The monument not only recognized the state's history but also acknowledged that the Mormons, who had been persecuted throughout the nineteenth century, had actually played a pivotal role in the settlement of the American West. As a minority group, then, the Mormons had to let go of some of their specific memories of persecution, had to accept a type of forgetting, in order to enter the American religious mainstream. The TITP monument proclaims triumph over an unstated enemy the group had to flee. After all, Young and his contemporaries are depicted as standing firm and anticipating the future, not running from their past. Because the nineteenth-century "Gentile" (non-Mormon) persecutors of Mormons were absent in the memorial, they could be easily divorced from the "Gentile" onlookers at the site. In the ritual unveiling activities, Mormons could be confirmed as leaders of their past enemies, precisely because their past enemies were not identified.[37]

In the same way that the monument demonstrated triumph without its preceding persecution, it also portrayed a triumphalist European American narrative in relation to Native Americans, representing another aspect of forgetting as part of collective memory. The sole Native American included on the monument was Chief Washakie, a Shoshone leader remembered for his friendliness to European American pioneers. The monument depicted the European American entry into the Salt Lake Valley as unimpeded, significantly forgetting those who originally peopled the land and who attempted to halt Manifest Destiny. Chief Washakie represents the "noble savage" who was friendly to the goals of civilization. On the monument Washakie stands, arms folded across his chest, holding a pipe in a dignified but passive posture, while all around him on the monument European Americans are depicted in action or holding tools of civilization, moving through space and time, forging a new future.[38] He stands as the only depiction of Native American traditions, and that depiction is a friendly one, as though he welcomed the settlement process that displaced so many indigenous peoples (see Figure 1.3).

Figure 1.3 Chief Washakie, This Is The Place Monument.

In the twenty-first century TITP Park sought to include Native Americans in the park experience in more substantive ways, yet the choices about representation still show echoes of the same displacements and erasures that occurred throughout the nineteenth and twentieth centuries. A brochure for the park reflects this in its description of the "Native American Village" that now stands off to the side of other park activities. It says: "when the pioneers settled this region, it was home to the Native American tribes. See their presentations at the Native American Village, make a take home craft and enjoy storytelling in the Navajo hogan. The Medicine Wheel will teach you about the values of Native American traditions." Failing to narrate the history of the settler's arrival alongside the presence of indigenous traditions, the brochure promises a simple display of indigenous cultures packaged for participants to take home with them. As Elise Boxer has noted,

> the rich histories of five Indigenous nations—Shoshone, Paiute, Ute, Goshute, and Navajo—are erased from the historical narrative and park. Only two tribal nations, Shoshone and Navajo, along with their typical primary dwellings (tipi and hogan, respectively), are included. The park has attempted to use authentic materials in the construction of the tipi and includes both female and male Navajo hogans. However, while both tribes lived within the boundaries of present-day Utah, they primarily lived in northern and southern regions. The park also selected dwellings that are decidedly "Native American." The tipi is arguably one of the most recognizable American Indian dwellings and further romanticizes Indigenous peoples. It also reinforces the notion that Indigenous peoples were nomadic, that they did not have ties to homelands.[39]

The village itself stands out at TITP Park not only for its off-the-mainroads location but also because it has the aura of timelessness that the rest of the park does not. There are no dates on any of the signs in the village; rather indigenous peoples are represented as out of time, allowing their histories of displacement and genocide, of survival and resilience, to go untold.

Instead, their culture is "put on display to attract tourist curiosity and further Mormon settler-colonial nostalgia." In Boxer's words, the village allows visitors to "consume Indianness without any meaningful conversation about the genocide and/or dispossession of Indigenous peoples of their lands and resources."[40] Thus, visitors to the park can "play Indian" for a brief moment without engaging the histories of how Mormon settlement disrupted the lives of the Utes, Paiutes, Shoshone, Goshutes, and Navajo. These activities happen as the park reinforces the narratives told about Washakie—that Mormon settlement happened without contest or conflict, and as part of some foreordained plan[41] (see Figure 1.4).

The final form of forgetting that had to occur in order for both non-Mormons and Mormons alike to claim the same history was tied to the aspects of Mormonism that made the Latter-day Saints an intolerable peculiarity in nineteenth-century America. Such traits include the practice of polygamy and the efforts of a communal economy, all part of a history of a

Figure 1.4 Tipi, Native American Village, This Is The Place Park.

prophet who was also governor, collapsing the relationship of church and state in nineteenth-century Utah. Instead of this narrative, Young and his counselors were remembered as men's men—full of vision, thrift, and stick-to-it-iveness. By stripping them of their peculiarities, the public memory could embrace them as civic ancestors for every Utahan. By forgetting aspects of their complex heritage, Americans could celebrate them as representative of western masculinity and American identity.

The monument's sculptor embraced a linear narrative of the region's history by his placement of the various scenes. Two significant bronze memorials appear on the back of the monument, indicating their position in Utah's *past*: Chief Washakie and the Donner-Reed party. The Donner-Reed party bas-relief, often identified as the most exquisite of the sculptures on the monument and which Mahonri Young called his "life's masterpiece," represents the failure of westward expansion, Manifest Destiny, and civilization itself.[42] That civilized European Americans would so quickly resort to such barbaric activities as cannibalism marred the function of the myth of Manifest Destiny, in which civilization inevitably drew the savage to itself and improved it. This story seemed to confirm the devolution of civilization.

The juxtaposition of the Donner-Reed party of 1846 on the back of the monument and the Mormon pioneer camp on the front is striking. The implication is simple: Where the Donner-Reed party failed, the divinely ordained, righteous Mormon party succeeded. The narrative of the monument as a whole, then, was also simple: Young and his fellow leaders facing the future of Salt Lake Valley and the other sculptures on this "future" side of the monument depict European American pioneers, eager to take on the projects of civilization and millennial fulfillment (see Figure 1.5).

What began as the memories of a specific minority group were portrayed and Americanized in such a way that non–group members, all Utahans, in fact, could lay claim to the memories.[43] The monument was an acknowledgment that Mormons were part and parcel of American civil religion—despite the fact that their entry into the valley was preceded by their persecution by other Americans and the murder of their prophet. The requisite for their membership in American civil religion was a forgetfulness of persecutions past, when they had acted as both the persecuted and the persecutors. Nonetheless, by the time of the 1947 centennial celebration of their entry into the Salt Lake Valley, the Latter-day Saints had claimed a piece of western America's civic memory.

Figure 1.5 Donner-Reed party, This Is The Place Monument.

This membership and leadership in western civic identity was reflected in two major ways. First, and perhaps a reflection of post–World War II ecumenism, several religious leaders served on the commission that selected the monument and planned the unveiling. Aside from a substantial Mormon majority, groups represented included Roman Catholics, Greek Orthodox, Protestants, and Jews. Interestingly, the individuals chosen for the committee charged with selecting the sculptor for the project and ensuring its timely completion was constituted of members of several of Utah's religious groups.[44] The selection of committee members according to their religious affiliations represented a tacit agreement that religious identity played a significant role in an individual's experience of life in the region. This was a state affair, after all, yet the representative membership were chosen, in part, by religious affiliation. In the same vein, the committee had a majority of LDS members. Here a message was sent to onlookers that Latter-day Saints were tolerant of other religious traditions, at least politically, as members of a multireligious state. At the same time, the narrative that Latter-day Saints were a majority who had been leaders building the state was also confirmed.

Second, the unveiling ceremony demonstrates, better than anything else, that the monument and the space it celebrated was both a sacred site of a particular religious group and a sacred site of the state. In order to participate actively in both narratives, the monument's artistic expression and the space surrounding it had to be symbolically flexible enough for multiple interpretations and narratives to be told about it.[45] These multiple narratives and diverse symbols were told and interpreted at the unveiling ceremony, where church and state leaders proffered an "official" analysis of the space. At the dedication, "each group of statuary, bas-relief and statue was shrouded in cloth." One by one, the statues were unveiled by "actual or spiritual descendants of the people depicted upon the monument." This meant that "a group of six brown-robed Catholic friars unveiled the Escalante group. . . . Chief Charles Washakie, the seventy-four-year-old son of Chief Washakie, came from Fort Washakie to unveil the statue of his well-known father. Various descendants of the Pioneers unveiled the statues or groups of their illustrious forebears.[46]

In the monument and ceremony we see joint processes at work: Mormon religious leaders were being claimed as pioneer leaders of all of Utah's people. We also see the Mormon process of remembering and forgetting and the negotiations that took place on the part of the other religious groups in Utah.

Non-Mormon Utahans consented to a narrative of the state's origins that was chock full of prophetic visions and promised lands. That this narrative was accepted as truth in the monument and the ceremony was a major concession on the part of the other religious groups present.

There was a theological concession made on the part of non-Mormon Utahans as well. Their conception of the God who oversaw the Manifest Destiny of the United States, and the American West in particular, expanded. According to this view, Mormons believed in the same God as other Americans, and it was for precisely this reason that they were able to be successful pioneers and role models for future generations of Americans.

At the ceremony itself, Bishop Moulton, a retired Episcopal bishop from the state, represented this concession. He proclaimed: "we dignify ourselves today, for we are associating ourselves with something more than a gala enterprise; we are offering to the world—upon the skyline for the world to see—images of mighty pioneers, rugged, sturdy, invincible and faithful men of 1847 who under God made possible for the men of 1947 to live in this good state in plenty, prosperity and peace." Not only did Moulton claim that *the same God* looked out over these Mormon pioneers as other Christians but also he claimed that Brigham Young had seen a corporate future for all of Utah: "these brave men look far back into the past and far forward into the future. They dreamed of what is real to us today."[47] By 1947 the narrative of Brigham Young's vision was expansive enough to include all Utahans and the landscape they had created together as "the place."

The tales of the pioneers and the monument that was built to convey them, in order to contribute to and confirm the role of Mormonism in Utah's civic life, also had to be part of a linear historical narrative. The monument celebrated Brigham Young's entry into the West as part of the progress of American civilization's movement westward. Interestingly, the land itself was celebrated and sacralized in a different way in the narratives of the state. The federal government donated much of the land surrounding the monument, which had initially been part of the Fort Douglas Military Reservation, to the state of Utah and determined that it should be protected. The area became "a historic state park" and was to be "left as far as possible in a primitive state."[48]

In fact, when one set of owners of land surrounding the site refused to sell, John D. Giles, the secretary of the commission and a member of the Boy Scout troop that had first marked the spot in 1915, articulated this complex understanding of sacred space.[49] When it was rumored that the owners were going to develop the area and had begun to cut down native plants,

Giles "expressed an opinion that this was a desecration of an area that is sacred to many thousands of people, not only members of the Church of Jesus Christ of Latter-day Saints, but of all religious denominations." Giles referred to it as a "desecration" of a "sacred and historic property." Later he wrote a letter to Noble Warren, editor of the *Salt Lake Tribune*, expressing this same sentiment that merged civil religion and LDS concern: "we feel too that we should use every proper means at our command to prevent anyone from capitalizing on the patriotism of the people of Utah and the West who have spent half a million dollars in that area, and also to prevent the commercialization of an area made sacred to the people of the West, regardless of creed, by the sacrifices of not only the Mormon Pioneers, but also that of the hundreds of others who had their first view of the Salt Lake Valley from that point."[50] In recognizing the site as one that could be ruined or defiled by the actions of a few who refused to accept the narrative being told about the land, Giles and others confirmed for themselves that it was indeed sacred for all Utahans. For in order to be sacred, a spot must have the potential to be profaned.[51]

Perhaps nowhere does the linearity of the monument's narratives come through more clearly than in its celebration of the West and progress. The narratives expressed in the monument were of pioneering, Manifest Destiny, and future fulfillment in the West. For the Latter-day Saints, and for Utah as a state (as told by its primarily Mormon leaders), the spot where Brigham Young stood was "to the civilization that lies west of the Mississippi river . . . the same kind of an emblem that Plymouth Rock is on the Atlantic coast. . . . the commencement of a civilization that has passed around the earth."[52] For Utahans, the pioneer entry into the valley, "which in large measure determined the destiny of the entire intermountain region and to an important degree that of Western America, is to be commemorated in a monument."[53] In these linear accounts, western history began at the moment when Brigham Young made his declaration that this was "the place": "when [it] was uttered, the destiny not only of the valley of the Great Salt Lake, but that of the entire intermountain region was determined. That declaration determined also much of the later history of Western America."[54] Thus the site of the 1947 monument was placed in the historical narrative as the Plymouth Rock of the American West: "the marker of a civilization that has subdued this entire country between the Missouri River and the Pacific Ocean."[55]

Returning to the Center, Seeing the Sacred

The TITP monument depicts two vying trends at a significant moment of change in LDS history. At precisely the moment when Mormons were deemphasizing a literal gathering in Utah, the monument memorialized the Mormon pioneers who envisioned themselves as living through the Israelite movement into their own promised land. The monument confirmed that that place was *the* place. At the same time, it placed Mormons at the helm of western civic identity and suggested that they embodied the values of American civil religion and identity.

Non-Mormons and Mormons alike have been increasingly encouraged to see the spot in Emigration Canyon as a point of origins—the place where an American prophet saw the future of Zion and the place where western character was forged. That "the place" was felt to be sacred space led to numerous efforts to enlarge its significance with the creation of the park and the later addition of its numerous monuments and activities. Later church members were told that they could have their own pilgrimage by following a path created to represent the trek of the pioneers. The Young Men's Mutual Improvement Association, the branch of the church dedicated to the cultivation of young men in proper, pious masculinity, helped to set up trails throughout TITP Park. The goal of creating a pilgrimage path was to "inspire respect and admiration for the courage and sacrifices of our Pioneer forebears, to have the present generation learn at least something of the toil, hardship, and determination which made possible the blessings we now enjoy." That they were not simply building a trail but preserving a sacred space was at the forefront of the project: "this trek is not intended to be a hike, a pleasure trip or simply an outing in the mountains," the Association's pamphlet stated; "it is in one sense a sacred pilgrimage. It should bring into the life of every Explorer. . . the utmost in experiencing satisfaction and inspiration from the adventure."[56]

The goal of establishing the trail system was to encourage in future generations a "Pioneer Trail Tradition" that would reserve the space's "stories and legends and its history spots." The purpose was twofold and a perfect reflection of the narratives offered at TITP Park. The park was to "reconsecrate" the space so "that it may live forever to commemorate the noble deeds of the men and women who laid the foundations of the great western empire and made possible the extremely favorable position our Church enjoys today."

This empire of the American West and the status of Latter-day Saints as a chosen people were to be memorialized and confirmed in a spatial way.

It was in the early twentieth century and particularly after the end of World War II that the church's leaders spiritualized the notion of gathering, interpreting it to mean that believers should gather away from the spiritual wickedness of the rest of the world, not literally gather in Utah. It was during this same time that the theological commitment to the idea that Zion was wherever the people of God were became popular among the Mormons. At precisely this moment, the church and state leaders' attempts to make visits to the TITP monument a pilgrimage experience increased. In fact, as part of the preparation of the area, the 1947 committee decided to remove an "obstructing knoll" and leveled the area that approached the monument. They wanted "a full view of the Salt Lake Valley as the monument area is approached from Emigration Canyon."[57] They wanted visitors to *see* what Brigham Young had seen in a vision (minus the "obstructing knoll"). Then the space might at one and the same time confirm the prophetic vision of a particular people and the success civilization had had in taming the wilderness. The sensory experience of seeing is the emphasis of both the park and the monument.

The idea that this was a special place was also memorialized in the new Utah state song written by Sam and Gary Francis in 1996 and officially recognized by the state legislature and governor in 2003. The song, "Utah, This Is The Place," has a refrain that affirms seven times: "this is the place!" The lyrics corroborate both the Mormons' narrative that the land was "blessed from Heaven above" and the claim of Utah's civil religion that its people have a "pioneer spirit" that "shows in everything they do." According to that civil religion, that pioneer spirit was inherited from the Mormon pioneers, who "suffered with the trials they had to face. / With faith they kept on going." That these narratives are still being told about this sacred space indicates their relevance to the lives of Mormons and their fellow non-Mormon Utahans today.

It was in the mid- to late twentieth century that efforts to build up the park increased. The first steps were to secure even more land for the park. The first expansion happened in 1959, and a second expansion, to 450 acres, in 1973. Efforts to create a "living history" followed in the wake. Various historical cabins and buildings were relocated to the park, and other replicas of well-known nineteenth-century buildings were crafted during the three decades from 1980 to 2010. Creators of the park added the modern visitors' center, more parking spaces, and replica trains to tote visitors around the park in order to foster a more "historical" aura for the space and make it "one of the most important tourist attractions in Utah."[58]

In 1947 the monument dedicated to Brigham Young's entry into the Salt Lake Valley celebrated Mormons' status as a chosen people and celebrated them as the leaders of a frontier pioneer identity that lay at the heart of civilization's success in the American West. The monument represents the type of memory Mormons embraced—one that included several forms of forgetfulness—in order to claim ownership of their place in the European American narratives of Manifest Destiny.

Figure 2.1 Pioneer View Monument (unveiled 1921).

2

A Lineal Temple

Mapping and Marking the Mormon Trail

Today, off the beaten path, up behind the main plaza of TITP Park, stands a simple white marker, perhaps five feet tall, with a buffalo skull carved into the front (see Figure 2.1). At the time it was placed, the marker represented the labor of many in the Mormon community to claim the church's history in Utah.[1] As mentioned briefly in chapter 1, a party of several men spent three days following the final portion of the Mormon Trail from Henefer to Salt Lake City, Utah. Two church historians, B. H. Roberts and Andrew Jensen, along with church leaders George Albert Smith, Hyrum G. Smith, Nephi L. Morris, Oscar A. Kirkham, and John D. Giles arrived above the Salt Lake Valley and, using five journals of the 1847 pioneers, tried to mark the trail, especially the last five miles. "Frequent stops were made at intervals of 100 yards or less," recalled Giles, "and these five journals were carefully checked noting each landmark, each crossing of the creek, or anything else that would serve to guide us."[2] Their careful efforts resulted in unanimous agreement that they had indeed found the place where Brigham Young stood when he looked out over the Salt Lake Valley and knew that it was the right place. On that trip in 1915, the men placed a wooden marker at the site.[3]

Later events made Giles even more confident that they had found the right spot. First, a man named W. W. Riter, who had arrived at Salt Lake not long after the first pioneer party and "had been taken to this site many years before and had it pointed out to him by those who were in the company," was asked to look for the place where he thought the events had occurred. His recollections led "us to within twenty-five feet of the site we had selected." After that, Robert Sweeten, a pioneer from 1847, also indicated the same spot.[4] Textual evidence from the journals along with "witness" accounts from men who had visited the spot later and had it pointed out to them by others, made Giles even more confident that they had found the right place. About six years after they placed the wooden marker, the buffalo skull monument replaced it as a more permanent recognition of where a sacred event had

Pioneers in the Attic. Sara M. Patterson, Oxford University Press (2020). © Oxford University Press.
DOI: 10.1093/oso/9780190933869.001.0001

taken place. The movement between the journals and the landscape, from pi-oneer accounts to the actual ground where the twentieth-century men stood, represents the movement one sees again and again in the spatial and histor-ical negotiations of Latter-day Saints with their nineteenth-century past.

Those early events profoundly shaped Giles's future. His interest in marking Utah's history blossomed as he became the executive secretary for a group called the Utah Pioneer Trails and Landmarks Association (UPTLA), begun in the 1930s, and earned him the nickname "Mr. Monuments."[5] The work of this association represents an important impulse in the LDS com-munity, one that echoed throughout the twentieth century. That impulse was to mark and to claim the landscape as a significant aspect of Mormon and western history. In order to do this well, the group employed methods sim-ilar to the ones described earlier, moving between text and territory to write history on the land. Their work was, in part, one piece of a project that was tied to their claim that the Mormons were as American as other Americans. The group's process was twofold: first, they marked the landscape as other Americans did, participating in rituals similar to those happening around the nation, and second, they claimed the landscapes of the American West as distinctly Mormon while also declaring that Mormon pioneers were the epitome of American values and empire-building.

That initial trip to find the spot where Brigham Young stood was part of the first phase of Mormons' attempts to mark the landscape. Mormon studies scholar Michael Madsen identifies this first phase, occurring in the early twentieth century, as "historical" and then argues that "this primarily histor-ical emphasis gave way to a more spiritualistic interpretation of Mormon his-torical sites."[6] The spiritualistic turn occurred in the late twentieth century. Although Madsen's characterizations of the two phases are accurate, I do not believe that they provide full pictures of them. First, I would argue that the early twentieth-century phase had an intriguing spiritual layer that arose in the attempts to mark specific locations as important or sacred.

Second, as Madsen asserts, the end of the twentieth century saw an em-phasis on more spiritual or metaphorical interpretations of the historical sites. To that I would add that this second phase, while spiritual, included an affective, experiential element as well. Late twentieth-century work along the Mormon Trail sought to ground Latter-day Saints in their history, but also to ground them in *experience*. Thus, the late twentieth-century activities made of the Mormon Trail a museum, a playground, and a temple—a "lineal temple," a sacred space, where members could come to experience their his-tory and theology under the umbrella of authenticity.

Phase 1: Marking the Trail, Defining the Lineal Temple

Why do people choose to place monuments in particular locations? Why decide to mark the natural world with narratives written in concrete, bronze, and granite? Certainly, that answer is in part contextually based, and I will explore that here, but there are also some aspects of monument-building that appear to transcend particular contexts and speak to general desires that monuments satisfy. Most monuments are made out of materials—metal, wood, stone—that people believe will outlast a human life. Thus, monuments often represent some type of hope for the future, the hope that what *we of today* believe is important will be meaningful and matter to the *you of tomorrow*. Monuments serve as a wish for the future, an attempt to pass on some narrative of identity that will (in the hopes of the monument makers) continue to inform who "we" are. Janet Donohoe suggests that one can think of monuments as "narratives written in stone," a description that includes not only the explanatory texts that accompany most monuments but also the sculptures and artistic representations themselves. These texts and physical markers help to form a symbolic narrative that not only recounts some set of events or people but also tries to tell viewers how to interpret them; they tell the viewer why they matter.[7] Monuments participate in the process of creating "tradition" and collective memory because they help to pass down narratives from one generation to the next. A monument demands that viewers " 'remember this!' " —and in so doing, demands that they carry that memory on into the future.

Mormons have participated in monument-making throughout the twentieth century but were certainly not distinct in their desire to mark the landscape. One of their earliest endeavors of the twentieth century was the creation of a monument to honor the birthplace of Joseph Smith Jr. The period surrounding the creation of this monument was one of rapid change in the LDS community. They had made a public declaration in 1890 that they would give up the practice of polygamy, an attempt to reconcile with their non-Mormon neighbors, who had increasingly pressured them politically, economically, and socially to give up the practice. The church was in an era of transition. In her work on turn-of-the-twentieth-century Mormonism, Kathleen Flake has noted that the dedication party who traveled from Utah to New York to dedicate the monument fulfilled an important function: to reassure Mormons that their foundations in divine revelation would remain secure, like the concrete and granite that made up the memorial, even while they were changing a practice, plural marriage, that had been declared by revelation. The concession to give up plural marriage allowed Mormons to be on a trajectory of becoming more like their American neighbors.[8] That trajectory was so successful, in part, because of the encouragement of church leaders. During the first half of the twentieth century, "Mormons became models of patriotic, law-abiding citizenship, sometimes seeming to 'out-American' all other Americans."[9]

In addition to generating more interest in monument building, Utah Mormons began in the late nineteenth century, very hesitantly, to ponder purchasing early historical sites. This idea first surfaced when they sought to acquire the temple in Kirtland, Ohio.[10] Courts became involved in the question of who owned the property and eventually determined that the COC was the rightful owner.[11] Individual Latter-day Saints focused their attention elsewhere and purchased lands and built monuments, but as an institution, the church did not actively pursue the purchase of historic sites and monument construction until the early twentieth century.[12] At that point Joseph F. Smith, the president of the church, began the process of acquiring some church properties, and subsequent presidents followed suit: Carthage Jail (1903); properties in Independence, Missouri (1904); Joseph Smith's birthplace (1905); the Smith family farm in Palmyra, New York (1908); Hill Cumorah in New York (1929); Winter Quarters (1936); the original temple site in Nauvoo (1937); and Liberty Jail (1939).[13] Of particular significance in this list is the purchase of Joseph Smith's birthplace, not only because of its importance in church history but because it was the first property that was developed with an eye to encouraging visitors and setting up a form of spiritual tourism.[14] It is important to note that the earliest attempts the church made to purchase and mark historical sites did not begin in the American West but focused on sites in the East, where the early church had formed.

Another way the Latter-day Saints changed the landscape was in the development of new temples. By 1900, the church had built temples in only six cities: Kirtland (1836), Nauvoo (1846), St. George (1877), Logan (1884), Manti (1888), and Salt Lake City (1893). At the turn of the century, the church controlled the four temples in Utah and had forty-three stakes and nineteen missions both in and outside the United States. Outside missions included Canada, western Europe, and the Pacific Islands. As the church continued to grow, its international presence became a focus of its leadership. David O. McKay, who became church president in 1951, saw building temples as a key aspect of his presidency and of making the church international. Not long after the mid-twentieth century, the church had temples in Hawaii, Canada, Arizona, and Idaho, and by the final quarter of the twentieth century in Switzerland, New Zealand, and England. At the same time, more temples were built in Utah and California. There are currently 164 temples, with thirty-one other sites in the works.[15]

Despite the growing number of temples, they do not mark the landscape in the same way the LDS historical sites do. What began very tentatively with historical sites in the late nineteenth century took real form in the early twentieth. While the first round of Mormons marking the landscape emphasized the historical nature of the sites, the method of marking incorporated an interesting admixture of the historical and the spiritual, the textual and *felt* religion.

On a national level, efforts to commemorate key American events took off in the early twentieth century as the United States was rapidly urbanizing and industrializing. Particularly in the American West, nostalgia for what was imagined as a simpler frontier life helped to spur the growth of monument building.[16] Americans wanted to narrate the West as the place where American values and identity were formed. At precisely the same time, Mormons were trying to prove to their fellow Americans that they were no longer an intolerable peculiarity but now an ideal neighbor. Following other Americans and taking up the activity of marking the landscapes, particularly in the American West, where Mormons could lay claim to that romanticized notion of pioneer life, helped them to claim a stake in American identity. Both the activity of marking and the message of heralding the pioneers emphasized their similarities to other Americans rather than their differences.

The endeavor to mark the landscapes of the American West, to sacralize and remember space, began in earnest for the Latter-day Saints with the creation of the UPTLA in 1930. Following in the footsteps of other groups around the country, the purpose of the UPTLA was "honoring the pathfinders and the pioneer builders of [Utah], preserving our historical heritage and developing our historical resources . . . [and] the teaching of the history of Utah in its all-American aspects and vital relations to the up-building of our west and our country."[17] In its stated purpose, the UPTLA heralded the founders of Utah and its history as "all-American," a claim to which the group firmly committed itself. From its inception, the UPTLA worked within church structures to further its causes. This commitment should come as no surprise given that George Albert Smith, then general superintendent of the church's Young Men's Mutual Improvement Association and later president of the church, served as president of the UPTLA, and John D. Giles, "Mr. Monuments" and an enthusiastic church member, was named executive secretary. The two, especially Giles, became wholehearted in their attempts to make the UPTLA's work thrive.[18] And so from the very beginning the civic organization was intimately tied to the LDS Church hierarchy and supported the public recognition of and display of Mormons' role in helping to build the nation.

The UPTLA was caught up in a national movement to preserve historical sites, particularly in the American West. The Association helped erect over forty monuments in its first five years. Taking inspiration from the Oregon Trail Memorial Association (OTMA), begun in 1926 by Ezra Meeker, leaders of the UPTLA sought to mark historical sites and create monuments that would help preserve public memory in Utah. A visit from Dr. Howard R. Driggs, a historian from New York who subsequently ran the OTMA, sealed Utahans' commitment to the new organization. Seven other western states had already participated in similar projects, and Driggs convinced Giles and other Utahans that they should join. Because of their connection, the OTMA authorized the UPTLA to sell Oregon Trail memorial coins to begin their first fundraising projects.[19] The first project the UPTLA undertook was funded by "Plains Dinners" held in local congregations, or wards, throughout the state, where attendees could enjoy a pioneer-type dinner and donate to the project of creating permanent markers at many church and state historical sites.[20]

"Our Pioneer heritage is to be preserved," claimed the 1931 UPTLA campaign. "After years of neglect we are now doing the things we should have done years ago." The Association's understanding of pioneer history included laying the foundation for "the great mountain empire."[21] Its constitution expressed a commitment to the pioneers by extending honorary membership to anyone who had come to Utah before 1869.[22] The Association carefully defined its role as to "coordinate the work of all other groups and to act as a clearing house for the activities" that fit with its mission. The Association also sought to "create interest among all the citizens of the state in this work."[23] And so the UPTLA worked with organizations like the Daughters of the Utah Pioneers and the Sons of the Utah Pioneers to help fund and support the celebration of Utah history throughout the state. While both the Sons and Daughters of the Utah Pioneers began to meet in the late nineteenth century, they gained momentum in the first few decades of the twentieth and have continued to this day. Their focus was also to remember the history of their ancestors and to find methods of retelling it to future generations so that they, too, would find meaning and value for their sense of identity. These two organizations did this in the form not of scholarly historical research but of ritual and monument.[24]

The UPTLA quickly got involved in a number of projects, especially in the state of Utah, but also along the Mormon Trail in other states. In a *Denver Post* article dated June 20, 1931, R. E. Evans, a writer for the *Post*, recounted the way Mormon officials were retracing the steps of pioneers and reported that a bronze marker would be dedicated at a campsite near Independence Rock, Wyoming. The dedicatory ceremony included the unveiling of the memorial, a speech by George Albert Smith, then president of the UPTLA, and John D. Giles, its secretary. There to accept the memorial was Howard R. Driggs, president of the OTMA, and former governor of Wyoming B. B. Brooks, then president of the Wyoming Historical Landmarks Commission. The group erected the marker near Independence Rock, a major landmark on the trail westward. "The reverence in which it is held by Mormons is explained by the importance it played in their migration," wrote Evans.

This marker was to join several others: one commemorating the 1862 first Masonic lodge ceremonial ever held in what became the state of Wyoming, one dedicated to Father Peter John De-Smet, the Jesuit missionary who carved his name on Independence Rock on June 13, 1840, and a tablet, dedicated by the OTMA, marking the spot as a key landmark on the trail westward. These monuments were part of a move to mark the spaces that were important to the history of the American West as several centennial anniversaries were approaching.

Just two years later, on June 22, 1933, George Albert Smith visited Martin's Cove, a site where many Mormon pioneers had perished, to set up a bronze memorial there. The memorial came after Smith and several others, including Joseph Fielding Smith, then the church historian, visited the area in 1932. The group wanted to find the exact location where many pioneers had died on the trail (discussed further in chapter 4). As one member of the group, Watson Loraine Rollins, retold the story, Joseph Fielding Smith became frustrated "because he couldn't get any inspiration or any feeling about where they were buried or where the graves were" and wanted to return to Salt Lake City. As they were leaving, one of the party members tripped and fell on his face. As he got up and went to see what had tripped him, he found part of the rim of a handcart wheel. Joseph Fielding Smith "stopped right there and said, 'I feel impressed that this is where the graves are.' " The men marked the spot, and Smith instructed the group to come back and construct a monument there.[25] Others in the party did not record the events with this much detail, but Giles later wrote that through this process, "which to many seems providential," they had also located the site of Willie Camp in Rock Creek Hollow.[26] Thus, the effort to be historically accurate and to find exact locations where historical events occurred was accompanied by a spiritual understanding that the divine would help them to *get it right*. These church leaders and landscape markers merged inspiration and prayer with historical accounts, believing that this process would yield the greatest accuracy.[27]

Interestingly, the process whereby church leaders found the site was not much different from their process for finding the site where Brigham Young presumably stood and looked out over the Salt Lake Valley. In both instances, they recognized the importance of historical research while also celebrating the movement of the spirit as the ultimate confirmation of a spatial truth. Historical memory and spatial politics intersect in intriguing ways in these instances. In this narrative, it was ultimately the material reality of a handcart wheel rim that confirmed for the party the spatial point where a historical event happened. Thus, the collective memory of the group did not hinge on the evidentiary requirements of professional historians but on the evidentiary requirements of a community of believers who understood the work of the Holy Spirit to be the confirmation of truth.

One of the concerns that arose again and again in the work of the UPTLA was the desire to be as historically accurate as possible about *where* important historical events occurred. Giles argued that this was difficult for nonmembers to understand: "before trails and landmarks can be marked correctly they must be searched out and the true history established. This is sometimes a more difficult and expensive task than the actual marking."[28] The desire to get it right, to know the precise latitude and longitude of certain events, stems from a number of impulses. First, accuracy was key to a community who wanted to preserve history for future generations, a community called to be a record-keeping people. Perhaps more important, though, the idea that the landscape itself might serve future generations in the appreciation of that history was tantamount.

The UPTLA also spent time developing a symbol that would mark historical sites not only as western but also as distinctly Utahan. They allowed that "the Oregon Trail has the covered wagon as its emblem. It represents all the migrations to the West." Wanting to be distinctive in their selection of an emblem that would tie the Mormons "most nearly with Utah's part in the winning of the West," the UPTLA chose the buffalo skull "as the most distinctive emblem of the Utah trail," likely because buffalo skulls were used as nineteenth-century trail markers and message posts.[29]

The UPTLA's members referred to the Association itself and Utah's history as "all American" and asserted that it was "confined to no group or sect."[30] Yet, unsurprisingly, the Association's leaders understood most of the history of the state to be Mormon history. "Because most of the early history of the Intermountain West was made by Mormons it is natural that most of the markers should be Mormon," declared Giles, "just as most of the markers in California are Catholic." And so even as the UPTLA marked spots important to the early history of trapping and exploration in the state of Utah, the Association's main emphasis lay on marking the path of the Mormon community westward and celebrating the Mormon pioneers as the founders of early twentieth-century Utah.

But it was not only Mormon or Utahan memory that the UPTLA sought to preserve, it was America's. Giles worried that the church or nation that forgot its story was "indeed lacking in vision," and he believed that the West was an especially important region in the nation's history. He maintained that the West had been neglected in national histories but the UPTLA's work would help right that wrong by preserving "the 'story spots' connected with the winning of the west for future generations" and bringing "to the attention of the present generation a realization of their responsibility to those whose heroic acts and sacrifices made possible the blessings we enjoy today."[31] Then the "story spots" could serve as locations where particular stories could be told to promote values deemed American, with the landscape serving as evidence. The landscape seemed to reinforce the facticity of the history, providing an aura of truth around the narratives and the values being offered at that location.

It was not just history, though, that the UPTLA wanted people to remember. That history had to be *marked on the landscape*. In an early edition of the UPTLA bulletin, this impulse received much attention. Paul Revere's ride was important, one author declared, but "it required that bronze marker on the spot to carry the light of that fact to this generation; to revive that historical event with living reality in our thought today!"[32] Without markers, the UPTLA claimed, history would recede from the collective memory of church members, and of citizens, and a subsequent loss of identity would accompany the loss of memory. Future generations would not know "the importance of [their] own destiny" because they would not understand their roots. "No community can afford to squander its historical resources. No community can afford to neglect its historical heritage. No community can afford to ignore the educational value of its history," claimed one bulletin.[33] But it was not enough to simply remember that history, it had to be *marked* so that the setting in which the history happened, the landscape itself, would not be "obliterated."

Marking had another important component to it that the UPTLA rarely discussed but that undergirded much of their work: inspiring tourism. The movement to create markers "further [capitalized on] Utah's climatic, and scenic attractions," formed it into a "truly storied empire," and ensured that Temple Square in downtown Salt Lake City would be "one of the greatest signal tourist Meccas in the world." Those claims were indeed hyperbolic, but the rhetoric the UPTLA employed was intended to inspire civic pride that would motivate donors. This effort to memorialize and mark the West was not the first or only attempt to claim Mormon sacred space. Yet the UPTLA's work was the first large-scale attempt to mark the entire journey West as *Mormon*. In so doing, Mormons claimed not only particular sites but an entire region as Mormon *and the founding of that region* as a Mormon activity. The UPTLA set up monuments all along the Mormon pioneer trail that merged church history with American history by asserting the significance of Mormon pioneers in the settlement of the West. In so doing, the UPTLA claimed a stake in American identity. All of the changes happening in the church, especially the struggle to maintain a sense of peoplehood while attempting to assimilate with other Americans, were, in part, worked out on the landscapes of the American West.

* * *

The same impulses embraced by the members of the UPTLA echoed throughout the twentieth century in various organizations. A more recent iteration, the Mormon Trails Association (MTA), formed in 1991. One leader described it as unique, but added that as "the successor of earlier trail associations going back to the '30s, the midwife of other current trail associations," it "must, should, ought, could, may, might be the mother hen of yet new and important associations."[34] The MTA formed, in part, in anticipation of the 1996 Utah Statehood Centennial and the 1997 Pioneer Sesquicentennial.

One goal was to work with the National Park Service to better preserve the trail.[35] The MTA's goal was to continue to accurately mark the westward movement of the pioneers an d to create monuments and materials that would celebrate that history. In the words of Stanley Kimball, a leader of the MTA, it was "not just a Mormon hobby" or a "Utah thing" but was "increasingly legitimate and important in US history."[36]

The members of the MTA, like the UPTLA, imagined their association as an umbrella organization that could "coordinate the efforts of interested groups and individuals, including the National Park Service and other government agencies as well as historic, civic and Church-related organizations." The MTA worked closely with the National Park Service to develop "a system of wayside . . . interpretive panels," "a system of auto tour route signs," and appropriate markers for the trail.[37] The Association also worked with the Bureau of Land Management, which managed some of the trail land and wanted to ensure the preservation of the viewscape along the route. Along with these governmental organizations, the Oregon-California Trails Association and the Daughters of the Utah Pioneers, two groups that had been friends of the UPTLA as well, also cooperated with the MTA.

As part of the effort, the MTA began its work by attempting to refine and standardize maps of the trail. In this, they faced a set of questions similar to those the UPTLA had faced decades before. How should they find the exact spots on the trail? "There are some fuzzy places where it's hard to tell if the trail was here or maybe a mile or two over there," recalled William G. Hartley, the MTA's chair and associate professor of history at Brigham Young University. He identified Iowa as the most difficult place to map the trail because, he said, "it does not have landmarks in terms of mountains and peaks and major rivers." Because the pioneers "didn't have landmarks to record as they went across the plains," Hartley and his fellow MTA mapmakers were hard-pressed to identify the exact trail in the terrain.[38]

After map-making and the development of guide books, the MTA focused its attention first on the state of Utah, so the markers could be placed along the trail before the 1996 and 1997 celebrations. The Association pursued these goals precisely because the members believed that the trail was significant in the lives of Mormons and the people of Utah more generally. The MTA recognized that the celebrations each year enabled "facts and myths [to be] repeated, and values . . . reinforced." Their hope was that following the trail would be an experience of "seeing the trail for the first time" and would bring a new and "expanded meaning" that would "be as important for most people as anything else done in celebration of the settlement of the valley."[39] Marking became an activity to honor the space for what had happened in it, and in marking, the MTA believed that they could enhance the experiences of visitors to the space. The MTA's goal was for visitors to have meaningful encounters with the space and its history, thereby reinforcing the values considered to be Mormon and American in the late twentieth century.

The MTA's members even imagined what the Mormon Trail might look like in 1997, as part of a goad to encourage members to work as hard as possible toward realizing their goals of mapping and marking. "It's early March," a visionary flyer read; "a family sits at the dining room table reviewing material on the Mormon Pioneer National Historic Trail." The family in this scenario decides to go and enjoy the entire trail. They begin in Nauvoo and then head off: "with a large envelope of state highway maps, trail maps and brochures in hand . . . [they] follow the well-signed *auto tour route* through Iowa." As the family travels, they encounter signs that show them the way, markers that identify particularly important sites, wayside exhibits that explain the history to them, and parks and museums that enhance their understanding of place.

As the family drives west, they listen to cassette tapes and CDs that explain the pioneer experiences. At the same time, they enjoy using their four-wheel-drive vehicle to explore the western landscapes. Even as they imagined making the trail meaningful for visitors, the MTA also noted and promoted recreational opportunities. Finally, the family enters Utah, and "the anticipation builds for the first glimpse of the Great Salt Lake Valley and they wonder what the anticipation must have been like after four months on the trail." Continuing on past more markers and appreciating the landscape, they finally arrive at TITP Park and spend their final few days sightseeing in Salt Lake City before heading home.[40] The MTA's imagined family trip explains much about its mission. The Association understood its primary goal to be providing the materials—the maps, pamphlets, and markers—that would enable a meaningful and enjoyable experience of the trail. The goal was to promote an *experiential* approach to the trail. That experiential approach merged religious and value lessons with sightseeing and recreation to create an all-encompassing experience for visitors.

This hope for an experiential knowledge of history is evidenced throughout the MTA's newsletters. In 1996, *Trail News* included an article that explained that the trail was "a living, breathing representative of our heritage." The trail was imagined as a character in the story, and visitors might experience "the power of place and the power of locale." The newsletter even referred to the trail as a "lineal temple." What might that name point to? That the trail was a sacred space, most obviously—that it was a place where people could, through engaging in ritual activities, learn the truth claims of their faith tradition. A lineal temple would allow Mormons to kinesthetically and spatially experience their tradition in a new way. It was map and metaphor, space and history.

Phase 2: Feeling Authenticity in the Lineal Temple

Describing the Mormon Battalion visitors' center in Old Town San Diego, California, historian Colleen McDannell calls what is going on there "heritage religion": "a set of generic religious beliefs, cast into the past, and translated into media and material culture." Both McDannell and Michael Madsen have identified a key shift in Mormons' understandings of space and history in the late twentieth century. While some movement happened in earlier decades, that shift took firm hold with the presidency of Gordon B. Hinckley, who believed that religious commitment could be inspired by interactions with Mormon history and taught that the LDS community needed to be bound to place and a geographical center.[41] This emphasis on rooting the LDS tradition in place happened alongside a larger interest in American culture in engaging history. Within the LDS community, engaging history intersected with an embrace of the idea that one could *feel religion*.

The shift within Mormonism toward history as a medium for engaging theology and religious experience was accompanied by an increased emphasis on space. As the church continued to become more globalized, the institution emphasized center spaces that could bind the people together.[42] Storying those spaces became a primary activity of the late twentieth and early twenty-first centuries, and storying became the process whereby the church and its members collectively sanctified those spaces. Yet, as Madsen argues, that sanctification process has been primarily in the hands of the institution, which is "currently engineering the creation of 'sacred space'" in a top-down process.[43] That sanctification has put the institution in a powerful position. It has enabled the institutional church to "*reinforce* the official history that acts as a centripetal force that binds members to the Church through the construction of Mormon identity." At the same time that these stories can function to bind insiders together, they also allow the church to "present a carefully constructed image of itself to the 'outside' world."[44] In so doing, the church crafts narratives that speak to insiders about who they are while confirming to outsiders that church members are fellow Americans with shared values and visions for the future.

Over the course of the twentieth century, Americans sought to experience history in new ways, becoming "avid and appreciative consumers of heritage."[45] This turn was accompanied by a desire for authenticity that is perhaps best represented by the development of Colonial Williamsburg into a massive living history site in the late twentieth century. At Mormon historical sites, missionaries function in the same role as the historical personnel at Colonial Williamsburg. In both instances these people on the "front lines" are reinforced by historians, curators, and librarians, who work to create the stories that are told to visitors.[46] For the LDS Church, missionaries, who fund their own missions, serve as inexpensive labor for the church's sites. Missionaries at the sites are also at the ready to make theological ties between history and belief.[47] The crafted historical narratives are made for public consumption and seek to provide an authentic experience for visitors while also presenting a rather romanticized notion of the simplicity of the past.[48] Because of the cues provided at such living history sites, visitors *feel* as though they are getting "just the facts" of history rather than an interpretation. In turn, that impulse to provide just the facts allows for "the teeth of critical history" to be pulled.[49] In the late twentieth century, the church developed a way of leading visitors through historical sites while promoting a particular theological interpretation through the sharing of historical narratives. The popularity of the sites grew, and the church decided to invest millions of dollars in historical sites, visitors' centers, and historical restorations. In the 1990s it developed a master plan that prioritized sites and purchases. The plan focused on major sites and then suggested that the church could then invest in more regional sites once the top tier had been completed.[50]

And so efforts by the MTA and the LDS Church have created a series of summertime activities that Mormon and non-Mormon tourists may explore. Between Nauvoo and Council Bluffs, Iowa, a road called the "Mormon Trail Auto Tour" marks a very twentieth-century space that follows the path the nineteenth-century pioneers traveled. Along the route, signs with the buffalo skull, the symbol of the Mormon Trail, dot the landscape. At times, a sign indicates that the modern road is actually crossing the Mormon Trail itself. Aside from these signs, businesses like the Mormon Trail Hotel in Omaha, Nebraska, help mark the space as Mormon space. On the road there are a few historical places that can be visited; one of these, Mount Pisgah, is a small park and cemetery in Iowa where several pioneers were buried along the way. Church member Oliver B. Huntington purchased the site in 1888, wanting to memorialize the pioneers.[51] A modern sign marks the spot, explaining that the biblical Mount Pisgah was the site from which Moses stood and looked down into the promised land. Why would the Mormons, then, call a place in Iowa Mount Pisgah? The sign explains that as Parley P. Pratt, a leader in the church, approached this area, "he saw the beautiful Grand River Valley below him and felt that he could see the Mormon 'Zion.'" Pratt had gone ahead of the main body of pioneers to find a place where they could camp after crossing muddy Iowa. "Perhaps Pratt was not actually viewing the promised land from this hilltop, as the name Mount Pisgah suggests. However, the beauty and abundance of this site provided a welcome respite for the Pioneers," the sign proclaims. Interestingly, the sign-makers seem to have wanted to assure visitors that Pratt did not actually believe he had found the New Zion and that Zion is a static, easily identifiable place.

Other signage explains that this was a way-station along the route, that thousands of Mormons passed through, and that somewhere between 300 and 800 died along the way. Another sign makes an intriguing connection between Native Americans and Latter-day Saints. The sign declares: "soon after the Mormons arrived here the renowned Indian Chief Pied Riche came to bid them welcome and tell them how the Pottawattamie Indians had likewise been driven from their homeland in what is now Michigan." Chief Pied Riche is quoted as having said to the Mormons: "we must help one another, and the Great Spirit will help us both. Because one suffers and does not deserve it is no reason he shall suffer always. We may live to see it right yet. If we do not, our children will." As a collective, the signs tell an interesting narrative. Mormons are likened to the Jews on their journey from oppressors to find their promised land and likened to an American people who were oppressed, whose members were run out of their land by others. Collectively, the signs promise a future that will be different from the past of oppression and displacement.

Further on, on the border between Iowa and Nebraska, is a modern-technological site built by the LDS Church to mark the place where the Saints wintered before heading west to Utah. The Winter Quarters site deserves a detailed look because it is a place that witnessed both of the phases this chapter discusses: first, the efforts to mark Mormon history on the American landscape, and second, the spiritual and aesthetic turn of the late twentieth century.

Brigham Young made the choice to stop at Winter Quarters on the way west because both the people and their livestock needed to rest. It was too late in the year for their journey to continue with enough time to safely arrive in the West. At Winter Quarters, the people built a community of huts and cabins, trying to set up a temporary life. Even with their crops and supplies, their diet was not particularly good; it consisted primarily of bacon, corn products, and milk. Because of this poor diet, many in the camp developed fevers, scurvy, tuberculosis, and malaria. From 1846 through 1848, more than 600 Mormons died at their camp at Winter Quarters.[52] The site is one of promise (they were on their way to Zion after all) and sorrow (for those who would never achieve that Zion).

The burial ground where the Mormons who died were laid to rest did not receive much attention for many decades. It was not until 1924 that the Daughters of the American Revolution first marked it with a board inscription and later, in 1932, a bronze plaque.[53] One of the visitors to the cemetery when it was in a state of decay was Avard T. Fairbanks, a Beaux Arts tradition sculptor. He was himself a Mormon and had family members who died at Winter Quarters. Because of his personal connection to the place, Fairbanks offered to create two sculptures—one representing sorrow and one hope, both symbolizing the same place. His *Tragedy at Winter Quarters* was one of the two sculptures at the LDS Church's exhibit at the Chicago World Fair in 1933 and 1934 (see Figure 2.2).[54]

Fairbanks first imagined what the sculpture would look like after his visit to the neglected cemetery. But that imagining developed further as he gave demonstration lectures in Utah and told the story of the grieving pioneers.[55] Each time he made a clay version of the sculpture, it grew in size. The completed sculpture shows a man and woman sharing a moment of grief, both wrapped in a cloak to shelter them from the elements. The man holds in his right hand a shovel, indicating that he has just finished digging a grave for a child the couple has lost. As Fairbanks developed the sculpture and raised support, church leaders signed a fifty-year lease for the land the cemetery was on in 1936; the lease required the church to beautify the grounds, finally gaining some attention for the place.[56]

The dedication of the monument and its surrounds occurred on September 20, 1936. John Widtsoe, a member of the Council of the Twelve, the church's governing council, attended the events and recalled that it was a celebration of "a courageous people [who] sacrificed life itself for the building of a western empire wherein they could assure to themselves and their children and their children's children the right to worship and the right to live peaceably." Emphasizing several times that Winter Quarters was about people

Figure 2.2 Tragedy at Winter Quarters.

seeking the freedom to worship, Widtsoe recalled: "now the representatives of Church and State from Nebraska and surrounding states and from the far west have gathered to honor the memory of the men and women who were once ejected by religious intolerance." Interestingly, he never named those who persecuted the Mormons but placed Mormons in the center of narratives about the meaning of "American." They could be celebrated, where once they had not been tolerated. They could be praised as American pioneers in the service of American values, freedoms, and empire.

Widtsoe noted that the initial marker read "Old Pioneer Cemetery. Here were buried 600 of Nebraska's first white settlers, 1846–47." Then he declared: "the 'First White Settlers' were Latter-day Saints who had been driven from their homes the year before."[57] Naming and claiming the dead as persecuted and Mormon, while at the same time placing them at the heart of American identity, Widstoe emphasized precisely why marking Mormon sites was so important to the church in this first phase. Most significant, the audience celebrating the sculpture was made up of both church members and authorities (including the church's president, Heber J. Grant) and nonmembers, including the mayor of Omaha, Dan Butler, the governor of Nebraska, Robert LeRoy Cochran, and members of the Omaha Chamber of Commerce.

Fairbanks worked with a landscape designer, Irvin T. Nelson, and a stone carver to design the cemetery and garner for it the respect he believed it deserved. His grandson describes *Tragedy* and its surrounds this way:

> it is situated on a high hill commanding a view of Omaha and the Missouri River. It was placed on a pedestal cut from granite quarried in Little Cottonwood Canyon, the same granite used in building the Salt Lake Temple. Immediately around the monument is a sunken enclosure, or court, set off in Utah sandstone masonry. A few yards in front of the solemn figure is a great bronze panel nineteen feet wide on which are listed names of about four hundred of the known dead. In the center of the panel is the striking figure of a young man symbolic of the resurrection, stretching out his hands and giving the message: "Life is Eternal." Behind him are concentric radiant beams of the resurrected glory. These rays continue divergent from this figure between the pavement blocks of the court crossed by concentric arcs. There are two areas where headstones of seven graves were found during the excavation. Spreading evergreen junipers were planted over the graves in place of concrete.[58]

Dedicated in 1997, the Winter Quarters of today has a visitors' center and represents the second phase in Mormon historical memorializing, with its emphasis on the spiritual and aesthetic, as well as the experiential aspects of engaging history and religion. In 2017, the website for Winter Quarters promised visitors that they could "witness glimpses of the great 'Mormon Migration' as you walk beside a covered wagon, pull a handcart, climb in the bunks on a steam ship, and imagine a railroad journey."[59] Approaching

Figure 2.3 Handcarts.

the entrance, visitors see a bronze sculpture facing westward. In *Handcarts*, sculpted by Franz Johnson, seven figures all lean in that direction as though ever pulling their handcart toward the future. A young boy with a rope in his hands leads the way, his rope tied to the handcart rail. Between the pulls of the handcart is a man flanked by a woman and a daughter. Further back, an older gentleman adds his strength to turning the large wheels, and another young woman walks along the mother's side. The sculpture communicates the essence of what the creators of the site want visitors to see inside, a narrative of people communally struggling to move westward toward their promised land, their Zion.

At the dedication ceremony on April 18, 1997, President Gordon Hinckley, standing in front of a log cabin display, declared that the visitors' center was "a beautiful structure designed to memorialize those who came here in 1846 and subsequent years." "What we do today," he said, "is celebrate . . . the beginning of that journey from here and memorialize those who participated." Drawing on themes Widstoe emphasized at the 1936 sculpture dedication, Hinckley claimed that the Mormon Trail "is fraught with nobility, courage, faith, loyalty, sacrifice, every virtue, I think, that one can think of." And so Hinckley stood in a line of church authorities who placed the traits of Mormon pioneers at the center of American identity. At the same time, Hinckley articulated a position about history that he took many times throughout his presidency: that history provides lessons for the future. "It is good to look to the past, to gird up and face the future." So it was to history that current Mormons should turn for examples of how to live. When asked how Brigham Young might feel about the church today, Hinckley declared: "I think he would be highly pleased to see what has become of the church." Describing a portrait of Young that hung in his office, Hinckley explained that "his eyes are on me," and that Hinckley had heard him saying: "do your best, boy. Keep going."[60]

In 1999, the institutional church announced that it was going to construct a temple in Winter Quarters, Nebraska. This choice was part of a larger decision that included building temples in Palmyra and Nauvoo. Built between 2000 and 2002 and under the presidency of Gordon Hinckley, these three sites do not represent a massive population boom of Mormons in their surrounding areas. While population density is the primary reason that new temples are built around the world, Palmyra, Nauvoo, and Winter Quarters represent something else. In the words of Michael Madsen: "the presence of these temples will serve to reinforce for generations of Mormons to come the understanding that the places in which the LDS Church's history unfolded are sacred places, and that they, as Mormons, are tied to them."[61] The temple at Winter Quarters serves as another step in the process of claiming that place as sacred space. When the temple was announced in 1999, the city of Omaha transferred the lands on which the cemetery sits, the lands the church once leased, to the church.[62] Now the church has sanctified the ground and owns it, reinforcing its claim to interpret and narrate the place.

The film visitors watch when they enter the visitors' center reinforces Hinckley's vision of history and a place anchoring contemporary Mormon faith. Two of the most common words used in the film are "gather," as both pioneer and immigrant Saints were told to gather together, away from the world, and "Zion." The film tells the story of the pioneers who used up their provisions crossing Iowa and were sick and near death when they arrived at Winter Quarters. Many people died in that spot of scurvy and other ailments that could not be cured, yet the Mormons continued "their search for Zion." Amid National Geographic–esque images of landscapes and sunsets, the film narrates pioneer and immigrant narratives. Once the narrative gets the Saints to Salt Lake, they have reached their "Zion" and are "home at last."

The exhibits throughout the center continue the themes set forth in the film. The first station, called "Beginning of an American Exodus," tells the story that Mormons "were forced to abandon their temple and city" in Illinois and "pressed west with courage and determination." Panels describe the pioneers as understanding themselves as "exiles cast into the wilderness, yet . . . buoyed up by their faith in God and the promise of an eternal life." Exhibits show the materials the Saints brought with them, along with the research Brigham Young did in advance of their departure westward. Once prepared for the exodus, the stations proclaim that the Saints entered "Into the Wilderness." Another station along the way explains that on April 15, 1846, William Clayton, on hearing of the birth of a son to his wife, who had stayed in Nauvoo to care for her ailing parents, wrote the most well-known Mormon hymn, "Come, Come Ye Saints." The signage explains that a marker stands at the spot where Clayton stood when he penned the tune and that visitors can go and visit that place today. The hymn instructs the saints to "with joy wend your way" even though the journey may appear hard. "Why should we mourn or think our lot is hard?" and "Why should we think to earn a great reward, if we now shun the fight?" asks the hymn. The final two stanzas promise: "We'll find the place which God for us prepared / Far away in the West, / Where none shall come to hurt or make afraid / There the Saints will be blessed."

Clearly embracing and crafting parallels between the biblical exodus and the Mormon journey west, Winter Quarters is referred to as "A Temporary Home in the Wilderness" where the Saints stopped and "paused only briefly on the way to their promised land." And stations throughout describe the departure from Winter Quarters as motivated by a focus on "locating Zion and designating a site for a temple": the pioneers "viewed their trek as a sacred journey to their promised land." The experiential emphasis appears throughout the visitors' center. One display, designed for children, encourages them to load small wooden blocks labeled as supplies into a covered wagon, trying to make them fit. As they are doing this, a missionary times them: "hurry up! You can hear the gunshots!" she says, as she tries to make the packing of a miniature covered wagon provide some sense of simulation of the past.[63]

Included in the narrative told at the center is an understanding that the first pioneers would not be the last and so those who went first marked the way, measuring the route, noting the landscapes, and establishing ferries, because as church leader Wilford Woodruff noted, "it should be understood that we are piloting the road for the House of Israel to travel for many years to come." Virtually every station repeats the concepts of exodus, gathering, and Zion. Finally, on reaching "a new home in the west," the Saints built temples "at the end of the trail for the thousands of Latter-day Saints who gathered to Zion."

One of the key messages of the Winter Quarters visitors' center is theological: the pioneers are models for us today; though we do not have physical hardships, we do have unseen ones, and we, too, can overcome them with faith in God. In order to promote this lesson, the site has a large chest full of pioneer clothes: bonnets, shawls, and skirts are available to women, and men can choose from vests and hats. Once dressed as the pioneers, visitors can pull a handcart across the room. Sensing that it is fairly easy to pull an empty handcart across a carpeted floor, missionaries then place small rocks underneath the wheels of the handcart, and visitors are asked to again pull it across the room. Missionaries remind visitors that the carts were full and the landscape was rocky: "just think of how many rocks *they* had to overcome," said our missionary guide in 2014.

One room in the center stands out from the others, set apart by the floor plan as a separate place. The room has windows on three sides that look out over the cemetery outside. In one corner of the room is a facsimile of a partial gravestone found nearby. In another stands a small copy of *Tragedy at Winter Quarters*. The room's purpose is to ensure that the sacrifices "never be forgotten." Our missionary guide offered an interpretation of both versions of *Tragedy* that was rather interesting. In the room with the small copy, the guide pointed out that the man in the sculpture stood with one foot in front of the other and that his front foot was pointed toward an image of Jesus standing across the room. "He is still moving in the right direction even after all that has happened to him," she noted. She encouraged me to look at the back of the sculpture at a tree that grows up the back of the couple. She noted that the tree represents hidden obstacles we can't see that grab us and try to hold us back. This was a particularly interesting moment for me because (1) had I been left to my own interpretation, I would have said that the tree was actually holding the couple up in their grief, and (2) more important, I had the artwork interpreted for me as I was moving through the site. Thus, the missionary was controlling both narrative and interpretation. She then commented that the original full-size sculpture also had significant placement: there, too, the man's foot was pointed toward the adjacent temple, again moving toward what was good in the world. Even though the sculpture was already in place when the temple opened in 2001, the missionary understood it to be symbolic truth: obstacles drag people down; faith and the temple will help them overcome. The room itself suggests to the visitor that it is a place set apart; it is neither fun nor historical but a place of sorrow, moving visitors through many emotional responses to the narrative it tells. And missionaries suggest to visitors that the room represents the sacrifice faith can require.

How scholars interpret *Tragedy* varies, even though only one interpretation is offered at the visitors' center. One scholar of American western monuments, Cynthia Culber Prescott, sees in the sculpture an emphasis on the man as patriarch of the family. He is holding his wife and is in an "active pose and proximity to the viewer," and his stance has "eclipsed both the honored mother and their young son, for whom the statue is named."[64] Prescott argues that the sculpture represents notions of the family at the time it was sculpted. Another scholar of Fairbanks's work, Kent Ahrens, argues that "seen from the back, the dead knurled tree against the man's great wind swept cloak heightens the sense of cold and despair."[65]

Winter Quarters embodies many of the themes I will explore further in the coming chapters. At one and the same time it is graveyard, museum, playground, and a link in the lineal temple, the sacred space the LDS Church and its members are creating in the twenty-first century. At Winter Quarters visitors can engage LDS history kinesthetically. They can do so in a visitors' center set up to distill history into simple and easily absorbable value lessons. At the same time, they experience messages saying that Latter-day Saints were and are part of the spread of the American empire westward: that Latter-day Saints embody the values represented in the quest of the nineteenth-century pioneers.

Figure 3.1 *Eyes Westward*, This Is The Place Park.

3

Eyes Westward

The Smithification of the American West

Standing on the banks of the Mississippi River in Nauvoo, Illinois, is a bronze statue of Joseph Smith and Brigham Young called *Eyes Westward*. Joseph has his right hand on Brigham's back, as though supporting him, as they look west, across the Mississippi River (see Figure 3.1). In Young's right hand is a scroll with the words "Map of the Rockies" written on it. Both men are gazing in the same direction, sharing a vision with one another. The statue marks several boundaries: the boundary between the eastern United States that was the Saints' past and the West that was their future; today's boundary between the Nauvoo lands owned by the LDS Church (the group that followed Brigham Young West to Utah) and the Nauvoo lands owned by the COC (the church that stayed in the Midwest and eventually came together under the leadership of Joseph Smith III, the prophet's son); and the boundary between the two religious communities' understandings of prophetic activity, sacred space, and historical memory. *Eyes Westward* is a statue that attempts to ignore the contested boundaries by asserting a confident and simple narrative—by suggesting that there are no historical ambiguities.

Over 1,200 miles away in Salt Lake City, at the end of the pioneers' 1847 journey in the place now called TITP Park, is a copy of *Eyes Westward*. This statue, placed in 2009, is the first thing visitors see as they get out of their cars and walk toward the visitors' center. Here, also, Joseph and Brigham lean toward one another and gaze out into the future. Perhaps nowhere else can we see the intersections of space and historical memory better. Two statues, over 1,000 miles apart, stand as bookends to the narratives told about the Latter-day Saints' journey. The statue on the Mississippi gazes toward Salt Lake; the statue in Salt Lake gazes toward the Great Basin, positioned so that the two prophets gaze toward the valley where the Saints settled. Thus, the setting of the Salt Lake statue suggests that the valley itself is the fulfillment of the shared prophetic vision of Joseph Smith Jr. and Brigham Young.[1]

Pioneers in the Attic. Sara M. Patterson, Oxford University Press (2020). © Oxford University Press.
DOI: 10.1093/oso/9780190933869.001.0001

Why wasn't one version of *Eyes Westward* enough? What might account for two copies of the same statue more than 1,000 miles apart?[2] These two statues point to a process begun in earnest in the twentieth century and coming to full fruition in the twenty-first that I call the Smithification of the American West. Joseph Smith never made it very far west of the Mississippi, yet the Mormons who followed Young built a home in Utah and began to call it Zion. The Smithification of the West refers to the process whereby Utah Mormons embraced and emphasized a historical narrative that proclaimed that the prophet Joseph Smith had known all along that the Mormons would wind up in Utah. The narrative asserts that Young inherited the prophetic vision as he did the prophetic office from Smith and that Smith understood in a prophetic, spatial, and kinesthetic way all that would transpire after his death. It suggests not only that Young was the rightful heir to Smith's prophetic office but also that Smith intimately knew the landscapes of the American West because he had seen them in prophetic vision. The narrative recalls that just as the biblical prophet Isaiah foresaw the movement to the Salt Lake Valley, so, too, did Joseph Smith. He saw the mountains and the valley just as visitors to TITP Park can today. They can stand not only in Young's spot but also in Joseph's, and they can read the evidence that "this is the place" on the landscape. Thus the narrative proclaims that the prophets from the biblical Isaiah all the way to Joseph Smith Jr. fully and physically anticipated the Utah valleys and mountains as the home of God's people.

The Smithification narrative retold over and over again highlights the prophetic rather than the practical aspects of the journey westward. It suggests that with the death of their prophet, Joseph, the Saints could only move westward *and* follow Brigham Young. The narrative has an air of inevitability. That narrative, though, is told over and against other narratives. It is asserted as emphatically as possible, and evidence is shored up against other possible narratives, including the ones told by the COC.[3]

The stories told during the process of Smithifying the American West allowed the Latter-day Saints of Utah to affirm that their exodus westward was divinely ordained. Not only that, but Smithification allowed them to see a continuity between the church's history before Smith's death and after. What might well have been read as a rupture in the historical narrative—the death of a founder and the sense that the people must leave the place where he died—was later reinterpreted as tragic, but a step in a larger journey. The spatial movement from place to place, from Zion to Zion, paralleled the first movement from prophet to prophet. And so a narrative developed that allowed for both those transitions to be understood as mutually reinforcing one another, as part and parcel of a divine plan—and of a God that moved in history and in place.

Thus, the Smithification of the American West has an important spatial component while also being about history telling. The legitimacy of the prophetic office is tied to spatial evidence, and there is much the Latter-day Saints have done to mark the landscape and interpret it for visitors so that they will conclude that the narrative told is true.[4] *Eyes Westward* claims that Joseph Smith Jr. knew that the Saints would end up journeying West and building a new Zion there. It asserts that he prophesied and endorsed that journey and the subsequent history-making and space-shaping that followed in the wake of that journey to a new Zion.

While this chapter is interested in the question of the narratives crafted in the late twentieth and early twenty-first centuries to cement the idea first promoted in the nineteenth century that Smith knew and anticipated the West, it will explore how that narrative is framed in terms of material memory along the Mormon Trail. It asks how monuments and places along that trail, which one group of memory-makers called a "lineal temple," mark the narrative on the material world so that pilgrims and visitors to the sites can see and touch the narrative.[5] With the 2005 bicentennial celebration of Smith's birth coming directly on the heels of the 1997 sesquicentennial celebration of the Mormons' arrival in the Salt Lake Valley, the joining of these two narratives—of a new prophet founding a new church and of a people's move to their promised land—became an especially important project. Even in the twenty-first century, as the LDS Church continues to expand globally, with more and more members living outside the United States, the memory work of claiming space and creating a seamless narrative of prophetic activity is still important to the collective memory of the people. Mormons today continue to mark the landscapes of the American West as sacred space and to invite pilgrims to physically engage the history of their people.

Latter-day Saints and the Community of Christ

Before continuing with an analysis of the intersections of space, historical narrative and prophetic office, I would like to further explore the differences between these two Mormon traditions that claim Joseph Smith Jr. as their founding prophet. Perhaps the most obvious and well-known of the differences is the argument about who would succeed Joseph Smith. Whereas the Mormons who went to Utah followed the majority of the Quorum of the Twelve and Brigham Young, the group who came to be known as the Reorganized Latter Day Saints (and later as the COC) stayed in the Midwest and eventually rallied around Joseph Smith III as the rightful successor to the prophetic office. The disagreements do not end there, though. Because of disagreements about the position of prophet, the process of history-telling began to develop quite differently. Perhaps most important, the two groups disagreed about the relationship of Joseph Smith Jr. in the practice of plural marriage. Although the Utah Saints embraced the practice and publicly announced it in 1852 as a core part of their religious lives, the midwestern believers refused to participate and suggested in their own historical narratives that Brigham Young had invented the practice and then lied about Joseph Smith's participation in plural marriage just to buttress his authority and legitimize polygamy. The COC thus emphatically proclaimed, to the extent that they hung aspects of their identity on the narrative, that plural marriage was a far cry from the orthodoxy of Joseph Smith. A key source of evidence for their claims was Emma Smith, the prophet's first wife, who maintained for the rest of her life that she had had a monogamous relationship with Smith and that Brigham Young had brought polygamy into the tradition.

One problem with the history-telling that still creates a palpable tension in modern-day Nauvoo is the issue of Smith's polygamous marriages and any other aspects of his life that would today be seen as less than desirable in historical narratives. As visitors walk through the Nauvoo spaces owned by both churches where Smith lived and moved in the final years of his life, they encounter much discussion of Emma as his wife, as well as several portrayals of him as a modern-day family man, but there is little acknowledgment of what that family consisted of, other than when visitor inquiries prompt a response. This absence/erasure has been called the sanitization of Mormon history, an action performed to recast the narrative so as to communicate that the Saints are truly American.[6] In similar fashion, narratives about Smith's destruction of the press in Nauvoo are sanitized as well.

Guides at Nauvoo do not acknowledge that the dissenting founders of the press arose from among the church membership. That Smith led the charge against the press and ordered it to be destroyed is softened by a narrative that recounts a government ordering the destruction of the press in self-defense. Why? Just as Smith's polygamy seems un-American to modern-day ears, so, too, does the destruction of a press. It appears antithetical to the First

Amendment values Americans hold so dear. Thus, the overall narrative is vague, who acted in which ways is unclear, and the passive voice is rife in each story; in this context, the history of Smith's life and death are simplified and sanitized for modern-day consumption.

Each group, away from the other, developed in the late nineteenth and early twentieth centuries its own ways of practicing rituals and of understanding the role and function of the temple. For my purposes, a significant difference developed between the two groups' understandings of the concept of Zion. In 1943, the presiding patriarch of the Reorganized Latter Day Saints, Elbert A. Smith, wrote: "we have come to differ over the question of location, at least temporarily so. Ever since their migration to Utah, the Mormons have designated it as Zion. We have held to the position that Missouri was designated as Zion."[7] Interestingly, in a demonstration of identity, history, and place being intertwined, this same church leader explained: "today the *Doctrine and Covenants* as published by the Utah Mormon Church contains nothing claiming to be a revelation coming through any of their presidents since they entered what is now the State of Utah; of such it is sterile and barren."[8] Here the patriarch suggested that landscapes themselves either promote or retard prophetic activity and that the Utah Mormons had moved to a place that not only was *not Zion* but was a revelatory desert as well. Such claims represent the ways both sides attempted to define themselves against one another based on the intersections of space and religious activity.

Carthage

It may sound odd to begin an exploration of the Smithification of the American West with a discussion of Carthage, Illinois; first, because today Illinois is not often thought of as the "West," and second, because it was the place where Joseph Smith died, not where plans about the future movement of the Saints were hammered out, not where future prophets were chosen, not even where many Mormons lived when the deaths happened. Yet today Carthage is an interesting site because it plays a role in the spatial narratives told by the Latter-day Saints who control the space where Smith was murdered and, by controlling it, get to begin the narrative westward there. Unlike Nauvoo, which will be discussed later, Carthage does not bear the burden of negotiating competing claims for the ownership of space and historical narratives.

Purchased in 1903, Carthage Jail is owned and narrated solely by Latter-day Saints. But it is an important beginning to the narrative of the American West told by the Utah Mormons. The narrative they tell might begin: "it all starts with the martyrdom of our prophet who stood in a long line of prophets."

The pamphlet the LDS Church offers visitors to Carthage supports this narrative. "Events Leading to Martyrdom" is the first heading; the second is "Martyrdom." The passages explain that "Joseph Smith was the subject of much persecution." They recall that the Mormons settled peacefully in Nauvoo but experienced much animosity and terrible treatment from the locals. When the city council, led by Joseph Smith as mayor, ordered the destruction of a newspaper press, many became angry and brought charges against the council. The narrative crafted here portrays Smith as an unsuspecting innocent who felt that he was " 'going like a lamb to the slaughter' " when he turned himself in at Carthage.[9]

That the site is understood and interpreted as a site of martyrdom is evident on arrival. When I arrived at Carthage in the summer of 2015, across the gardens and grounds, people were praying, some silently weeping, while others sat intensely involved in their prayers. It was clear that they considered this site a sacred one. A walkway lined with plaques bearing quotations from Joseph Smith leads toward a central bronze statue of Joseph Smith and his brother Hyrum that was created by D. J. Bawden, a member of the LDS Church whose religiously themed artwork is popular among his fellow members.[10] These statues were made part of the Carthage Jail block and dedicated in 1989. Joseph stares confidently ahead with the Book of Mormon in his right hand. Hyrum stands a bit behind his brother, appearing to support him as they journey forward. The two men are remembered in this place as men "who sealed their testimonies of the restored gospel of Jesus Christ with their lives." The two men look off into the distance, confident in their gaze, their faith, and their fate (see Figure 3.2).

The tour of Carthage Jail begins with a film, "Impressions of a Prophet," and played in a room with a dozen Kleenex boxes scattered about. The Kleenex boxes serve as gentle promptings, suggesting to visitors the weightiness of the historical narrative they are about to hear and the gravity of the place. As discussed before, the boxes serve a symbolic function, letting viewers know that the appropriate emotional response to the film is to cry for what was lost and to wish that Smith's life had not ended at that time or in that way.

The film includes contemporaries' memories of Joseph Smith. The narrators offer the perspective of Smith's mother on who he was as a child

Figure 3.2 Statue of Joseph and Hyrum Smith outside Carthage Jail.

alongside the accounts of other family members. Once Joseph is older, the recollections are from others outside the family. A carefully constructed narrative is shaped for modern-day visitors through the use of historical figures' recollections. First, a Catholic priest remembers that Smith helped him across a river when he needed to get to a sick parishioner, thus communicating a message that Smith participated in religious pluralism (an interesting juxtaposition with the message that his testimony was "the truth"). Second, the film tells the story of an ex-slave. When Smith was mayor of Nauvoo, he encountered this ex-slave and was supposed to charge him with a fine. Knowing that the man was trying to buy his son out of slavery, Smith gave the man his own horse and told him to sell it and use the proceeds to pay the fine and to increase his fund for buying back his son. The messages of these encounters are clear and meant to draw in modern-day viewers: Smith recognized the importance of families, appreciated racial diversity, and knew that his religious message was for everyone even while respecting others' belief systems. The film portrays Smith as a family man who was kind to everyone, loved children, and never hurt a soul. Thus his death comes as a mysterious, surprising tragedy—no explanation is offered as to why people would be angry at him or want him dead. He was an innocent lamb led to slaughter by unfair and jealous neighbors.

After the film, the tour of the jail snakes its way through the kitchen, living room, and dungeon. It was in the jailer's home that Smith and his friends first received a bit of kindness when the jailer moved them into an upstairs bedroom without bars. It was in that room that they were shot at, and then pursued by a mob.[11] After realizing that both Hyrum and Joseph had been fatally wounded his friend and fellow church leader, Willard Richards, pulled John Taylor into the dungeon to hide and to nurse Taylor's own gunshot wound. The tour of the Carthage jail ends in the room where the angry mob murdered Joseph Smith. Several benches are in the room along with a bed and a nightstand. Kleenex boxes are again scattered everywhere. On the mantle of the fireplace the visitor sees a clock, a copy of the first edition of the Book of Mormon, and lamps that flicker with a dim light. My missionary guide asked us to sit quietly, pray that God would let us know what was in store for us, and "feel the power of this place." As we sat in silence, the guide then played a soundtrack of the final scenes of Smith's life. The soundtrack, full of gunshots and confusion, ends with the story that many non-Mormons fled Carthage that night for fear of Mormons' vengeance and retribution against those who had killed their prophet but that the vengeance never came. Silence. The message: Smith was an innocent man martyred, and the Mormon people were an innocent people wronged—they would have been justified in taking vengeance but did not.

Nauvoo

Just over twenty miles from Carthage is the town of Nauvoo, where nearly 10,000 Mormons were living when Smith was killed. Nauvoo is not far from

Carthage, but the relationship between historical memory and space is much more complex in Nauvoo. Unlike Carthage, Nauvoo offers many histories, not a singular one. In Nauvoo, visitors must navigate competing narratives and competing claims about the appropriate response to the history and the space.[12] The town, which was one of the most populous in Illinois at the time Mormons lived there, has a population of just over 1,000 today, about one-tenth of the population it had in its nineteenth-century heyday. Parley Street, which runs east and west through the historic part of Nauvoo, signifies a key division there, an invisible but obvious line for visitors to the site. The street marks the boundary between the northern portion, owned and run by the LDS Church, and the southern portion, owned and run by the COC. Each church has its own visitors' center and its own maps. Each has its own way of telling history and interpreting the space. As visitors cross back and forth over Parley Street, they can feel the different interpretations of space and time, of prophecy and theology.

For 3 dollars, visitors to the "Joseph Smith Historic Site" get a tour of the COC's property and a sticker to wear that says: "I'm helping to preserve Joseph Smith's Nauvoo." Interestingly, the sticker suggests that the area explored in the tour was *Joseph Smith's* Nauvoo and that this portion of Nauvoo is the *historic* area. Guides tell visitors about the archeological digs going on at the site, and a flyer encourages visitors to come and help with the digs: "the hands that laid these bricks held Joseph's hand. Now you can hold a piece too." The flyer offers visitors a chance to touch history and interact with that history in a material way. That sentiment seems to exude from the site—tour guides are careful to enumerate all the items that are historical in nature: "this is Emma's walking stick"; "that is a replica of an item from Missouri." The COC tour includes a visit to the Nauvoo House, the Homestead (Smith's first home in Nauvoo), the Smith Family Cemetery (free, open to the public twenty-four hours a day, and containing the important graves of Joseph, Hyrum, and Emma Smith) and the Mansion House.

The COC first obtained the Nauvoo House from Charles Bidamon in 1909. Over the following ten years, Frederick M. Smith deeded the lots that held the Homestead, the Smith Family Cemetery, and the site of Joseph Smith's Red Brick Store to the COC. By 1918, the COC had created the position of caretakers and guides for these Smith family properties and had opened them to the public. In the coming decades, the COC consolidated its control in Nauvoo to these Smith family properties. In addition, it exchanged a parcel of the Nauvoo temple lot that the LDS Church did not own for three parcels of property in Independence, Missouri. In 1939–1940, the COC landscaped their Nauvoo properties and decorated the homes with furnishings from the nineteenth century.[13]

The COC tour emphasizes the COC's ownership of the main buildings where Smith lived during the final years of his life. Thus, a spatial claim to legitimacy bubbles up throughout the town: *we* have his home, *we* have the graves of Joseph and Emma; these are assertions that don't need to be stated boldly yet are palpable throughout Nauvoo. Religion scholar Lee Wiles has argued that the bodies of Joseph, Hyrum, and Emma Smith have been the sites of identity negotiations in Nauvoo. Owning the property of the Smith Family Cemetery and therefore the bodies of these three key figures, Wiles notes, the COC situated and memorialized the bodies of Joseph and Emma Smith so that "they could be gazed upon by different publics as a monogamous couple." Wiles also observes that Lewis Bidamon, the man Emma married after Joseph died, is listed as an "other" in the family cemetery, "indicating he was not a relative."[14] Thus, the cemetery space is marked in such a way as to promote a version of history in which Joseph was always in a monogamous relationship. This portrayal, while initially defining the COC over and against the LDS Church during the period when its members practiced plural wifery, is now a narrative that both churches prefer to embrace in Nauvoo.

Emma Smith plays a particularly significant role in the history-telling of both groups in Nauvoo. Her choices after Smith's death—to stay in Nauvoo, to maintain that Smith did not practice polygamy, to remarry, and to openly critique the LDS Church in Utah—have made her a troubling figure for the Utah Mormons, and nineteenth-century Latter-day Saints critiqued her often. In the late twentieth century, decades after the LDS Church had given up the practice of plural wifery, however, LDS depictions of Emma have focused on portraying her as a model of femininity and an active participant in a loving, companionate marriage with Joseph.[15] Historian Christopher Blythe extends the discussion of portrayals of Emma in Nauvoo by noting that for Latter-day Saints, she is at various times portrayed as a hope-filled young woman in love or a suffering widow mourning her husband's death.[16]

The COC tour begins with a film showing the history of the Mormons. There is a shift partway through the film from the historical to the contemporary, marked by a statement that claims that Nauvoo was the point where "we" were arguably the most powerful but not the most peaceful. The "we" is then clearly defined as the ancestors of the COC. The film emphasizes the ways the COC is distinct from the LDS Church without ever naming the latter: assertions that the COC has an "open temple" and that women can hold the priesthood play significant roles alongside an emphasis on world peace. Near the end of the film, Wallace Smith, president emeritus of the COC, appears and states that he is a great-grandson of Joseph Smith, thus making a claim to legitimacy through ancestry, a claim that would be quite meaningful read through an LDS lens given the LDS emphasis on ancestry in understandings of identity.

Where the COC tour ends, at the reconstructed Red Brick Store, visitors are handed a pamphlet about it that recognizes the site as a particularly important one, as the site of prophetic activity, and as a sacred space. On the second floor is Smith's combined office and study, which "has traditionally been associated with one of Smith's several formal prayers of blessing on his son Joseph III, given during the winter of 1843–1844. By the terms of those prayers of blessing, Joseph III was designated to become his father's prophetic successor in the church presidency at some indefinite time in the future." Aside from an assertion about prophetic succession, the site is also remembered as the place where endowments (a key ritual for church members) were introduced and where the Female Relief Society met. Paradoxically, the COC does not practice the endowments, nor does it have a Female Relief Society.

Another pamphlet offered by the COC, titled *Nauvoo: "City Beautiful,"* makes several similar claims and recounts the historical narrative the COC offers of Smith's death. This narrative is quite different from the LDS version told in Carthage and north of Parley Street. The pamphlet marks June 27, 1844, as the date when "a mob stormed [Carthage] jail and assassinated the two brothers. The church's leaders were dead." Not only does it declare that the brothers were assassinated, a claim to be explored further, but it also recounts that after the deaths of Joseph and Hyrum, there were "rival claimants to leadership of the church." The pamphlet names Brigham Young, Sidney Rigdon, and James J. Strang as among those claimants. "Others remembered that Smith had designated his son Joseph III to be the presidential successor by a prayer of blessing in the spring of 1844," the pamphlet recounts. Thus, the narrative the COC has embraced tells of many rivals for the prophetic office with Joseph III emerging as a prophet because of the blessing he had received from Joseph Smith Jr. in the Red Brick Store. The place serves as evidence of the prophetic claim and lineage.

The COC embraces the narrative that an angry mob *assassinated* Smith, and that narrative appears throughout the literature of the community. On my visit, the tour guide emphasized the assassination element of the narrative as we sat in the main room of the Red Brick Store. The guide noted that *Times and Seasons*, one of the church's publications at the time, had called the murder an assassination, adding: "which is a political term." The guide then went on to offer three points of evidence that Smith had angered other Americans. In Smith's bid for the presidency, the guide recounted, his platform had encompassed the abolition of slavery after 1850, turning all prisons into schools and releasing their prisoners, and reducing the pay of politicians in Washington, D.C., to the pay American farmers earned. After enumerating the political stances that made Smith undesirable, the guide reminded us that the Nauvoo Legion had consisted of 3,000 men with guns as well as one canon. To the people in the surrounding towns of Carthage and Hamilton who did not have as many weapons, that was scary. To the Saints, it was assurance against an unknown future, because "they didn't want what had happened in Missouri to happen again." And so on the south side of Parley Street, the COC narrates Smith's death as the assassination of a political threat, while the LDS Church recalls his death as the slaughter of an innocent lamb, a martyrdom. Both groups pin their identities to their versions of the story, and they tell those stories over and against one another in their efforts to assert their claims to the space and to the status of being *the* legitimate heirs of Joseph Smith Jr.

The LDS portion of Nauvoo is about seven blocks long and five blocks wide. I began my visit to Nauvoo in the summer of 2014 at the LDS visitors' center, where I was welcomed by a missionary and given a map. She pointed out Parley Street and the COC visitors' center, telling me: "*they* charge a 3 dollar entrance fee, but everything *here* is free." And thus the line was drawn, her implication being that the COC was driven by other-than-godly reasons. In so doing, she marked the boundary and marked the beginnings of how the two groups defined their identity over, against, and with one another. The spaces themselves wore the markings and narratives the two groups used to distance themselves from each other.

The LDS space is filled with restored historic buildings and new buildings fashioned to resemble historic buildings. In the 1950s, the LDS Church opened its Bureau of Information, where visitors could learn more about the area. At the same time the institution purchased the homes of Brigham Young, Wilford Woodruff, Orson Spencer, Orson Hyde, and Lorin Farr. In the 1960s, the LDS Church financially supported archaeological activity at the Nauvoo temple site and sought to renovate many of the above-named structures, along with the blacksmith shop, the gunshop, and the Lucy Mack Smith home.[17] In addition to the historic restorations, the LDS Church built its visitors' center in 1971.

In 1962, the LDS Church created Nauvoo Restoration, Inc., a nonprofit corporation that would work to restore Nauvoo. This followed on the heels of the 1961 designation of Nauvoo as a National Historic Landmark.[18] The nonprofit's articles of incorporation included a few telling goals: "to provide an historically authentic physical environment for awakening a public interest in, and an understanding and appreciation of, the story of Nauvoo and the mass migration of its people to the Valley of the Great Salt Lake"; "to interpret and dramatize that story, not only as a great example of pioneering determination and courage, but also as one of the vital forces in the expansion of America westward"; and "to engage in historic and archaeological research, interpretation and education and to maintain, develop and interpret historic landmarks and other features of historic, archaeological, scientific or inspirational interest anywhere in the United States and particularly along the Mormon Pioneer Trail."[19] Here one can see that this work, while focused on Nauvoo, was undertaken as part of an effort to highlight the entire Mormon Trail and, especially, its terminus in the Salt Lake Valley. It was an effort to legitimize the LDS Church's narrative of its movement westward. In addition, the work was done in order to make the pioneer effort meaningful to Mormons and non-Mormons alike.[20]

In the LDS-owned portions of Nauvoo, visitors can travel from building to building and learn some of the town's nineteenth-century history. The history in this portion of Nauvoo is told by missionaries dressed as nineteenth-century Mormons. Each building in the town has activities that allow people to act out the history as they hear it being recounted. So, for example, visitors can participate in rope-making, bread-baking, newspaper-pressing, and game-playing.

The style of history-telling north of Parley Street is quite different: there, rather than giving the suggestion that the tour guides are simply conveying the facts, the history is told in order to relay a theological message that takes primacy in each place, with the spaces and material objects serving as evidence of the truthfulness of the theology.[21] When visitors enter the Newspaper and Print Shop, they hear some of the history of setting type. They learn the origin of such sayings as "coining a phrase" and "cutting to the chase." As they do, they can hear about how the press worked and that it was a cooperative endeavor shared by the typesetter, the person who inked the plates, and the person who hung the pages up to dry before folding them. The historical lesson points to the theological message: everyone is important to the workings of the church, and all are responsible to one another, just as Jesus taught. Similarly, in the Post Office, visitors learn how nineteenth-century Mormons sorted mail, how much it cost, and how they wrote letters. They hear how Joseph Smith managed all of the mail he received from around the country from both admirers and detractors alike. Missionaries end with the theological point: the importance of writing and journaling today so that future generations will know how faithful people tried to create Christian lives. And missionaries remind visitors that both the New Testament Paul and Joseph Smith also sent letters so they should as well, including the "letters to God" that are sent in prayers.

Running along the primary north–south street in historic Nauvoo, Main Street, is a trail that communicates a key aspect of the LDS historical narrative told at the site. The sign marking the trail calls it "The Martyrdom Trail." It explains that on June 24, 1844, Joseph and Hyrum Smith and a few of their friends set out from Nauvoo, traveling to Carthage. "It was the last journey that Joseph and Hyrum would ever make. . . . [in Carthage Jail, following the brothers' arrest] a band of armed men stormed the jail with guns blazing and ruthlessly martyred the Prophet Joseph and his brother, Hyrum." For those interested in walking the last path the two brothers walked, a map is available along with trail markers.

Visitors can spend hours walking, bicycling, or riding a covered wagon up and down the streets of historic Nauvoo. The southernmost part of their journey in the LDS Church's territory is set off by two markers: first, the northern side of Parley Street, which is called the "Trail of Hope," and second, the statue *Eyes Westward* at the end of the Trail of Hope, near the Mississippi River. On the map handed out at the LDS visitors' center, this spot is marked as the Pioneer Memorial and as "Exodus to Greatness." The Pioneer Memorial, built in 1978, lists the names of those who followed Brigham Young west but did not make it to Salt Lake City. "Upon these walls are the names of those who died before their journey's end," the memorial explains. "In addition to these, others died who are lost from our records but are remembered unto the Savior." A bronze marker is part of the memorial, and with the name "Exodus to Greatness," it makes a dramatic claim, as it stands at the spot where the lands of the two churches meet: it is the starting point of the Latter-day Saints' journey west. "Exodus to Greatness" asserts that the journey was a religious exodus (suggesting that the participants were God's chosen people carrying out a divine plan) and was one that would bring about greatness. The bronze marker briefly narrates the story of the Latter-day Saints: "near here, the Mormon exodus to the Rocky Mountains began on February 4, 1846," the story begins. The marker reminds visitors that these seekers were "under Brigham Young" and "seeking freedom to worship God as they believed." Here the narrative ends. What begins with the martyrdom of a prophet ends with the movement of a people westward seeking relief from religious persecution. The statue *Eyes Westward*, so close to the boundary with the COC territory, suggests that Young was the prophet who was to be followed as the legitimate heir to Smith's legacy.

There is a great deal of text at the base of *Eyes Westward* that asserts the Smithification narrative of the LDS Church. The inscription begins: "Joseph and Brigham are depicted standing on the banks of the Mississippi River with a map of the westward trek that Joseph had seen in vision. The two conversed regarding the relocation of the Saints to the Rocky Mountain. Many other saints also were privileged to hear Joseph's prophecies concerning the exodus." These words are followed by several quotations, worth repeating here in their entirety:

My people shall become a numerous and mighty host in the vastness of the Rocky Mountains. —Joseph Smith

We have come here according to the direction and counsel of Brother Joseph before his death. —Brigham Young (Salt Lake City, July 20, 1847)

The Prophet came to our home and stopped in our carpenters shop and I got my map for him. He said, "Now I will show you the travels for this people." He then showed our travels through Iowa and said, "Here you will make a place for the winter and here you will travel west until you come to the valley of the Great Salt Lake. You will build cities to the north and to the south and to the east and to the west and you will become a great and wealthy people in that land." —Mosiah Hancock

Joseph Smith, just before he was killed, made a sketch of the future home of the Saints in the Rocky Mountains and their route . . . to that country as he had seen in a vision. Levi Hancock drew a copy of that map . . . and told them that there were 4 copies of that map taken; one of which Brigham Young kept and one that was carried by the Mormon Battalion by which they knew where to find the Church and Salt Lake Valley." —Oliver Huntington

While he (Joseph Smith) was talking his countenance changed to white . . . a living, brilliant white. He seemed absorbed in gazing at something at a great distance, and said: "I am gazing upon the valley of these mountains . . . Oh the beauty of those snow-capped mountains! The cool refreshing streams that are running down through those mountain gorges." Then gazing in another direction, as if there was a change in locality (Joseph said) "Oh the scenes that this people will pass through!" —Anson Call

And thus *Eyes Westward* narrates the Smithification of the American West. Notice the order of the various prophecies and confirmations. The first quotation states that Smith saw the group strong and in the Rocky Mountains. Next, the Brigham Young quotation affirms the prophetic nature of the first: it suggests that Young was merely playing out what Smith had known all along. In doing so, it legitimizes Young as Smith's successor to the prophetic office. The third quotation, Mosiah Hancock's, affirms the spatial significance of the previous two. Joseph Smith had a map, the story suggests. It wasn't just that he saw mountains and knew of persecution that would lead the Saints westward in some vague sense; the addition of the map to the narrative inserts a sense of just how precise Smith's vision was—he knew exactly where they would be. The fact that Smith had a map implies that he had an ownership over not just the space the Mormons would traverse but also their history. The massing of these particular quotations leads toward the conclusion that Smith knew the future that was coming for Mormons. The map concretizes the narrative and thus places power in Smith's hands as he hovers over the map and explains to others what will happen in the space. Thus, the journey of the Mormons becomes sacralized in the narrative: a prophet traced his finger over the topography and knew the landscapes they would traverse, could see them with his prophetic eye.

The fourth quotation, Oliver Huntington's, adds more detail to the narrative. Not only did Smith have a map, but he could draw a depiction of where the Saints would end up. The detail about the copies indicates that the depiction was so clear that many could use it to find their way to Zion. The narrative also confirms that not only was the prophetic vision passed on to Young but also a literal image, one he could see, touch, and consult, was left in his possession. Thus, the materiality of the West is introduced to the narrative in a new way.

The final quotation, attributed to Anson Call, furthers the kinesthetic message of the prophetic activity. In this portion of the narrative Smith first *feels* and *sees* the West. That this quotation rounds out the narrative is not surprising. The quotation returns the vision to Smith, thus reinforcing his role as prophet (with the change in countenance marking what followed as a genuine vision), and then indicates that not only did Smith know the West in an embodied way, he knew the kinesthetic experiences of his followers before they did. He knew the horrors they would face. Thus, the senses confirmed the divine activity; visions of the American West announced the truthfulness of all Smith saw then and the Mormons would see in the future.

Anson Call

When visitors get out of their cars in the parking lot at TITP Park, the first thing they see is the duplicate of *Eyes Westward* with the same texts just quoted. For Latter-day Saints, the pairing of these two men when the movement west is discussed is of the utmost importance. The statue promotes a narrative that is retold again and again in the LDS community, especially in the time surrounding the bicentennial celebration of Smith's birth and the sesquicentennial celebration of the Saints' movement to their Zion in the West. The narrative claims that Brigham Young stood where Joseph Smith stood and that Joseph stood where Brigham did—that the two had the same vision of a promised Zion fulfilled in the American West.

Sunday school materials in 1997, the sesquicentennial year of the Mormon pioneers' entry into the Salt Lake Valley, taught church members to "see the pioneers and themselves as important participants in the gathering of Israel and the establishment of Zion."[22] The lessons reminded students that "the move west from New York would eventually culminate in the settling of the Salt Lake Valley." The materials listed such key points as "the coming forth of the Book of Mormon to clarify the doctrine of Christ," "the restoration of the priesthood keys for the gathering of Israel and performing saving ordinances," "the organization of the Church and its government to administer the kingdom of God on earth," "a place of refuge where the Church could grow and be firmly established and freed for a time from the persecution of the wicked," and "that place of refuge . . . was located in the Rocky Mountains, in the western United States." Thus a *place* was part of and central to the playing out of the divine plan for the Mormons. And the American West was celebrated as the place where the fulfillment of prophecy happened and continues to happen.

The lessons quote a passage in the *History of the Church* that recollects Smith having a prophetic vision that the Saints would be persecuted all the way to the Rocky Mountains.

On August 6, 1842, Joseph Smith prophesied that the Saints would go to the Rocky Mountains. His own account of this significant event is as follows:

> passed over the river to Montrose, Iowa, in company with General Adams, Colonel Brewer and others. . . . I had a conversation with a number of brethren . . . on the subject of our persecutions in Missouri and the constant annoyance which has followed us since we were driven from that state. I prophesied that the Saints would continue to suffer much affliction and would be driven to the Rocky Mountains, many would apostatize, others would be put to death by our persecutors or lose their lives in consequence of exposure or disease, and some of you will live to go and assist in making settlements and build cities and see the Saints become a mighty people in the midst of the Rocky Mountains.[23]

In the context of the sesquicentennial celebration, the passages support the idea that Smith knew all along of the Mormon move to the Salt Lake Valley. Like the Anson Call quotation on *Eyes Westward*, this account foretells oppression and suffering and the eventual discovery of peace and home. Those same materials quote a recollection offered by George Albert Smith in 1869. The father of a future prophet of the church recalled:

> After the death of Joseph Smith, when it seemed as if every trouble and calamity had come upon the Saints, Brigham Young, who was President of the Twelve, then the presiding Quorum of the Church, sought the lord to know what they should do, and where they should lead the people for safety, and while they were fasting and praying daily on this subject, President Young had a vision of Joseph Smith, who showed him the mountain that we now call Ensign Peak, immediately north of Salt Lake City and there was an ensign fell upon that peak, and Joseph said, "Build under the point where the colors fall and you will prosper and have peace." The Pioneers had no pilot or guide, none among them had ever been in the country or knew anything about it.[24]

On the heels of the previous quotation, this recollection serves as an interesting verification. In the first, Smith foresaw the West, and in the second Young envisioned Smith pointing to the place. The second offers the idea that the Mormons would not have known where to go had their prophets not both envisioned the same future in the American West.

That message, that prophetic activity and the loop of prophetic activity, where prophets share their visions with one another, is also affirmed when the prophecies of Smith and Young are lined up with the prophecies of Old Testament prophets, particularly Isaiah. Throughout Sunday school materials, TITP Park, and many of the Mormon Trail historic sites are quotations from Isaiah 2:2: "and it shall come to pass in the last days, that the mountain of the Lord's house shall be established in the top of the mountains, and shall be exalted above the hills; and all nations shall flow unto it." Church publications and Mormon material culture teach modern-day Mormons to see the prophecy of Isaiah fulfilled in the hills and mountains surrounding the Great Salt Lake. Isaiah foresaw the American West. Joseph Smith foresaw the American West. Brigham Young foresaw the American West. Prophetic visions always confirm previous visions, these messages suggest—Old Testament Isaiah knew about the restoration of the gospel in the Americas, knew that Mormons would face persecution by their neighbors, and knew that they would find safe haven in the hills of the Salt Lake Valley. The narrative asserts that the westward trek to Utah was the plan all along—of both God and the prophet—one can just look out over the valley and see it.

That understanding of space and history is confirmed later along the TITP Park sculpture walkway with a monument to Anson Call. The monument, dedicated by Elder Dallin H. Oaks of the Quorum of the Twelve Apostles in September 22, 2007, serves as yet another step in the Smithification process. On the monument, Call is remembered as being present "when the prophet Joseph Smith uttered the Rocky Mountain Prophecy" (see Figure 3.3). Below the bust of Call is the text of one of his memories, clearly reinforcing the significance of this monument:

On the 14th July [1842] in company with about 50 or 100 of the brethren. . . . Joseph . . . told us of many things that should transpire in the mountains. After drinking a draught of ice water, he said, Brethren, this water tastes much like the crystal streams that are running through the Rocky Mountains, which some of you will participate of. There are some of those

Figure 3.3 Statue of Anson Call, This Is The Place Park.

standing here that will perform a great work in the land. . . . There is Anson. He shall go and shall assist in building cities from one end of the country to the other, and you shall perform as great a work as has ever been done by man so that the nations of the earth shall be astonished . . . and Israel shall be made to rejoice.

The monument's text operates in a number of ways. It confirms the message of *Eyes Westward*, of the two prophets who imagined and mapped the West together, *and* it suggests that Smith intimately knew the West—that he had *tasted* its water and imagined its cities. At the same time, the text links Smith's visions and work to the promises made to Israel, placing him squarely in the prophetic lineage from the ancient to the modern.

The historical accuracy of Call's recollection has been questioned over the years for several reasons. First, as the publisher notes indicate in the published version of Call's journal, only a small portion of the journal was written in Call's hand. The vast majority of it was written by his wives. Second, some of the accounts in the journal were written years later, and so events were recalled through the lens of later events.[25]

Finally, Call's account was rewritten by Edward Tullidge in his book *History of Northern Utah and Southern Idaho*. Tullidge modified the narrative to make it more dramatic, writing: " 'with the tumbler still in his hand he prophesied that the Saints would yet go to the Rocky Mountains; and said he, 'this water tastes much like that of the crystal streams that are running from the snow-capped mountains.' "[26] Tullidge's version provides an even more detailed picture of Smith's confidence about his knowledge of the Saints' future in the American West. These varying versions, written by different hands, years after the event mean that no one is quite sure whether what is recounted happened at all or happened the way Call's journal records.

Why would an account that has been questioned so often be cast in bronze, remembered for the ages? As the final project of Shann Call, one of Anson's descendants, the purpose of the marker was "to honor Anson's good name and accuracy in documenting church history events and finally to bring to light the major role Anson played in church history."[27] Through the medium of the monument, Shann Call was attempting to restore the good name of Anson Call, who he felt had been much maligned, in that his account of the Rocky Mountain Prophecy had been called into question. And those words were etched in bronze on the monument as an attempt to permanently settle the controversy and assert the veracity of both the account and the prophecy itself. The monument rescues Anson Call from historical neglect, as it is this account for which he is remembered, and places him as the sole person who remembered the time when Smith foretold the American West in this way. In the words of one biographer, "Anson Call emerged for one brief but significant moment in the prophetic life of Joseph Smith."[28] The map of the West on the back of the monument, the one that shows the lands and settlements Call helped create, reinforces the idea that Smith saw the map of the West, that he understood and knew its landscapes, and that he even knew where the people would settle (see Figure 3.4).

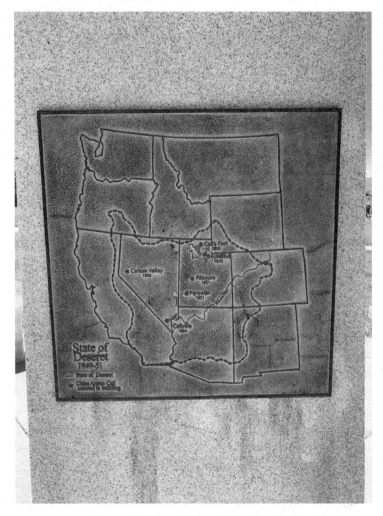

Figure 3.4 Statue of Anson Call (rear), This Is The Place Park.

The reminiscence operates on another level as well. A description of the
Rocky Mountain prophecy first appeared in print in the *Deseret News* in
1855 and then in the *Millennial Star* in 1857. This account appeared as the
Reorganized Latter Day Saints/COC were forming; they were part of the milieu of competing succession claims, and Call's biographer reminds us: "this
was after a group of members split off and became The Reorganized Church
of Jesus Christ of Latter Day Saints, now named Community of Christ. This
Church did not go to the Rocky Mountains."[29] The story then functioned
as an assertion that Smith had known all along that the Saints would go to

the Rocky Mountains; it made this assertion over and against the narratives being offered by another church who claimed to be the rightful heirs to Smith's prophecies. In the Call account, space plays a significant role in determining a legitimate heir to Smith's legacy. If Smith saw the West in a vision, if he knew that it was Zion, if he had seen and tasted and felt the West, then those who followed Brigham Young had built that Zion, had fulfilled the prophetic visions of Joseph Smith Jr. In its silence, the narrative also asserts that Smith moved on, knowing that Salt Lake was the future of the Saints rather than Independence, Missouri.

And that narrative remains significant today precisely because it challenges competing claims to the inheritance of Joseph Smith. It suggests that the move to Utah, the choice of Brigham Young as the successor to Joseph Smith, and all that happened later was precisely what Smith saw in a vision, thus confirming that it was precisely what God had wanted and planned all along. Another text at the base of *Eyes Westward* reads: "may those who read this message today and the countless thousands who will read it in the future be blessed in the knowledge that The Lord of Hosts has once again delivered His people and has restored His glorious gospel to the eart

h in these latter days." Here the words accompany the message of the material object. They claim that Brigham Young and his movement to the American West were a reiteration of a longstanding function of the biblical God as deliverer. The narrative of delivery here offers a divinely ordained leader, a new, promised land, and the movement of a chosen people toward their promised land.

It is therefore no surprise that *Eyes Westward*, by the sculptor Dee Jay Bowden, stands at two locations over 1,000 miles apart. The first, requested by then president Gordon Hinckley, stands on the banks of the Mississippi River on the border between COC Nauvoo and LDS Nauvoo—where it operates as a statement that the Saints who followed Young westward were the legitimate heirs of Joseph Smith and that their movement west was a movement to build up his imagined Zion. The copy commissioned by the Sons of the Utah Pioneers in TITP Park completes that narrative. Here the statue stands on soil that, while officially owned by the state of Utah, is decidedly LDS territory.[30] Visitors to the duplicate are invited to stand where the two prophets stood and to see on the landscape what they had seen with their prophetic eyes: to see the material realm as confirmation of prophetic office.

Whether or not the Rocky Mountain prophecy happened is not a question that can be answered with certainty, but the question of whether or not it happened is similar to the question of whether or not Brigham Young actually said "this is the place" when he first gazed out over the Salt Lake Valley. On the level of mythology, of stories told by a people that transcend historical accuracy and point to a larger value or truth for that group, the message is clear: Call's recollection is significant precisely because it ties Joseph Smith, the founder and visionary of the church, to all that transpired after his death. The monument makes the contemporary American West evidence of Smith's prophetic office. Here the West is confirmed in prophetic vision and also confirms prophetic vision. Smith's declaration encourages readers to think about the West as only a portion of all that would happen in the future. The declaration beckons Anson Call to build cities across the country, suggesting that the West is just a starting point, just the first step in building the Zion foretold by the first Mormon prophet.

Figure 4.1 *Journey's End*, This Is The Place Park.

4

"The Price We Paid"

A Theology of Suffering and Place at Martin's Cove

At the very beginning of what TITP Park calls the Statuary Walk is a bronze sculpture made of two separate parts; together the two make up Stan Watts's work *Journey's End* (see Figure 4.1). *Journey's End* represents the nineteenth-century handcart movement in a few different ways. The first sculpture is a bronze handcart. No humans accompany it; it alone is the symbol meant to call forth a set of narratives and feelings in those moving around the park. Next to the handcart is a second sculpture that depicts a family of five kneeling on the ground. Their eyes lowered as if in prayer, the family looks downward, indicating to viewers who gaze at it that the land itself is important, maybe exactly what they have been praying for. In fact, the base of the sculpture offers an explanation that the family is in the midst of a "humble prayer of gratitude" because they have reached their "journey's end." The text goes on to explain that "between 1856 and 1860 some 3,000 members of The Church of Jesus Christ of Latter-day Saints eagerly started their westward journey to Zion by handcart." It further describes the journey westward, saying: "hardships and trials tested the faith of the men, women and children as they pushed and pulled their handcarts over rugged trails, mountains, rivers, deserts, plains through heavy snow, drenching rain, and fatiguing heat." They did this because of their faith and hope that they would "gather with the early settlers in Zion where they would have religious freedom, live in peace, and help build the kingdom of God."

The resilience of all of the handcart pioneers is juxtaposed in *Journey's End* and in Mormon collective memory with the story of those who died on the way to their Zion. Martin's Cove, Wyoming, the site of the handcart trage-dies, sits around 320 miles from TITP Park and is a distinct type of sacred ground for Mormons: the handcart pioneers are remembered as losing their lives for the faith, sacrificing self for the greater values of gathering and Zion. The ground is marked so that the people of the church can remember the high stakes of being faithful. In so doing, the Wyoming site and *Journey's End*

Pioneers in the Attic. Sara M. Patterson, Oxford University Press (2020). © Oxford University Press.
DOI: 10.1093/oso/9780190933869.001.0001

reinforce for viewers that the faith they hold may be tested and is ultimately worth the greatest sacrifice.

At Martin's Cove, Latter-day Saints gather together to remember the people who died on the journey westward. Martin's Cove may be considered sanctified ground by Mormons, but that understanding of the land has not come without its contestations.[1] As mentioned in the introduction, David Chidester and Edward Linenthal have argued that religious groups ritualize sacred space, creating a meaningful world for their participants. At the same time, Chidester and Linenthal recognize that sacred space is "inevitably contested space, a site of negotiated contests over the legitimate ownership of sacred symbols. . . . Power is asserted and resisted in any production of space, and especially in the production of sacred space. Since no sacred space is merely 'given' in the world, its ownership will always be at stake. . . . In this respect, a sacred space is not merely discovered, or founded, or constructed; it is claimed, owned, and operated by people advancing specific interests."[2]

Martin's Cove is one of the sites along the Mormon Trail where these interests and contests are most evident. In the early twenty-first century, contests over the land came to a head when the Bureau of Land Management (BLM), a part of the U.S. Department of the Interior, first attempted to sell and eventually leased the land on which Martin's Cove sits to the LDS Church and allowed the church to take control over what happens in the space. The twenty-five-year lease had nearly automatic renewals built into it.[3]

Detractors were angry. Concern about the lease raised questions about whether or not a legal precedent was being set. The BLM and the National Park Service had made accommodations for religious groups who considered particular sites sacred before, but they had never set up an agreement that turned over a sacred historic site to a private, religious group.[4] Did this mean that any religious group could claim that it considered a portion of federal land "sacred" and get special rights to that land? Did the lease represent a collapse of the establishment clause of the First Amendment, which states: "Congress shall make no law respecting an establishment of religion"? Was the lease an example of the U.S. government showing preferential treatment to one religious group over others? If it was still technically federal land, who would get to interpret the landscape and the significance of the land for people who visited?

The events surrounding Martin's Cove show the LDS process of sanctifying sacred space and the spatial exploration of Mormon theologies of suffering.

The deaths near Martin's Cove raise the question of how a good God, one who called the chosen people to Zion, would allow those same people to die so close to their journey's end. In the space around the cove, Mormons offer a theology of suffering through the storying and ritualization of space. There the LDS Church articulates a theology of suffering that is meant to connect believers today to their nineteenth-century community. From the LDS perspective, that theology of suffering justifies why Mormons should have exclusive rights to Martin's Cove. The theology of the site takes a historical narrative of collective suffering and repackages it so as to encourage twenty-first-century believers to connect to their own individual sufferings. Through the creative interplay between narratives of collective and individual suffering, contemporary Mormons are reminded of their history of hardship and oppression, a narrative that affirms the high stakes of their religious affiliation. At the same time, they are taught that suffering is part of a larger divine vision and that suffering ultimately leads to a greater good. Not only is this theology communicated verbally throughout Martin's Cove, but the theology itself has been written on the landscape through various interpretive sites, monuments, and activities.

At a time when Mormonism is more broadly experiencing a loss of common place and common experiences, Martin's Cove suggests that suffering is a common experience all Mormons throughout the centuries have shared. In proclaiming such a theology, the Mormons' interpretation of Martin's Cove asserts a collective history of suffering that reinforces the history of the group as an oppressed and beleaguered people. Contemporary Mormon visitors to the site are encouraged to connect to that collective history of suffering as part of their identity formation while also understanding their own personal trials as being shared with other group members. Thus, the Mormons' collective memory recalls the story of the Willie and Martin handcart company members as "the price we paid" for Zion.[5]

The Willie and Martin Handcart Companies, 1856

Even the history being told about the significance of Martin's Cove is a contested history. Not everyone agrees on what happened or where it happened, and still others are concerned that with the LDS Church gaining control of the space, only one story will be told about that land. As Tom Rea, a historian of the place, has put it, the lease of the land represents the victory "of the one story over the many," and he declares that "Martin's Cove is now a Mormon somewhere, and will remain so."[6]

Before exploring the contours of the Mormon "one story" and the theologizing that accompanies it, it will be helpful to get a general outline of what happened in 1856 in order to explore the battles over history-telling and space-making at Martin's Cove. Handcarts were not part of the Mormons' initial journey to Utah in 1847; in fact, they only used handcarts from 1856 to 1860. During that brief period they built only about 650 handcarts; prior to the transcontinental railroad, their other modes of transport included covered wagons and walking. Of the 70,000 Mormons who came to Utah before the completion of the transcontinental railroad, only 3,000, a relatively small percentage, came using handcarts.[7]

Why did Latter-day Saints begin to construct and rely on handcarts at all? First, they were a cheaper form of travel than wagons. Once out on the trail, not only did the wagons require continuous upkeep but also the animals who pulled them needed to be fed and watered. Because humans were the physical labor for handcarts, there was less of a concern for the well-being of livestock. Second, handcarts were easier to build and repair than wagons. And so, in 1856, the church began to use handcarts as a cheap form of transportation. Missionaries abroad were converting thousands of new church members, and these members believed that they should literally gather together at Zion with other church members. If the church leadership did not help them, did not fund their journeys, then it might appear that the leadership wasn't as committed to the concepts of Zion and gathering as it claimed to be.

At the same time that the leadership faced the need to help bring these new converts to Zion, things were not ideal in the Salt Lake Valley. Drought and insects were ruining crops, and people were going hungry. This meant that the institutional church was not able to contribute to church funds the way it might have during more robust times. And so the leadership turned to the handcart as a solution to its problems. Alongside this move to reduce expenses, the leadership used what it called the Perpetual Emigration Fund to help fund those emigrants who could not afford the cost of traveling across the world to arrive in the Salt Lake Valley. This fund required that on their arrival in the Salt Lake Valley emigrants would work off any debt incurred on the journey westward.[8]

The people just kept coming. Several successful handcart companies made the journey with relatively few problems along the way, and these reinforced the idea that the handcarts were an ideal solution to the expense of migration.

Yet in 1856 two companies met with great failure. The Willie and Martin handcart companies left Florence, Nebraska, in late August, even after several warnings that no one should make the journey after June. During the meeting where it was decided that they would embark despite the time of year, one person cautioned against it. Levi Savage, who had made the journey before, suggested that they stay in Florence for the winter and then head off in early spring. His caution was met with much disagreement. Several men countered that they should leave Florence immediately; these believers were filled with religious zeal and wanted to race to Utah to be in the midst of what was called the Reformation, where Brigham Young was calling people to return to the tenets of their faith with renewed vigor. Yet others just wanted to make it to their point of rest so that they could begin their new lives. Savage ultimately lost the argument; the Willie company left Florence on August 17 and the Martin company on August 27.[9]

The two companies encountered much hardship along the way. Their handcarts had been hastily made and so required a lot of repairs. They also experienced severe storms and blizzards, causing hypothermia and other weather-related health problems. Pioneers in 1856 faced physical exhaustion while having to survive on small rations.[10] All told, the Willie company had a death rate of 13–14 percent and the Martin company about 25 percent. In a particularly bad stretch of Wyoming, where they endured rugged terrain, starvation, and blizzards, both companies lost many members. As I will show, just how many and where has been a question of debate. Having heard that the two companies had set out so late and had had so much trouble in Wyoming, Brigham Young sent rescuers who journeyed from Salt Lake City to Wyoming with provisions. If not for the rescuers, the death rates would surely have been much higher.[11] The rescuers helped the survivors take care of the bodies of their dead and then helped them make their way to Salt Lake City. There they were taken into people's homes and nursed back to health.

Once in Salt Lake City, though, other events immediately demanded people's attention. In 1857, President James Buchanan began to show concern over what was happening in Utah and appointed new territorial officers, taking away Brigham Young's political positions in an attempt to limit the church's power in the region. In response to hearing that U.S. troops were on their way to Utah to enforce the new order, Young called on the Nauvoo Legion to protect the territory. The U.S. army traveled slowly and ended up wintering near Fort Bridger. By the time they arrived, a compromise had been reached; and so the escalation did not end in bloodshed, even though it put many Mormons on high alert.[12] Further contributing to people's anxieties, that same year the Mountain Meadows Massacre occurred in southern Utah: a massacre of the members of a wagon train heading through Utah on the way from Arkansas to California.[13] The question of whether and at what level the institutional church was involved in the massacre, and later how the federal government would hold church leaders accountable, drew a lot of attention.

Because of these other events, what happened to the Willie and Martin companies was not recorded much and did not immediately become the stuff of Mormon collective memory. Historian Tom Rea explains: "aside from one remark that fifty-six members of the Martin company died in the ten miles between fording the Platte and their discovery at Red Buttes, none of the diaries, letters, and reports written at the time bothers to note how many other people died, or where. Only after the turn of the twentieth century did the folk tradition arise that most of the dying was done at the place that came to be called Martin's Cove." As more and more stories accrued about what the emigrants had faced, the more popular ones used Martin's Cove as their setting.[14] The narratives began to braid around the site and the name of the place, cementing its spot in the collective imagination.

Why did Martin's Cove become the site of all of the stories of tragedy? To answer this question, I must start with an analysis of the lure of the story of the Willie and Martin handcart companies. Mel Bashore, a scholar of the Mormon exodus, has noted that the overall mortality rates of Mormons moving westward were not that much greater than the national averages of other pioneers. Bashore worked with other scientists at Brigham Young University to study the records of 56,000 pioneers. Of these, around 1,900 died on their way westward or within a year of their arrival, a 3.5 percent mortality rate. In 1850 the overall pioneer movement westward had a mortality rate of 2.5–2.9 percent. Bashore argues that Mormon youth who experience the ritual of reenactment of the Mormon Trail called trekking and visit places like Martin's Cove assume after their experiences that many more Mormons died along the route. With the Willie and Martin handcart companies as the focus of the Mormons' narratives of the pioneers, especially at Martin's Cove, it is easy to see why one might come to believe that many more Mormons died on the trail than actually did: those two companies together experienced a 16.5 percent mortality rate because of their late departure.[15] Mormons visiting the site, then, can leave with a misperception of what the toll on Mormon lives actually was. As historian William Hartley suggested, at a conference panel on the Mormon Trail, the Mormon Trail story has been "hijacked" by the Willie and Martin disasters.[16] A glorification of the deaths of those along the trail and a disproportionate emphasis on them has resulted. The emphasis on the fate of the Willie and Martin handcart companies, while skewing visitors' perceptions of the overall Mormon experience of westward migration, enforces the theology of suffering narrated at Martin's Cove. Thus the function of the space is not to communicate accurate history per se but to connect believing visitors to a narrative of sacrifice and in so doing to reinforce group identity. The greater the number of deaths, it seems, the greater the sense of sacrifice and suffering for the cause of Zion.

Visiting Martin's Cove

Each year about 35,000 people travel to a middle-of-nowhere area in Wyoming to push and pull handcarts around a series of trails on the ranch now called Martin's Cove (see Figure 4.2). Two hours away is a second site, the Willie Center at Sixth Crossing, where visitors can also engage in a handcart experience. According to one missionary at Martin's Cove during my visit in the summer of 2015, only about 20 of the 300 or so daily visitors to the site are non-Mormons. It is clear that the experience is designed primarily to enhance the spiritual life of the faithful and secondarily to educate non-Mormons about what happened at Martin's Cove. It is a site where "Zion" is often discussed; the physical Zion served as goad and goal for Saints in the nineteenth century, and those reenacting the Martin's Cove catastrophe today are now offered a spiritualized version of Zion tied to a theology of suffering and sacrifice.

Most visitors are Mormons who have planned to do precisely the pushing and pulling of handcarts the site promotes. The majority of those who come are young Latter-day Saints coming to trek or take part in a camping, reenacting faith experience that has been plotted out for them by the elders of their church. Reservations for groups to come and push handcarts and participate in three-day or six-day treks have been made years in advance. But a few handcarts are set aside for those who drop by for the day and want to take a handcart for a spin. In an interesting example of interreligious exchange, the handcarts are crafted by two groups. First, Amish carpenters fashion the axles and wheels. Then, Mormon missionaries craft the cart beds and everything else.

Figure 4.2 Entrance to Martin's Cove, Wyoming.

Some youth who come to participate in reenactments prepare for their trips by sewing their own pioneer clothes, getting them "in the mood" for a nineteenth-century experience. When the youth arrive, they pull and push handcarts during the day to designated spaces across the ranch owned by the church and then across land leased from the Bureau of Land Management and cared for by the church. In the evenings the missionaries at the site, retired couples who have donated their time and money to the church, come out to share a special evening with the young people. These adults might gather around a fire and read firsthand accounts of the pioneers who moved through that space over 150 years ago, or they might teach the youth how to square dance.

Whether or not daily visitors wish to push the handcarts, they are invited into the visitors' center, an interactive site where they can learn the stories of the place. Off to the side is another building that holds a museum with two rooms full of items from the ranch and the surrounding area. The building was once the homestead of a rancher named Thomas Sun, a French Canadian who changed his name from Thomas DeBeau Soleil. He built his homestead in 1872, not long after the Martin and Willie handcart company disasters, not far from Devil's Gate.[17] At the time Sun owned the ranch, it encompassed about one million acres. Today the ranch is owned by the LDS Church, who purchased it in 1996. Part of the land is used for the trekkers; the other part is ranched, with over 1,000 head of cattle. These cattle are raised and then slaughtered, and their meat is sent to the church's "bishop's pantries," which are part of the church's welfare program. Individuals can donate their time to the church and in return receive food and material goods they cannot afford to buy.

Throughout the visitors' center are various stations where missionaries can pause to tell the stories of the fateful Martin and Willie handcart companies. What is the "one story" offered at the visitors' center and how is it told? The tour begins at the hearth of the ranch. Early on, a map of the United States outlines the key nineteenth-century trails across the country: the Mormon Trail, the Oregon Trail, the Pony Express Route, and the California Trail. While incorporating the other trails, the map begins to tell a narrative about the Mormon people being a special, divinely chosen group. Over the Oregon Trail looms an interpretive box that, in its largest letters, declares: "Lured by Land: The Oregon Trail." Next to the Mormon Trail is another interpretive box that claims: "Moved by Faith: the Mormon Trail." Thus, from the beginning, Mormons are set apart from others moving westward as having a higher calling or purpose. The California Trail does not merit its own interpretive box, though the missionary who led me through reminded me that those who followed the California Trail were "after all the gold." The interpretive text describing the Mormon Trail goes on to say that between 1847 and the 1869 completion of the transcontinental railroad, about 70,000 Saints went west to the Salt Lake Valley: "they were a devout and visionary people. Unlike others, they came seeking refuge from the lash of religious persecution, a place where they could worship God and live in peace." Alongside the map is another explanation that claims that thousands of people went westward and that among them "were the Latter-day Saint, or Mormon, pioneers bound for the Valley of the Great Salt Lake in response to a call from their prophet leaders to 'gather to Zion.'"

The next station of the center continues a religious interpretation of the movement westward and communicates further that the Saints were a people set apart. Under the heading "The Gathering Begins" a text describes the missionaries who went out into the world to preach the message of the Book of Mormon. The next text calls the movement west an "exodus." Thus, within a few feet, two key theological concepts shape the theological message and narrative being given at the site: first, the Saints were to gather together, and second, their journey was an exodus—a parallel with the biblical exodus; they were a persecuted, chosen people led by their God. The next station explores the economics: "Assisting the Needy Saints" and "Financing Emigration to Zion." Here the kiosks recount the church's history of funding those who could not afford the journey. Thus visitors are prepared to hear how handcarts played a role in Mormon movement west, and the station suggests that the "poor welcomed less expensive travel." Indeed, the handcart allowed many to travel west more cheaply.

The next stations outline what happened to the Willie and Martin handcart companies, explaining how their late departure put them in a precarious position early on. One display holds a small bowl containing a few ounces of flour, the ration for each person when things were at their worst. Handcarts made of uncured wood, poor wheels, and the bad luck of a thunderstorm scaring off the cattle the Willie company used to pull its provision wagon put the companies in a difficult position. The interpretive stations lift up Levi Savage as a heroic figure because he warned the Saints when they reached Florence, Nebraska, suggesting that they wait a year to depart. Because he had made the journey before, he knew the trail well. He argued that God wanted the Saints to use their good judgment and delay their departure. The heroic Savage was outvoted by the other members of the companies.

Calling these pioneers "Winter's Helpless Victims" once they began their journey through Wyoming sets up the narrative for what comes next, the story of those who left the Salt Lake Valley to take provisions to the stranded companies and lead them back to Utah. Just as several dozen people died on the journey and it appeared that rations would run out, the rescuers arrived. One panel quotes a speech given by Brigham Young on October 5, 1856: "that is my religion; that is the dictation of the Holy Ghost that I possess, it is to save the people. We must bring them from the plains." Missionaries then ask visitors to consider how the rescuers might be a model for their lives today; how they might help others in need as they go through winters in their own lives.

Visitors reach the end of the narrative journey about the movement west when they get to the station declaring "Zion At Last." This station describes how crowds met the wagons when they entered the Salt Lake Valley and all of the pioneers were taken into people's homes and cared for. Once again, the missionary hosting me noted how much generosity of spirit there was in taking strangers into their homes. The account told on the walls of the visitors' center ends in two ways. First, it quotes Francis Webster, a member of the Martin handcart company who survived. The quote ends: "was I sorry that I chose to come by handcart? No. Neither then nor one moment of my life since. The price we paid to become acquainted with God was a privilege to pay and I am thankful that I was privileged to come to Zion in the Martin Handcart Company." Thus, the narrative ends with this assertion: human misjudgment and bad luck may have contributed to these disasters, but it was the hand of a loving God who guided these seekers through obstacles. The experiences of suffering and hardship were part of the price paid for a larger divine narrative about humans coming to better know God.

Second, the station suggests that the pioneers have left a "Legacy of Faith" from which visitors to the site are to learn. The handcarts show that faith comes with many trials and obstacles but will also carry one through anything. The final room of the center bears the names of those pioneers who made it to their Zion and those who did not. Above the names of the members of the handcart company are the words "faith," "obedience," "sacrifice," and "charity," all carved in wood.

Off the final room is a theater where visitors can view a film about the handcart companies. The room is littered with Kleenex boxes, and the missionary showing the film when I arrived told the audience that we "were going to need them." The film, *Tongue nor Pen Can Never Tell the Sorrow*, follows the journey of the McBride brothers, young immigrants from Europe who were members of the handcart companies headed toward Utah. The trip was fun on the boat across the Atlantic Ocean and as they took the railroad to Iowa City. When they got to the Missouri River their mother got sick, and things began to get worse. On their journey their father died along with thirteen other men in one night. The McBride brothers continued to suffer many hardships along with their siblings and mother and were part of the group rescued at Martin's Cove. The film ends with their arrival in Salt Lake City, where they were cared for by others. The final message of the film suggests that viewers should look to the past to gain an appreciation for what they have and inspiration for the future. Gordon Hinckley's voice ends the 1997 film with an encouragement to reflect on the pioneers' work and benefit from their story. "Each of us is a pioneer in his own life," he suggests, calling on viewers to see themselves as the spiritual descendants of the pioneers and the inheritors of their vision.

As visitors leave the center, a sign reads: "An Invitation to Walk in Hallowed Footsteps." It promises that visitors will "better understand the heroic efforts of the handcart pioneers by pulling and pushing a handcart . . . over portions of the trail they actually traveled." Those who do take handcarts set off from the visitors' center but quickly move away from modern buildings and into the terrain of Wyoming. One of the first stops is a series of bronze statues, dedicated in 1992, that memorialize the rescuers who left the comfort of the Salt Lake Valley and risked their lives to help others. No specific rescuers are portrayed in the statues because, as the missionary I toured with said, "they all were helping and risking their lives." One statue portrays a rescuer in river water up to his knees carrying a small infant and a toddler across the raging water. The next portrays two rescuers carrying a third man across the river, unable to walk for himself. A third depicts a rescuer carrying a teenage girl across the river; her feet, bound in cloths because she has no shoes, are severely damaged by the winter weather. My guide told me that visitors were meant to stop at this site and reflect on what it means to sacrifice self for others. Not far from the statues is a bathroom stop and water station, along with a handcart parking lot (see Figure 4.3).

Moving away from the statues, visitors journey through grasslands and follow trails, pushing and pulling handcarts all the way. The camping sites are designated; trekkers are not to stray off of the trails. Perhaps what stands out most is how regulated an experience the trek is. Prior to their arrival, Martin's Cove encourages church youth groups to visit a website that breaks the trek down into fifteen-minute, half-hour, and one-hour increments. For example, one of the plans suggests that between 1:00 and 2:00 on the first afternoon trekkers can arrive, and then "use restrooms, orientation, pick up handcarts—60 minutes. Option to stop at Fort Seminoe for Daniel W. Jones story—add 30 minutes." Evening activities include "Ephraim Hanks—30 minutes. 7:00 or 8:00 only Square dancing—1 hour. Pioneer Express—10 minutes."

The trail rules contain many instructions; a few of them indicate how visitors are expected to understand the site as a sacred space. They are encouraged to walk in groups of about twenty, because that size "promotes reverence for this sacred site." Later the instructions promise trekkers that the "walk through Martin's Cove is a reverent experience." Visitors to the Willie Center at Sixth Crossing are told that they will cross the Sweetwater River at least once and that "your first water crossing should be silent to allow your group to feel the Spirit." The instructions encourage group leaders to prepare

Figure 4.3 Statue in the Rescue Sculptures series, Martin's Cove, Wyoming.

themselves spiritually because they "are especially in-tune with the Spirit in knowing what to and how to share with your youth." Furthermore, iPods and CD players are prohibited unless "used for appropriate musical numbers for devotional purposes." In Martin's Cove, trekkers are instructed to remember that "it is *not* what you will *see or hear*, but what you will *feel!*" The emphasis on feeling here as the primary sensory experience—an embodied awareness of the spirit—stands out. The instructions suggest that it is physical movement through this particular place that will allow visitors to find spiritual lessons and truths and to *feel* them in a new way.

All of these activities are meant to concretize believers' testimonies, the narratives of the individual believer about the truthfulness of the LDS message. Missionaries encourage "testimony meetings" throughout Martin's Cove —meetings in which visitors share what they *know* to be true about the gospel message and the teachings of the church. So are "firesides," where speakers present a faith-promoting message to listeners. Yet both of these activities are prohibited on the BLM portion of the property, suggesting that the church's intentions for the space and the federal government's are decidedly different.

Discussing a version of the trek reenacted at Martin's Cove, participant-observer Megan Sanborn Jones described participants' ability to interpret the meaning of the trek as "tightly controlled."[18] Rather than remaining open to experiential interpretation, church leaders and missionaries craft and maintain a "one story" interpretation of the trek. They shape the trekker's movement through space and interpret it for them. These leaders want participants to realize that "[they] are the chosen of Israel . . . the descendants of these pioneers either by blood or adoption . . . [and] have an obligation to serve the Lord the rest of the days of [their lives]."[19] Church narratives about how believers are still pioneers today suggest that rather than physical obstacles, church members face obstacles such as "spiritual indifference," "self-indulgence," "greed," "pornography," and "drugs." Believers are counseled that they are "not working to physically push handcarts over steep mountains and through deep snow drifts . . . [but] working to spiritually push ourselves to overcome discouragement and complacency."[20] And so trek experiences at Martin's Cove and beyond are designed for trekkers to learn kinesthetically a message about spiritual attitudes and obstacles. Their physical movement, while profoundly tied to the lesson, is also profoundly regulated—movement and message are designed to be one.

There is an interesting balance between church attempts to control the ritual activity and to make the ritual efficacious for believers who participate. Movement and activity are highly regulated. Visitors often hear the same stories, follow the same paths, stop at the same spots along the route. At the same time, the hope is that they will use their spiritual imaginations along the way. In the hearings about H.R. 4103, a proposed bill to sell Martin's Cove to the LDS Church, Bishop David Burton explained that at the cove visitors are provided with handcarts, can follow trails, and can take a "bridge back across the Sweetwater Crossing where they can imagine the events of the young rescuers carrying weakened pioneers across the icy river." Here Burton emphasized the role of religious imagination: visitors are supposed to use their spiritual imaginations to place themselves in the shoes of nineteenth-century pioneers so that they might "know and remember the handcart pioneers who suffered there and the men who rescued them."[21] Thus, no matter how regulated, scripted, and ritualized the space may be, it still relies on visitors' active imaginations to connect the dots—to see the suffering of *their people* on the landscape.

Also included and celebrated in the handcart reenactments, both at Martin's Cove and at other sites on the Mormon Trail, are the suffering and sacrifices the pioneers made throughout their journey. Reenactors are encouraged to meditate in silence on those sacrifices and to reflect on the ways that they, too, might suffer or sacrifice for their faith. Participants read biographies of the pioneers; they pause at various points and remember someone who died at a particular time and place and, in so doing, remake the "pioneer dead . . . through performance as they live again and again in re-enactments in which no one ever dies."[22] These performances give the character traits an eternal quality, suggesting that Mormons today have automatically inherited such traits from those who came before. One 1997 trekker wrote a poem titled "To My Pioneer Brothers and Sisters." Its numerous stanzas communicate her belief that she is connected to those who have gone before: "We have never met, Yet I know you. / I have read the stories of pain and sorrow / Of love and joy, That were yours. / I have not buried loved ones in shallow graves / or billowed seas./ Yet, today I felt some of your pain."[23] Another 1997 trekker explained: "I truly believe that if you believe in something so much, you should be willing to die for it. The pioneers were. I know that I am too. Many of us, if we did not know it before we do now, would die for the gospel."[24]

In the survey I conducted about trek experiences, which I will discuss in greater detail in chapter 7, the respondents who trekked at Martin's Cove had responses that carried a more somber tone than others. They emphasized sacrifice and suffering in ways that other trekkers, who certainly recognized those themes, did not. One participant recalled: "we had a lot of historical and spiritually uplifting information shared with us along the way. My husband had relatives who were in the Martin Handcart Company and it was poignant to be in the place where they had been and had sacrificed so much."[25] For this respondent, it was the specific place that made the experience and the consideration of suffering more profound. Reflecting on the past in that space shaped her experience.

The testimony that is concretized at the Martin's Cove site is about sacrifice and strong faith, but it is also tied very much to a Mormon theology of suffering. It is at this disaster site that one can see the Saints working out their theological understandings of why bad things happen. Events like those the Martin and Willie companies faced—rocky ridges, blizzards, and depleted rations—could challenge a theology of a powerful and good God. Surely a God who loved faithful people would not leave them stranded out in the cold with nothing to eat. Surely a God who wanted Zion to be built would not let believers die so close to their destination.

Surely a good God would not let this happen. As one journalist, Peter Fish, put it, "most modern Americans are not used to considering suffering as exaltation."[26] At Martin's Cove, suffering is narrated as a necessary part of a journey closer to God. And so this rather common Christian theological explanation of suffering—that a good God can see the greater good that can come from human, finite suffering—is given a distinct LDS brand at Martin's Cove. The explanation feels satisfying enough to some. As one believer recalled, "it's a miracle any of them lived. The only way was that their heavenly father was watching over them."[27] One LDS historian of the disaster put it similarly, writing that the shock was "not so much that as many as two hundred died, but that more than a thousand lived."[28] Both individuals reversed the question, allowing survival to be miraculous and death assumed. Therefore Martin's Cove could be for them a place to make sense of the suffering of the 1856 expedition while maintaining faith in the goodness of God.

Through the ritual of trekking and the ritual of setting out to overcome obstacles, through the careful storying of that place, the theological problems presented by the disasters are ritualistically overcome. The suffering and death of the pioneers is explained in their example for Latter-day Saints on into the future. A good God saved *some* from sure death, they claim, allowing them to achieve Zion. The others, those who died on that land, sacrificed for the broader value of Zion. Mel Bashore's observation that teen participants leave the trek believing that many more Mormons died in the handcart journey than actually did is intimately connected to William Hartley's claim that the story of the Martin and Willie handcart companies has hijacked the narrative of all of the handcart companies, the rest of which were highly successful. It is in service of a theology of suffering that the narratives have been hijacked and the teens believe that so many died. And so the "one story" told at Martin's Cove can be read as evidence that the hand of God is at work in the world and that God intimately cares about human lives, even when disasters strike.

Leasing Sacred Land

While early in the development of the Mormon imagination of today little interest was shown in Martin's Cove, the place took on meaning and significance for other communities. As mentioned earlier, in 1880 a man named

Tom Sun claimed a section of the area near Devil's Gate under the Desert Land Act, which allowed Americans to claim a square mile of land for $1.25 an acre as long as they brought water to it and grew a crop there within three years of making the claim. The Act did not describe how much land needed to have crops or water, so Sun made the claim with the plan to graze his cattle there and eventually take ownership of it. From there, he continued to acquire land in the surrounding area.[29]

In the 1990s, the LDS Church started an earnest effort to purchase historically significant land along the Mormon Trail, and that effort included purchase of about 16,000 acres in Wyoming.[30] In 1992, Scott Lorimer, the bishop of the Riverton stake (a stake being an area similar to a Catholic diocese), attempted to purchase the Sun Ranch from the Sun family.

Lorimer sought out the sale because church members wanted to purchase a spot on the dune above the cove in order to enable visitors to "pinpoint the story spot."[31] The plan was to erect a monument there. The BLM did not support the idea, saying that it would cause environmental harm and potentially ruin the view of the area for other visitors. And so the participants in the exchange decided that the best idea was a smaller monument that would be more out of the way. In August 1992, the church dedicated that monument along with two other sites along the Mormon Trail.[32] Talks continued between the Suns and the church, with the Suns acknowledging that they were allowing more and more Mormons wishing to visit the site to cross over their land. After the dedication of the monument church publications wrote about the site, and soon more Mormons believed that it was theirs to visit.[33] The growing number of visitors encouraged the Suns to sell, and in 1996 the church purchased the Sun Ranch, a huge boon for the project to claim the site as sacred and to mark it as uniquely Mormon. At that point, the church began its plans to develop a visitors' center within the ranch buildings; the center would be run by missionaries and would allow faithful visitors to learn the tragic history of the place and appreciate its significance to Mormon history. The next year the church entered into a collaborative agreement with the BLM "that placed Martin's Cove under the stewardship of the Church, subject to certain conditions, including a public access easement." That agreement paved the way for the church to build a two-mile path across federal lands in cooperation with the BLM; they constructed the path in such a way as to cause the least amount of damage to the environment. The agreement was scheduled to expire in 2002, but efforts on the part of the church and government officials led to new plans.[34] What the agreement allowed was visitation for historical activities, including pulling handcarts, but it did not allow for other recreational activities such as hunting and fishing, an interesting delineation I will discuss further later.[35]

In 2001 the movement toward the church's claim to the land reached new heights. James V. Hansen, a congressperson from Utah and member of the LDS Church, proposed that the federal government sell Martin's Cove to the church. That proposal (H.R. 4103) was not met with much support in Wyoming; in fact, polls demonstrated that a majority of residents were against the sale. So the church suggested a ninety-nine-year lease, a plan that also met with some resistance. More congressional meetings resulted in a proposal to lease Martin's Cove to the church for twenty-five years for about $17,000 a year.[36]

Attached to the Energy and Water Development Appropriations Act of 2004, the lease said that the church had to rent the land at fair market value (which was determined based on the land being categorized as grazing land rather than as a tourist site), provide public access to the ranch, and protect the environment of the site and any artifacts found there; in addition, the church would have the rights of leasees (which meant that it could prohibit people from entering the site based on its own criteria).[37] The legislation allowed the secretary of the interior to renew the lease based on terms found acceptable to both parties. In response, the American Civil Liberties Union (ACLU) sued Gale Norton the secretary of the interior, and Kathleen Clarke, the director of the BLM, claiming that the lease contradicted the establishment clause of the First Amendment. Because of the suit, whose arguments I will discuss later, the church took down all religious signs from the cove and made it possible for visitors to hike to the cove without going through the visitors' center.[38]

Why did the church make so many attempts to acquire or lease Martin's Cove? Why didn't it seem right or appropriate for the land to stay in BLM hands with the knowledge that the faithful could visit whenever they wanted to? In the process of negotiating the purchase of Sun Ranch, attempting to purchase Martin's Cove, and the subsequent lease, the church made clear that from its perspective, only Mormons would be able to properly care for the site because only they knew its actual worth. And so the church made several arguments as to why it needed to *at the very least* have oversight of the land if not outright ownership.

In formulating their claims, church members constructed a narrative, their "one story," about why the place was sacred, thus validating their rights to ownership. The church argued that the land at Martin's Cove was sacred to its membership for several reasons. Eni F. H. Faleomavaega, a delegate to Congress from American Samoa and an LDS convert, explained it this way in the hearings: "as far as I am concerned, any burial site is sacred ground." For him, the questions of exactly how the bodies were buried or exactly where people actually died were meaningless and were attempts to challenge the idea that the cove was sacred space.[39] Lloyd Larsen, then president of the Riverton, Wyoming, stake, made a similar argument. In the hearing he recalled that "when we came here yesterday, I brought my 17-year-old son, Jared, with me on this trip. This being his first trip to Washington, D.C., we tried to take in some of the sights yesterday afternoon. We were the most touched as we went into Arlington National Cemetery. The signs there state[d] that we were on hallowed ground. We felt that, and rightfully so. It was made hallowed by men and women who gave their lives protecting the freedom and the civil rights enjoyed in this country." Larsen suggested that the fact that the people died for a cause made the burial sites sacred. Then, in a parallel move, he declared: "Martin's Cove . . . is also hallowed ground, made hallowed by people who gave their lives, committed to a religion that they believed in, and in pursuit of the freedom that is the cornerstone of this nation."[40] And so, he suggested that those who died at Martin's Cove in 1856 were collective martyrs, of sorts, examples for how to live an ethical life. He also affirmed the sacrality of the land by suggesting that it was similar to a cemetery for American war heroes.

Other church members claimed that the deaths sacralized the land as well as other events that happened there. There were some pioneers who survived that tragedy, and that was because of the sacrifices made by the rescuers. The church's presiding bishop, H. David Burton, who oversaw the church's temporal affairs, explained: "the story of the Martin and Willie Handcart Companies of Mormon pioneers is one of dedication, determination, and death, a story of suffering, of selfless sacrifice, and above all, a story of great faith. The courage and sacrifice of those marooned pioneers in 1856 and their rescuers is one of the great historic events in the American pioneer era."[41] Acts of valor and rescue, then, too, came to be viewed as evidence for the sacrality of the land. At the same time, Burton suggested that the LDS history of the site was a model history from which other Americans could learn. Here he sought to make Mormon history part of a larger story of American identity.

The narratives of rescue resonated within contemporary Mormonism precisely because they had been taught specifically through the stories of the rescue of the Martin and Willie handcart companies. Historian Scott Orton has shown that the story of the rescues is much more complicated than the one often taught to LDS members; that story tends to have only three rescuers who managed to carry the entire company across the Sweetwater River and subsequently died early deaths because of related health concerns. Instead, Orton has demonstrated that there were a number of rescuers who helped many in the company cross the river (probably more than one time) and lived for quite some time afterward (and died for various reasons). Orton points out that the Sweetwater rescue story transforms the story of the handcart disasters into one that is also about the "triumph of human spirit under adverse conditions." Because of this overarching theological message, a much more complex story has become simplified in the Mormon imagination. In Orton's words: "it is not *the* rescue story, but *a* story of the rescue effort."[42]

Nonetheless, the weight of the theological message found in the rescue story is a powerful one today. It functions to connect believers with their nineteenth-century history. One participant in the modern-day ritual of trekking recalled: "during the first day of my second trek a major storm forced us to evacuate the mountain and people from Heber came up in the mountains to ferry us down in their trucks to a barn where we spent the night. The next day a local burger joint opened early to feed us all breakfast. To me, the whole experience proved that the same spirit of charity which we often talk about regarding the Martin and Willie handcart rescue was still possessed by members of the church."[43] In order for twenty-first-century Mormons to make these kinds of connections, the narratives of rescue at Martin's Cove have to be accessible and often told. In this instance, avoiding a storm and providing a breakfast, charitable acts indeed, could be connected to historical events precisely because of the significance of the nineteenth-century narratives to the trekkers today. Suffering and sacrifice *paired with narratives of redemptive rescue* mark Martin's Cove and its history for modern-day Mormons.

Not only did the historical events at Martin's Cove sacralize the space for the LDS community; the activities at the site carried on by modern-day believers also do. Caring for and about the site, then, is portrayed as more than just historical preservation. It is an act of acknowledging the land itself because of what happened there. Through the rituals of caretaking—of making the trails, creating the monument markers, pulling shrubs—Latter-day Saints also mark the significance of the site to their history and demonstrate their understanding of the land as sanctified ground. In participating in rituals in that space, both the handcart reenactments and the rituals of tending the site are acts of respect and acts that reinforce the understanding of the site as sacred.

And so underlying every LDS argument for why the church should have oversight has been the assumption that the ground is sacred for Mormons. The other component of that argument is that that particular land is *more sacred* for Mormons than for any other groups or individuals in the country. As I will show, this argument has not been readily accepted by others. With the foundational argument of the sacrality of the land, the church also made several practical arguments as to why it should have oversight. First, the church claimed that because the BLM was underfunded and understaffed, the church with its seemingly endless supply of volunteers who wanted to tend to a sacred site would be a better steward of the place.[44] Lloyd Larsen, president of the Riverton, Wyoming, stake, explained: "Martin's Cove is an integral part of this nation's treasured pioneer story, and should be accessible and appreciated by all." In this statement he acknowledged that the land had significance beyond the LDS community. He also declared: "without the church's willingness to make this remote area accessible to visitors and tell the story of those who died there, it would still be isolated and unappreciated."[45] Similarly, James V. Hansen said: "given its uniquely religious significance, it is difficult to conceive how the Federal Government could ever care for and interpret the land in a better manner than the Church and. . . . give it the exemplary stewardship it deserves."[46] Here Hansen made even more ardent claims. Not only was the church best suited for tending the land because it understood the land's sacrality best but also it was uniquely qualified to interpret the space for others. The "one story" offered by the church served as evidence that the space was sacred and as justification for why Mormons should be given special rights to it.

Hansen also critiqued other groups who sought to "portray Martin's Cove as broadly significant to anyone they can think of." He wondered where those people had been when Mormon volunteers had "spent literally tens of thousands of man hours making the site accessible, building trails, building footpaths and bridges across the river to the site. . . . Why did we not hear from them about how they would like to help with their time and their money because the site was of such broad significance to them as Americans?"[47] Hansen's logic here is intriguing. He argues that the church is the correct institution to care for, narrate, and interpret the land because it understands the significance of the site. Then that tending and care is justification for the church's claim to some special ownership/oversight position. In the end, he dismissed other claims that the site was significant for other reasons: "the fact is that they were nowhere to be found because this site is not very significant to any group except the LDS Church." Not having shown the care that Mormons had, when they had, became his evidence that other claims are not as valid as the LDS claim. He also dismissed any argument that the land should have multiple interpretations: "no one should feel that if the Martin's Cove site is devoted to the interpretation of a single event, that this somehow undermines what took place by other great American pioneers along historical trails located really not too far from this site."[48] One of the church's most vocal defenders in the debate, Hansen was convinced that the deaths that occurred near the cove made the spot uniquely Mormon even though three of the major westward trails passed by the place. While some argued that fellow Americans might learn from the Mormon narratives of migration, Hansen defended the Mormons' right to offer their "one story" as the predominant narrative at Martin's Cove.

Opponents to the initial proposal to sell the land and the later proposal to lease it varied in their responses but were unified in their argument that both the possible purchase and the lease violated the establishment clause of the First Amendment. They believed that the lease constituted the government favoring one religious tradition and set up a dangerous precedent that would allow other religious groups to claim that they believed portions of federal land were sacred and therefore should be put under their oversight and care. In these predictions about precedence, Native American groups were most often cited as those who might do so, particularly for places where many of their members had died. That could mean that places where the U.S. military massacred indigenous peoples could be declared sacred as well.[49]

Others wondered whether Native American groups would use the agreement to push for the oversight of lands like Mato Tipila, or Devil's Tower, a site sacred to Native American groups that lies at the heart of many land contestations in Wyoming.[50] This conversation serves as another episode in the erasure of indigenous experiences, identities, and spatial claims. While the hearings focused on Mormons' claims to Martin's Cove, the question that lay under the surface in several discussions, the one that should alert us to these erasures, was the question of Native Americans' rights to sacred lands and to sites where colonialism led to massacres. Such questions were raised only briefly: a sign that power over narratives and access to legal means to seek out rights to lands combined in this instance. Whose suffering matters, and which communities get public recognition of past and present suffering, points to the structural power systems at work. In the words of claimant Holdsworth: "imagine if an Indian tribe or band wanted to acquire land that it considered sacred or was the site of a battle or massacre where many dozens of its members had died or been killed. Does it seem likely that Native Americans would be successful in such an endeavor? Probably not; history does not suggest success. . . . Native Americans seem to lack the political influence and representatives in Congress as well as the government agencies that the LDS Church enjoys."[51] In this instance, Mormon access to white and Christian privilege participated in shaping the legal and public discourse around Martin's Cove and sacred space.

One of the groups opposed to the initial bill to sell the land to the church was an organization of atheists who saw H.R. 4103 as an instance of the LDS Church pursuing its efforts "to expand its sprawling system of religionized historical trails and sites." This group attempted to mobilize its members to urge their congressional leaders to take a stand against the bill.[52]

The most vocal opponent to the later proposal to lease the site and hand control over to the LDS Church was the ACLU. Its 2005 lawsuit against the secretary of the interior and the director of the BLM was filed on behalf of four Wyoming residents: Jennifer Sorensen and Kevin Holdsworth (professors at Western Wyoming Community College and both descendants of Mormon pioneers), who claimed: "even though they repeatedly told [their LDS guide at Martin's Cove] that they did not wish to talk about the LDS Church, the guide persisted in asking them about the Church and about their religious beliefs" and that "the story of Martin's Cove and its surrounding areas is one of both Mormon and national significance . . . the official LDS explanation of the Martin Handcart tragedy does not tell the whole story." Sorensen and Holdsworth were named alongside Susan M. Wozny, of Laramie, who recalled that during a visit to the site she "was repeatedly asked by LDS guides about her religious affiliation and was prevented from accessing an area of the trail because Mormons had died there and it was 'sacred' and 'hallowed ground,'" and William Young, of Medicine Bow, who as a Quaker felt that the lease constituted preferential treatment of the LDS Church by Congress. The four Wyoming residents were joined in the suit by the Western Land Exchange Program, an environmental organization.[53] Overall, the suit argued that non-Mormon visitors to Martin's Cove felt as though they could not avoid proselytization and the narrow Mormon "one story" even if their only goal was to hike around the cove.

The ACLU's legal claim contained several arguments. One of the aspects of the lease agreement identified by the ACLU was that it gave the church "the right to exclude visitors based on their viewpoints (such as wearing an 'I Am Pro-Choice' t-shirt)." The ACLU argued that this gave too much power to the LDS Church, a religious group, on federal lands where no one should be excluded for acts of free speech.

Second, Mark Lopez, an ACLU attorney, argued that the history of Martin's Cove was not one story but many; it "is part of a much larger history of the American westward migration that is not limited to the religious significance that the site has for the church." He went on to suggest that Congress had, in effect, "singled out the LDS Church for special treatment by allowing the Church to act as gatekeeper and steward of the property." By granting this power, the church had been given the ability to historically interpret the landscape; here, he claimed, the government was abdicating its responsibility "to preserve those lands as part of the national trust."[54] In his arguments Lopez suggested that the land had a broader significance to the American people and because of this significance the federal government had a responsibility to properly care for the land and provide multiple narratives about what had happened there. Instead, the complainants believed that the church "has been given the go-ahead to create on federal property a Mormon shrine that incorporates the Church's own historical and religious interpretation of the events that occurred in Martin's Cove." And so complainants identified history-telling and space-making as two activities that should not be handed over to a religious organization. They argued that the "church can not constitutionally act as gatekeeper or storyteller for property that everyone agrees has historic value beyond its significance to the LDS Church."[55]

In the congressional hearings, Kirk Koepsel, the Northern Plains regional representative of the Sierra Club, also made several arguments against the lease. In a similar move to that of the ACLU, Koepsel asserted that the land had broader significance and Martin's Cove was "one of the best areas to view the intact trails and experience the history of westward expansion."[56] Another argument offered by opponents was that Mormon trekkers were harming the fragile environment in Wyoming. In 2005 estimates suggested that about 70,000 people were visiting the site annually and 12,500 people participated in some form of trek that included the public land near the visitors' center.[57] Koepsel wanted to preserve the area as a spot "of exceptional beauty and scenery . . . composed of an ancient mountain range whose smooth pink granite is the backdrop for the Sweetwater River and for the four national historic trails which pass close by."[58] Here Koepsel shifted the discourse about why this area should be preserved. He aligned with the ACLU and others who claimed that the site was of broader significance to the history of the United States. Yet at the same time he portrayed a landscape that was worthy of preservation simply because of its inherent beauty and pristine nature.[59]

In 2006, the BLM, the ACLU, and the LDS Church reached a compromise of sorts. In the nonbinding agreement, the church agreed to set aside a parking area that would be marked "public access" and would allow visitors to bypass all church-owned sites. The church also agreed to create nonproselytizing guidelines for its missionaries, who worked at different points along the trail into the cove. As well, the church agreed to post signage that stated that visitors to the cove had the same rights as "visitors to any other Department of Interior site that is open to the public." Finally, the church's logo was removed from several signs near the cove. If the agreement is not kept, the ACLU can refile its suit.[60]

When the arguments of all of the opponents—the ACLU, the Sierra Club, the complainants—are collected, they amount to challenges on several fronts to the LDS understanding of Martin's Cove as sacred and distinctly Mormon. First, the argument that the land is significant for all Americans as a site where the four major westward trails converge complicates the narrative about the site's significance that focuses solely on the Mormon deaths that happened there. It makes of the "one story" many stories. Second, what happened with the church's lease of Martin's Cove calls into question whether any religious group should be allowed exclusive claims to federal lands when they are significant historical or spiritual sites for the group—and, if so, why not allow claims to all groups equally? Finally, the next challenge, which I will discuss further, is a battle over accurate history-telling that raises questions about the narratives about the site.

Battles over History

One of the key questions in the debates over the lease of Martin's Cove was who would get to write the history of the space and tell its stories. Control of the place means control of its storytelling. Some, including the Holdsworths, were concerned that the narrative offered by missionaries at Martin's Cove would leave out certain aspects of the history and spin others into faith pro-motion. In fact, they feared that the goal of recounting the history was faith promotion rather than historical accuracy. Holdsworth identified what he considered to be three different types of history-telling about Martin's Cove. One is the scholarly version. The second is the institutional church's story as presented in the visitors' center, which leaves out "the idea of responsibility, that is, who made the decisions in question, but it does present selected in-formation in an accurate way." Finally, there is the folk version of the history that missionaries offer to promote the faith of church members.

Holdsworth argues that there are several errors in the second two versions of the story. First, he believes that the church has put a gloss of benevolence over the Perpetual Emigration Fund, which he likens to a "system of partial indenturement" whereby emigrants struggled to pay off their debts to the institutional church after arriving in Salt Lake City. Second, he sees an avoid-ance of the question of who was actually responsible for the late departure. Finally, he questions the number of deaths asserted in the church narratives. "The missionaries at Martin's Cove routinely claim that 200 emigrants died there," he writes; "this is patently and demonstrably false." He argues that the number is off by several dozen because company members died across Wyoming and all along the Mormon Trail but are remembered as having all died in one spot. He asserts that the church focuses on only one site, the bravery and sacrifices of the pioneers, and the efforts of the rescuers, in order to let Brigham Young "off the hook."[61] "Because I have an ancestral connec-tion to the handcart disasters of 1856," he writes, "I am troubled by both the lack of historical accuracy in the portrayal of those events, as well as an ap-propriation of the events—and particularly emigrant deaths—for narrow purposes."[62] Interestingly, Holdsworth draws on the cultural power of having pioneer ancestors to make his claim here, asserting that he has a stake in how the narrative gets told.

Critics of the church's version of history note that the history being told at the cove is different from that told on government-sponsored monuments and the BLM-designed museum displays in Casper, Wyoming. In these places, "God is conspicuously absent and the tone is grim. The pioneers were late, the displays say. They struggled and died." The director of the displays, Jude Carino, has said that the museum's job was not to put the history "through the filter of the believer."[63] These storytellers also remind visitors that the history of the site is the story of four westward migration trails and are concerned that through telling the narrative in order to inspire faith, the church lost some of the complexities of the historical narrative are lost.[64]

In contrast to this narrative, Latter-day Saints portray a different view of the history of Martin's Cove and the broader movement westward. Gordon B. Hinckley summarized this position well when he said: "ours was a united movement crossing the plains. It was an organized, methodical thing. It was not a motley crew. It all worked according to a well-thought-out and well-executed plan—except for those two ill-fated handcart companies of 1856. But other than those two companies, everything just seemed to be well-planned and it went very well. It was a test of their faith. They knew they were risking their lives to make this long journey, and they made it. Some of them died—they paid that price. It was a tremendous test of their faith."[65] Hinckley's brief narrative conjures the image of the beehive, so prominent in nineteenth-century Utah, where each individual is working towards a larger, communal, divinely ordained plan. In this narrative the 1856 tragedies operate as a blip on a much larger map. Yet in that narrative the handcart company members' untimely deaths still serve a purpose; they gave their lives, the ultimate sacrifice, for Zion and for gathering. And so, where the BLM and its history-makers recount a grueling and grim story of poor and flawed human choices, the church has instead found a redemptive narrative of human suffering, of faithful pioneers who gave their lives for the concept of Zion and who are models of sacrifice for believers today.

Figure 5.1 Statue representing Bodil Mortensen, This Is The Place Park.

5

The Sweetheart of the Riverton Stake

Martyrdom and Rescue in the Lives of the Saints

Not far from the entrance to the living history portion of TITP Park is a bronze statue commissioned by the Bountiful Sons of the Utah Pioneers and crafted by Stan Watts; it portrays a small girl standing next to the wheel of a handcart (see Figure 5.1). The wheel is just a shade shorter than the girl but at the same time appears to dwarf her, taking over the bulk of the sculpture's space. The wheel is upright but unattached; it is just the wheel and the girl. She gazes up at the sky with a questioning look on her face, and in her arms she clutches a bundle of branches. The statue represents Bodil Mortensen, a ten-year-old member of the Willie handcart company. A child from Denmark traveling toward Zion, she was one of the many people who died along the route in 1856. Bodil's legacy has increased since the 1990s, as Latter-day Saints have come to understand her history and claim her as a modern-day martyr.

The text at the base of the statue reveals a lot about Bodil's role in the modern Mormon imagination. It reads: "Bodil Mortensen. Once lost never again forgotten. Symbol of the children who walked toward Zion. Inspiration of the Riverton Wyoming stake's 'Second Rescue' and above all an example for those who have yet to walk to their own Zion." In some aspects of Mormon culture, Bodil Mortensen has come to represent what was lost along the route westward, affirming for audiences of her story just how much the journey was worth. In addition, she inspired a renewed ritual incorporation of the nineteenth-century pioneers into modern Mormonism. Her story framed their genealogical computer research and temple rites in honor of the pioneers as its own type of rescue, allowing recent Mormons to read themselves back into the nineteenth-century exodus in more direct, ritualistic, and tactile ways.

One church leader, M. Russell Ballard, remembered Bodil Mortensen in a 1996 General Conference speech, "Faith in Every Footstep," that prepared

Pioneers in the Attic. Sara M. Patterson, Oxford University Press (2020). © Oxford University Press.
DOI: 10.1093/oso/9780190933869.001.0001

the Saints for the 1997 sesquicentennial year. He described her story, along with that of Jens Nielsen, as one of the most touching stories of sacrifice, faith, and loving charity. "Nielsen, a Danish farmer, contributed all of his money to the church except for the funds he needed to purchase a handcart and stock it. Nielsen, his wife and son, and Bodil Mortensen set off to Utah—Nielsen had promised to care for Bodil on the journey. The same night that Bodil Mortensen froze to death, the Nielsen son Niels did too."[1] Ballard quoted Gordon Hinckley, then president of the church, as he described the Wyoming portion of the journey: "a trail of tragedy, a trail of faith, a trail of devotion, a trail of consecration." The blood that was shed on the trail was imagined as consecrating the land and serving as some sort of spiritual purchase. It is remembered still today as an important sacrifice for gathering and for Zion.

Bodil Mortensen lay buried at Rock Creek Hollow, Wyoming, for many decades without anyone remembering her name. In the late twentieth and early twenty-first centuries, Mormons "discovered" Bodil, made her the focus of ritual and storytelling, and fashioned her into a modern-day Mormon martyr. Members of the Riverton stake discovered her bones when they pushed to purchase the ground on which she died. During the process of trying to legally purchase the ground, stake members learned her story and imbued it with meaning for their own context. The story of Bodil the martyr then served to sanctify the ground where she was buried. This chapter will explore the process whereby Bodil became a martyr, the way her story was ritualized, and then the way the presence of her bodily remains (along with the remains of fourteen others) sanctified the ground at Rock Creek Hollow. Examination of the creation of Bodil the martyr will illuminate the way the slippage between metaphorical and literal interpretations happens in modern-day Mormonism. The inscription on the statue of Bodil seems to en-compass the tension between the metaphorical and the concrete and to embrace the slippages that happen in the spaces between. The text declares that Bodil is a symbol of "the children who walked toward Zion," suggesting that she is a symbol of the children (those she led as well as those led by others) who made their way through the hardships of the trail to achieve their Zion in the Salt Lake Valley. At the same time, the text projects that she is inspiration "for those who have yet to walk to their own Zion." Here, Bodil's journey is metaphorized in order both to make it accessible to all believers and to unmoor it from a particular place. The literal, geographical Zion is precisely where Bodil was headed when she lost her life, yet it is also anywhere—the goal and goad of believers today.

Bodil's Life and Death

Bodil Mortensen's name wasn't even on the books of the fourth handcart company led by Captain Willie. Her status as a child traveling without parents meant that her journey and her life were never very well documented. It was not until the 1990s that Latter-day Saints rediscovered Bodil and began to piece together what her experiences might have been. It was then that they decided to "rescue" her. That rescue included a sense that they were rescuing her from historical forgetfulness, embracing her as a spiritual ancestor worthy of remembrance and honor, and performing temple rites for her so that her future spiritual life would be secured. What they found out about Bodil was just the skeleton of a story, yet from those glimmers of a life, they fashioned her into the "sweetheart" of the Riverton stake.

What was the historical framework for the sweetheart story? Bodil Mortensen was born on August 5, 1846, in Systofta, Maribo, Denmark. Her father was a Danish weaver. When she was nine years old, her parents decided to send her on ahead to Zion, as they had done with her older sister Anne the year before. They planned to bring the entire family and join the sisters there soon. They left Bodil in the care of their friends Jens and Else Nielsen, who were also making the journey. With the Nielsens and their son, Bodil spent six weeks traveling to New York City from Denmark.

It was then up to this small band to make their way westward to Zion. It was in that process that they joined the Willie company in Nebraska. As discussed in chapter 4, the company's journey was catastrophic. In the midst of some of the worst weather they encountered, the group had to make its way across Rocky Ridge, one of the highest points on the trek. Bodil had been charged with caring for the children younger than she was; as the adults struggled with the handcarts, she shepherded the children over the ridge during blizzard-like conditions and with a foot of snow already on the ground.[2] Once arrived at the campground, Bodil went out to find kindling for a campfire. The next day, her frozen body was found; she had died clutching sagebrush and was huddled against a handcart wheel. Thirteen people died that night, and the next day a grave was dug for them at Rock Creek Hollow. Two more people, who helped to dig the mass grave, also died and were buried there.

One other child also receives a good bit of attention in Mormon narratives of Rock Creek Hollow, though it seems no one can outdo Bodil. James Kirkwood was eleven when he went on the trip with his mother and three brothers, one of whom, Thomas, was physically unable to walk on the journey and so rode in the handcart. When they arrived at the camp before summitting Rocky Ridge, Joseph, James's four-year-old younger brother, had frozen feet and could not walk. The Kirkwoods were told that they could either carry Joseph or wait for rescue wagons. So James carried his brother over Rocky Ridge to Rock Creek. Once he arrived, he died. Joseph, though, made it to Salt Lake City.[3] These types of tragic stories populate the imagined and actual space of Rock Creek Hollow.

Bodil's tragic death continued to affect the community. The Neilsens, with whom Bodil had traveled, did not have the address of her parents, so it was not until they arrived in Salt Lake City the following year that they found out that their younger daughter had died. Her mother, Maren Kirstine, "never fully recovered from the loss of her little child. She suffered a nervous breakdown and died in 1862."[4]

It is on these scraps of evidence that Mormons have constructed a modern-day martyr narrative.

The Martyrdom of Bodil Mortensen

The death of Bodil Mortensen and the fourteen other pioneers at Rock Creek Hollow was a tragic event remembered in narratives of the pioneers' movement west. It was not until the early twentieth century, though, that church members began to ask where the gravesite was, expressing interest in marking it in some way.[5] It was, after all, the site of a terrible tragedy, and church members felt that it should be a part of marking the Mormon experience on the landscapes of the American West.

In the late twentieth century, the site once again began to receive attention. Wendell Bunnell, who had been a member of the Riverton stake presidency (the presidency having three members, the president and his first and second counselors), served as the chair for the 1979 Pioneer Day celebration. On July 24, the Riverton stake organized an "authentic pioneer dinner" that consisted of wheat bread, milk, and raw onions.[6] Though not an appealing meal for most, the dinner points to how this space was understood, an understanding that continued into the late twentieth century. Mormons viewed Rock Creek Hollow as a place that demanded attention. The stake continued to return to that spot for their Pioneer Day celebrations—proximity to the place encouraged an understanding that their modern-day activities were somehow more authentic. The Pioneer Day celebrations began the modern-day attempts to make Rock Creek Hollow a sacred space.

The members of the Riverton stake returned to the site on other days of the year. Area stake presidents suggested that youth conferences be held nearby to save expenses. The leaders of the programs for young men and women developed their own handcart trek, one that would allow their youth to connect in meaningful ways with the spaces in Wyoming. The treks occurred every four years, and the youth built their own handcarts and spent their time singing, dancing, and remembering the suffering and joys of the pioneers.[7]

The activities surrounding Rock Creek Hollow cemented its importance for the members of the stake. The stake's leadership encouraged the institutional church to purchase the property. In 1989, the owner of the land, Ken Ballard, rejected an offer from the church to purchase 160 acres at $2,000 an acre. The church was not willing to pay more, so Ballard "constructed a fence blocking entrance to the site during the summer of 1989." Thereafter, stake members were not able to hold their Pioneer Day celebrations there.[8] The fence, however, actually served to further confirm to stake members the importance of the site. That someone else would attempt to halt the activities they wanted to perform, to keep them away, confirmed its sacred status. That someone would "profane" it, by monetizing its sale at a seemingly unfair advantage, served as evidence in the narratives that the site was fragile, in need of protection and Mormon care.

The desire of the stake leaders to acquire the land continued, and in 1990 they found themselves defending the importance of the land to others in the church who said that the "the project had no merit." A letter from Glen Leonard, then part of the Museum of Church History and Art, to Scott Lorimer declared: "it would not be appropriate to acquire property in the area for historical purposes. There are many places along the Mormon trail that come under consideration as historic sites. Most of the sites are burial sites or important campgrounds. We do not feel that it is an appropriate expenditure of Church funds to acquire and maintain such places as Church historic sites." Frustrated and defensive, the stake leaders responded by suggesting that their own historical research told them that this site was significant and special because it was the "exact location of a mass grave along the trail" and "historical and spiritual happenings of the location are paralleled only by the Martin site in all of Church History."[9] Despite the stake leaders' arguments, they were not given the funds to purchase the site and were told to wait in the hope that the landowner would lower the price.

As Lorimer recalled, "as we got into it, it became very apparent that we were not going to be able to buy Rock Creek. The man who owned it wanted an exorbitant amount of money for it."[10]

Even though the stake was unable to purchase the property at that time, the stake presidency became even more firmly convinced that the site was significant to the identity of its members and the members of the global church. They asserted that a divine force was encouraging their actions, "almost forcing us to continue the project." They asked stake members to "remember the project in their prayers and . . . to understand the promptings we were receiving."[11] In so doing, in positioning themselves as defenders of a space in jeopardy, one not fully recognized as it ought to be, the stake leaders further declared that the land was central to the narratives of who church members were and who the spirit was "prompting" them to be.

Eventually, the stake presidency put its drive to purchase the land on the back burner and shifted its focus. According to their accounts, it was further prompting of the Holy Spirit that convinced them to change gears. Desiree Lorimer, Scott Lorimer's wife, recalled that her husband had received a spiritual nudging that told him their project should focus on temple ordinances rather than land, at least for a short time. She recalled: "I rejoiced with him when the answer finally came that it was not the land, but rather it was the temple work. Goose bumps covered me as I realized that he had indeed received a revelation and knew that what was happening was bigger than we had ever imagined. Did I ever doubt it? NO! For I know the man!"[12] In 1991, Scott Lorimer recalled that he had learned the lesson that the land was not as important: "I've asked my counselors a hundred times if I've asked them once—what is so important about a piece of worthless sagebrush land? Why won't this leave us alone? . . . There is a far greater purpose than that land. The land is very, very important. It is a symbol to those of us who yet live today of the courage and the devotion of those who went before us; the dedication and the conversion to the gospel. But there is yet a far greater purpose for which the Willie people have come."[13] As I will show, the relationship between the land and the narratives, between space and memory, is much more complex than Lorimer suggests here. Yet the members of the stake and their leadership began to reframe the narrative, at least for a time, suggesting that memory and history might have to take precedence over space.

Shifting their focus to the spiritual lives of the pioneers was a crucial step in making a martyr of Bodil Mortensen. It may sound strange to refer to her as a martyr because the popular imagination often understands martyrdom as applying only to those who die by way of a state that rejects the belief system of the martyr. Yet martyrdom has also been applied to those who die in service of their beliefs, whether or not the death is caused by a state agency. Martin Luther King Jr. is one such example. King died as part of a larger cause; he was killed because of what he believed in and worked for. Told by communities over and over, martyr narratives describe people dedicated to a cause for which they are willing to pay the ultimate price, often in a dramatic, out-of-the-ordinary fashion.

It is the community that makes a martyr a martyr. In the telling of life and death narratives, the community creates meaning out of a tragic death. As Elizabeth A. Castelli, a scholar of early Christian martyrs, has noted, martyrdom "can be understood as one form of refusing the *meaninglessness* of death itself, of insisting that suffering and death do not signify emptiness and nothingness, which they might otherwise seem to imply."[14] While asserting meaning in the face of the meaninglessness of death, martyr stories also imply that the universe works in a particular way, that even though life may seem unfair and capricious, there is an ultimate and cosmic meaning to things. Martyr stories confirm that there is order in the cosmos. What this tells us is that martyr stories are about the meaning-making practices of the community "rather than a matter of unmediated experience." Martyrdom is in the eye of the beholder, and martyr stories play a significant role in the shaping of community identity. Martyrdom valorizes suffering to some degree and suggests that the death of the individual is worth it—that death supports the bigger picture and the value system of the community.[15] In its celebration of the exemplar individual, the martyr story actually celebrates communal values and encourages individuals to take on the traits of the martyr in order to honor the community.

If it is the community that makes a martyr a martyr, it is the Christian community that has made martyrdom a core aspect of its identity. That central story began early in the Christian community. When the Roman government crucified Jesus, a template was created. As the Christian community matured, members came to understand martyrdom as a form of imitating Christ. Not only would martyrdom mark one as a true follower of Christ, but early Christian theology taught that it would also gain you immediate salvation and entry into heaven.[16] As well, you would be remembered in history as one of those who gave their lives to the cause. Thus, the narrative affirmed that you could take comfort in knowing that you would be immortal in the collective memory of the community.

Martyr stories provide an account that endorses "the realms of aesthetics, piety, and narrative."[17] When martyr stories are told, the teller and the audience are able to connect to a narrative that endorses their faith and explains its values and significance. Castelli, writing about the Catholic practice of taking on a saint's name at confirmation, explains the significance for Catholics today: "*their* lives were *not* ours, but we could bask in their reflected glory by taking their names and copying out their stories. . . . Our fledgling 'research' [to choose a confirmation saint] was an attempt to reach across time, to acknowledge the yawning abyss between their 'then' and our 'now' and to find a way, however provisionally, to bridge the gap."[18] In the Mormon community, a similar set of activities surrounds the research and "rescue" of Bodil Mortensen and her fellow travelers. The Riverton stake members imagined themselves extending their arms across a yawning abyss between the pioneers' then and their own now, encouraging Bodil and the others to reach out and cross over.

Castelli's observations about the Catholic practice can help to clarify what is at work in the Mormon community. As young Catholics sought out the story of a saint or martyr to whom they could connect, Castelli notes that they weren't participating in professionalized history-telling, where evidentiary claims are of the utmost importance, but taking part in "an important form of collective memory work." That memory work "linked in our imaginations undeserved suffering, heroism, violence, religious conviction, gender, and identity."[19] Young Catholics were "laying claim to the past" and at the same time individually connecting themselves to the group's chain of memory through a story of a particular saint or martyr. The stories they chose were, in part, individual stories, yet they also followed known patterns of martyr stories, making it easier for modern-day believers to connect to the stories themselves. Castelli explains: "that the stories often bore remarkable structural similarities to one another . . . raised no historiographical suspicions. The fact that these repetitions bordered on the formulaic was indeed telling, but only in the sense that it confirmed what we were already sure we knew: that the story bore within itself a deep-seated truth."[20]

Believers interpreted the stories within a cosmic framework, based on patterns that they had already seen and knew by heart. In one of the first biblical texts written about the Christian church, the author of Luke-Acts "made the predictions of persecution an organizing feature of the triumphant story it told." That narrative was also reinforced in the book of

Revelation, with its "gruesome portraits of righteous suffering" and its in-terpretation of that suffering within the framework of the cosmic battle between good and evil. And the narratives about martyrdom continued to accrue because the popular stories were about "embattled enclaves of right teaching and innocent practice positioned amidst profound and hos-tile error."[21] In setting that context, the narratives affirmed for believers the idea that good would always triumph over evil, that in the end *their* side would win out. The weakness and innocence of the martyr were particu-larly appealing qualities precisely because the martyr's story affirmed the power of the good.

While cementing the community, martyr stories also served an important function in the relationship between insiders and outsiders. Martyrs die for their beliefs, the story goes, and those stories make the belief system *feel* true. Martyrs became the heroes of Christianity and served as witnesses that the truth claims of the new group were, in fact, truth itself.

The formulaic nature of the story, then, confirmed the truthfulness of the message, which was then solidified in the aura of historical facticity. Thus, the narratives of martyrdom participated in a type of "culture making, whereby Christian identity was indelibly marked by the collective memory of the re-ligious suffering of others."[22] This thesis can extend to the world of modern-day Latter-day Saints. Though they do not accept the idea of a special group of believers beyond death who can serve as intermediaries for living members in the same way modern Catholicism does, the stories of Mormon martyrs play a significant role in the community. As discussed in chapter 3, in the narratives of the LDS Church, Joseph Smith is understood as a martyr. Thus, martyrdom is a central concept to the community both as a Christian com-munity, with the example of Jesus, and as a restoration movement, with the example of Smith. Martyrdom continues to function as an affirmation of be-lief, and Latter-day Saints access the stories of martyrs to confirm their belief system and create community.

Maurice Halbwachs was interested in how collective memory shaped in-dividual identity and how groups mapped their collective memories onto landscapes. In his studies, he noted that collective memories must remain sufficiently fixed to give a sense of unchanging tradition while at the same time being sufficiently flexible to provide meaning as the community changes over time. The telling and retelling of a story ensures that the story becomes a part of the community's collective memory.[23] Halbwachs's key contribution was his ability to show how individuals connect their individual stories to larger group narratives and how that then shapes their understanding of a meaningful world.

Because collective memory is about identity, there is not necessarily a direct connection between historical events and the narratives people tell about those events. Though participants in the group *believe* that the events they are recounting are historically accurate, the meaning that is communicated in the events, rather than the historical narrative itself, holds the most significance. For this reason, one can look to the function of the various pieces of the story and consider how they play a role in collective memory and group identity formation. One can ask why the story of Bodil Mortensen would appeal to modern-day Mormons. What aspects of the story provide the Mormon community with a sense of group values, cohesiveness, and meaning?

Historically speaking, there is little substance to Bodil's story. Perhaps it is in the gaps themselves that modern-day Mormons can find the most meaning and connection to their pioneer past. In fact, we could read Bodil's story quite differently from the way it has been recounted. She was a young girl sent to America by her parents. She may not have understood the language spoken by the majority of the people with whom she traveled. She may not have felt a commitment to the religious ideals that propelled many of the Mormons westward and shaped her parents' choices. She may have been largely a victim of circumstance. The loss of her life on the journey westward could be attributed to the foolhardy choices of the adults under whose care she was placed. Her death could be read as the bad luck of a group who could neither predict nor adequately prepare for the weather patterns of a land they had never visited.

Yet the framework of Bodil's story now carries the shape of the collective memory of late twentieth- and early twenty-first-century Mormons. In her, they have found a sweetheart, or in the words of the stake's second counselor Kitchen, "a special friend." She is remembered as a heroic child of "tender years."[24] In her story, the whim-like nature of the natural world that caused a blizzard during the journey serves as the background, the setting of suffering in which her story was written.

Something about Bodil's story and the way it is told continues to draw modern Mormons back to it. Perhaps part of the draw of the story is that Bodil represents the immigrant community who traveled to the American West from around the globe to gather to Zion. She is an immigrant and a pioneer, thus merging two narratives the church is attempting to balance today.

That her story was considered "lost to history" until modern Mormons rescued her also makes her story appealing. The audience is connected to her precisely because they are playing a role in her rescue. "She's not listed anywhere as part of the company. . . . She's not listed anywhere. She's in some journals, and that's where we started running into her," recalled Scott Lorimer. Thus, each time her story is told, the teller and the audience can sense that they are participating in her rescue again, infusing her tragic death with new meaning.

Lorimer narrates Bodil's death in a way now common in Mormon circles. It is a narrative imbued with an understanding of principled sacrifice and suffering: "and this little girl shepherded those little kids through this blizzard, snow up to her knees, for twenty-seven hours. They got to Rock Creek, and she went out to gather firewood. That was her job when she got to Rock Creek. They found her frozen the next morning leaning up against the wheel of a handcart with her arms full of sagebrush." Bodil was bound by her duties and responsibilities, the narratives recall. She did not question her job but knew it was for the greater good. She died caring for the weaker members of the community.

Lorimer's telling does not end at Bodil's death. Instead, he describes her as present, watching over and encouraging the Riverton stake to do temple work for her, to remember her. He recalled: "she has worked very heavily on us in a spiritual way." Because of that spiritual connection, members of the stake "have become completely enthralled with this little girl." "We all love her dearly because of what she means to us," he explained. Even at Rock Creek, evidence can be found of her significance: "when you go to the grave at Rock Creek, there's always flowers next to her name. People pick them and put them there. She means so much to all of us."[25] Lorimer's "all of us" even included then president and prophet of the church Gordon B. Hinckley. Lorimer remembered that early on in the process, he had a conversation with Hinckley in which Hinckley said he was upset. He asked Lorimer why the pioneers' temple work had not been done for them. "He said, 'president, don't you stop until it's finished,' " Lorimer recounted. "And then I told him of Bodil Mortensen our young friend and President Hinckley wept. He said that he was truly sorry that the Church had not had the ability to do her work prior to this time."[26] When Hinckley visited Rock Creek Hollow, he saw Lorimer placing flowers by Bodil's grave. Hinckley said, " 'You can't get away with that.' He went and pulled a bunch of flowers out of the ground and put them down next to her name. He said, 'She's my friend, too.' What an honor for a little, forgotten, nine-year-old girl who was in a foreign country . . . to have a prophet of God put some flowers down to remember her."[27] Here we see an interesting narration of events. Bodil's significance comes, in part, after her death, when a prophet honors her by remembering her. She was rescued from forgottenness and remembered by the central figures of the community as a very special person.

Lorimer further recounted that Bodil's work on the other side of the veil of physical death continued: "she wanted her work done and she got it done. Neat person. I really look forward to the day when I can meet her. . . . But she has done so much for us, and we felt her spirit. We've all just been really touched by this little girl who was a nameless person until a year ago, completely forgotten." Explaining the significance of Bodil's narrative, he continued: "she gave all that she could to the kingdom of God, even her life, and she was promised, like we all are, that if she would do all that she could, that she would be blessed and taken care of. She had to wait 136 years, but it got done."[28]

Lorimer was not the only one who believed that Bodil's influence and mission extended beyond her short life. In a book titled *Follow Me to Zion*, a descendant of one of Bodil's siblings, Dorothy Bottema, writes:

> many times in this earthly life we think of our mission coming to an end when death comes to claim our physical body. Our family's experience with Bodil has proven that one's mission, even the most valuable part, may continue long after one's earthly passing. Bodil's body lay in an unmarked grave for over 130 years, with her Mortensen family knowing little of her struggles, courage, and sacrifice. Then in 1991, the story of this 11-year-old girl touched the hearts of the Riverton Wyoming stake presidency to ignite the Second Rescue, which caused thousands of temple ordinances to be performed for members of the Willie Handcart Company. The fire of Bodil's story continues to burn in the hearts of all who hear it. We as a family have felt of her strength and help. We view her as our rescuer.[29]

Bodil's family later dedicated a monument to her, at Parowan Heritage Park in southern Utah, titled *Tribute to Bodil Mortensen*. It includes these words: "welcome home, our dear and beloved Bodil. Not to the big valley where your sister anxiously awaited your arrival, but to this small peaceful valley which is now your spiritual place of rest here on earth."[30] And so Bodil's life and death are imagined as speaking to a larger theological truth in the present-day Mormon community. She is remembered as a martyr—a model of the character traits the community wishes to promote in its members. She is also remembered as one who continues to show perseverance beyond the veil of death, demonstrating how important individuals are even beyond their physical existence. Bodil's story tells modern-day Mormons that they, too, can achieve immortality and that immortality comes in different forms. It comes in the performance of temple rites for others, and it comes in influence. Bodil's story, rescued from historical forgottenness, serves as evidence that individuals can continue to influence the community in a positive way beyond their physical lives.

Bodil's story is retold in fireside chats (faith-promoting talks), testimonials, trek reenactments, and Sunday school classes. Her story has become a treasured narrative as some modern-day Mormons continue to find meaning in it and incorporate it into the communal, collective memory. She is also remembered in several film narratives. Those films range from locally produced YouTube videos in which young women retell her story to more polished church productions meant to promote faith on a larger scale. She is also remembered in song.[31] One song, "Remember the Journey," has a young girl's voice singing: "I can't feel my feet / there is nothing left to eat." That voice is joined by an adult woman's voice that sings the majority of the lyrics about Bodil, responding: "You didn't know your journey would end before you'd see the valley / but you left such a legacy / You didn't know that your faith changes me."[32] The song's message is that Bodil's voice would speak beyond her short life and that there was a larger value system that needed confirmation. In the song, she is assured that she is an example and an inspiration. In another song, "Bodil's Theme," which is part of a Mormon Handcart Pageant, a piano duet tells most of the story. Only one lyric segment appears in a much longer melody: "And should we die / All is well!"[33]

This song reduces Bodil's life to a simple message, but one that speaks to modern-day Mormons and encourages them to understand life as extending beyond physical existence. Her life had meaning for them, the narrative recalls. Her death may have been painful, but the narrative told by Mormons today declares that in the face of physical death, "All is well!"

In narratives of Bodil told by modern Mormons, one can see an example of the slippage between the metaphorical and the literal, the conceptual and the concrete. In his book *The Price We Paid*, Andrew D. Olsen tells the story of the Willie and Martin handcart pioneers. The title indicates the ultimate purpose of Olsen's narrative: to celebrate the pioneers as the ancestors of a modern "we" and thereby to cement the group and its collective memory around the narratives of sacrifice. Olsen speaks of Rock Creek Hollow and Martin's Cove as "places made sacred by the sacrifices of the Willie and Martin handcart pioneers." Narrating Bodil's story and the stories of the others who died at Rock Creek Hollow, he writes: "reflecting on these scenes, I sense a change in my feelings. More than suffering and death, I see sacrifice and faith, perhaps unparalleled, within these few sacred acres. The feeling that the earth mourns gives way to another feeling that is more subtle but just as real—a feeling that the earth rejoices. For what cause? Because of the sacrifices these people were willing to make for the gospel, for Zion. Because of the heroism of their rescuers. And even, perhaps, because of the power of these stories to teach and inspire."[34] Here one can plot a significant shift that occurs in modern discussions of Bodil Mortensen and Rock Creek Hollow. Olsen suggests that his feeling changes from grief to joy because people were willing to sacrifice for Zion—both as a place and as a central commitment of their faith. From the life comes the message of sacrifice for Zion. From the land comes the seemingly stored memory of these forgotten martyrs who sanctified the land with their deaths.

Why are narratives of suffering and rescue so important to modern-day Mormons? These narratives work on both the individual and the communal levels. C. Vinn Roos, who wrote a study of gravesites of the Martin and Willie handcart companies and their rescuers, described what was, for him, a personal enrichment from the experience of getting to know the stories of these people. "I have found and written about those who have inspired me," he explains. "It has been an exciting, difficult, and spiritual experience. Whenever I came to dead ends or didn't know what to do, there were miracles after miracles waiting for me."[35] For Roos, the stories of the pioneers allowed him to experience new miracles in his own life. And so, on an individual level, the stories can speak of model lives, dedicated to faith and a willingness to sacrifice. They can remind believers of the obstacles the pioneers willingly faced in order to find Zion.

On a communal level, Bodil's story, as well as the stories of James Kirkwood and others who died at Rock Creek Hollow, allows the community access to twinned narratives of piety and innocence. Dying for the causes of Zion and gathering, moving westward away from persecution by their fellow Americans, and participating in their own exodus are narratives that enable Mormons to embrace a story of their own innocence. At the same time, narratives of martyrdom allow the community to claim a type of moral authority that stems from those twinned themes—the death of the martyr authorizes that claim to authority and to spiritual truths.[36] Access to these narratives serves several functions. First, in an age when Mormons are increasingly tolerated by their fellow Americans, stories of pioneer martyrs allow them to tap into narratives of persecution. Such narratives affirm the exodus story—of a persecuted minority fleeing to its divinely promised land—and redeploy the symbolic system of that story in the present-day community. This function is especially important at a time when the LDS Church is no longer a gathered community but a generally tolerated and scattered community; such martyr narratives reinvigorate central stories of exodus and of promised lands. Paradoxically, at the same time that the martyr stories of the pioneers allow broad access to narratives of suffering and persecution for the Mormon community, they also allow Mormons to affirm their centrality to American narratives of westward expansion. Mormon martyrs can be fashioned as symbols for all Americans of the character and sacrifices made to forge a region and a nation.

Second Rescue

Once the members of the Riverton stake started to unearth the stories of the people who had died at Rock Creek Hollow, their attention shifted from acquiring the land to saving the future spiritual lives of the people buried there. Bodil's story stood at the forefront of this movement, which came to be called the "Second Rescue." "Second" because the first rescue had been of the Willie pioneers themselves: the party Brigham Young sent from Salt Lake City.[37] While the first rescue was physical, the second rescue was often referred to as a spiritual one. The pioneers no longer needed food and shelter but needed help proceeding to the highest levels of heaven. As one documentarian of the Second Rescue described it: "the rescue effort initiated by Brigham Young in October of 1856 brought the surviving pioneers safely to the Salt Lake Valley. Now, a 'Second Rescue' was needed to provide the sacred ordinances of the temple for those faithful pioneers. With the clearing of temple ordinances for those buried at Rock Creek Hollow, the Second Rescue of the Willie and Martin handcart pioneers, a very sacred and spiritual rescue, was just beginning."[38]

In order to see how members of the Riverton stake as well as Mormons more broadly came to see the Second Rescue as a significant event, it is necessary to understand certain aspects of Mormon cosmology. In a eulogy offered not long before his own death, Joseph Smith laid out a theology of eternal progression. In this plan of salvation, spirit beings become enshrined in bodies and enter into this world. During their time in this world, their goal should be to better understand God through study and the performance of various temple rites. After death, individuals continue to have free will and are able to make active choices. While awaiting the Second Coming of Christ, after which individuals will be assigned to various levels of heaven based on the choices they've made, these beings can still walk the path toward salvation.

For this reason, Mormons have embraced the idea that they can perform proxy rituals for people who have died. They might perform baptisms, which will allow those who are dead to choose whether or not they want to embark on the path to salvation. Baptism for the dead can be performed both for believers who for some reason were unable to be baptized and for nonbelievers. For dead believers, living Mormons can also perform "endowment" ceremonies and "sealings," which means that those believers will be tied to their loved ones, whether it be spouses, parents, or children, for eternity.

Along with several others who died on the Wyoming plains, Bodil Mortensen was one of the first to be "rescued" in a spiritual way through the performance of temple rituals. Like Bodil, many of the adult pioneers on the westward journey had not yet received their temple ordinances because they had not yet had access to a temple. Part of the draw of making it to the Salt Lake Valley was the promise of doing their temple work. As the members of the stake started to do research, they "began to feel like [they] knew these people." Scott Lorimer had several mystical experiences and realized that the purpose of the nudgings he'd been having wasn't just about acquiring the land, though that desire did not disappear. As a part of a shift in focus, his second counselor, Kim McKinnon, decided to go to Salt Lake City and acquire some of the new genealogical computer programs for the stake. In their discussion of the programs, Lorimer recalled: "in a form of communication that I had never before experienced nor since, I was told that it was because of the Willie people [that they needed the programs]. . . . 'Their temple work isn't done.' That was impossible. I mean, their story is told throughout the Church, all over the world. They are heroes. How in the world could their temple work not be done?"[39]

In response to these spiritual promptings, the stake leaders called a special meeting on July 21, 1991. Describing that meeting, Lorimer recalled that "the stake was just completely overcome with a spirit of love for these people and a desire to get [their temple ordinances] done." In order to satisfy the desires of stake members to find out the stories of individual pioneers, the presidency "divided up the Martin and the Willie Company and the rescuers so that each unit in the Stake had names from all three groups." The leaders then met with the temple recorder to discuss how they might submit names. The recorder suggested naming the entire file after Lorimer for organizational purposes. Lorimer interpreted this as a fulfillment of his patriarchal blessing, a blessing provided by a priesthood-holder in the role of patriarch and thought to provide information about the person's gifts and future use of those gifts: "in my patriarchal blessing it says, 'Many will bless your name as a Savior upon Mount Zion.' Not me personally, but my name. I'd always wondered about that, 'what does that mean?' But it was really a fulfillment of that patriarchal blessing, because through that name all of the Martin and the Willie work was done."[40]

When the members of the stake began to do research on the dead, they could not find records of Bodil's baptism or several of the ordinances for other pioneers. Once they figured this out, they came to believe that perhaps there were many pioneers who had never been able to participate in the rituals themselves, nor had proxy rituals been performed for them. This possibility was especially strong because several of those who died en route to Zion did not have direct descendants who might perform the rituals.[41]

After their research was complete, the stake members concluded that ordinances needed to be performed for about 83 percent of these pioneers.[42] Bodil's story was used as a symbol for the Second Rescue. Stake leader McKinnon told Bodil's story to the stake members and recalled: "she was not a member of the Peter Mortensen family. She did not have any descendants to research her line. She is not even listed on the roster of the Willie handcart company. She was a forgotten little soul all alone in a foreign land, perhaps not understanding the language and what was going on, caught in a terrible snowstorm. She has waited 135 years for all of this to come together, 135 years to . . . finally join the Church, to finally receive the blessings of temple ordinances."[43] For the stake members, Bodil and her peers were "lost souls with no one to do their work."[44]

To the members of the Riverton stake, their role was clear. Through the gifts of modern technology, they were able to do for the dead what no one had been able to do up until the late twentieth century. From a distance of over 130 years, they could metaphorically help the pioneers reach their destination even if they had never actually seen the physical Zion: "these pioneers were eulogized for their courage and sacrifices. Until recently we have not understood the real need of their memory being so well preserved. They have been remembered and will receive their eternal blessings as a result of modern technology. A Second Rescue is now underway. Through the modern miracle of computers, these brave pioneers who pulled handcarts will receive their eternal rewards for which they sacrificed so much."[45]

The Riverton stake's work of finding the spiritual ancestors of these Mormons served as a ritual in and of itself. Yes, temple work was done on behalf of those pioneers who were found not to have their temple ordinances. Yet the Riverton stake members had participated in a prior set of rituals tied to record-keeping when they received a name of a pioneer to research. Just as Joseph Smith Jr. had revealed in 1830 when he founded the church— that Mormons were to be a record-keeping people—these Mormons were keeping important records. Kim McKinnon captured the drive to perform this ritual when he told his stake members that they had "an obligation to read and research and share."[46] Though their work may not stand up to the scrutiny of professional historians, just like the work of Catholics researching confirmation saints, Riverton stake members believed that the act of finding Bodil's name, of rescuing her story from historical forgottenness, was a ritual in and of itself. They were participating in the formation and development of the collective memory of their people.

In the summer of 1991, the family of Scott Lorimer performed some of Bodil's rituals for her. Scott's daughter Sarah Lorimer carried out a proxy baptism for the dead girl. Later that day, Scott and Dee, along with Ruth Mortensen Hauck, sealed Bodil to her parents for eternity. Scott wrote about that day: "there were times when I knew if I would just look up I would be able to see the pioneers."[47] On that day, Bodil was baptized, received the initiatory and endowment ordinances, and was sealed to her parents for eternity.[48] In part because she served as a central figure in the narrative of the Second Rescue, several members participated in the ordinances, and Diane Ison McKinnon, the wife of Kim McKinnon, performed Bodil's initiation and endowment rituals. She recalled that during the process she felt "so close to Heavenly Father, Jesus, Bodil, and especially my dear husband, Kim."[49]

After stake members performed temple ordinances for those who perished at Rock Creek Hollow, they expanded their work to include all of those in the Willie and Martin handcart companies who died en route. Once the Second Rescue was complete, more than 4,200 temple ordinances had been performed on behalf of the pioneers.[50]

Lorimer also claimed that the Second Rescue brought more spiritual attention, both natural and supernatural, to the stake. "We've had some trials and will continue to have some," he said, "because Satan doesn't want us to have the blessings that are really ours. We received three apostolic blessings from Elder Faust and President Hinckley . . . and Satan doesn't want us to have them, I'm sure, and so he's trying us."[51] Because of their work, as Lorimer interpreted the situation, the members of the stake were at the center of a cosmic battle between good and evil. The work they had done was, from his perspective, so important and qualitatively good that Satan now had it out for them.

There was also a sense that the work they had done had elevated them to an important status and affected them spiritually. When James E. Faust, a member of the church's First Presidency, visited Rock Creek Hollow on July 25, 1992, he told stake members that what they had done for the pioneers was "a spiritual service" that "they could not do for themselves." But that spiritual service required even more from the stake members: "that imposes, I think, upon you a responsibility to be worthy to one day greet them and let them express their appreciation to you for what you have done for them."[52] When Susan Madsen wrote a glowing recollection of the process of the Second Rescue, she described it as a story of "courage, personal revelation, and divine providence. It is the story of how the hearts of living Saints were turned by the spirit of the prophet Elijah to those who had gone before, bringing blessings to both the living and the dead."[53]

The revelations and miraculous events described in the narrative of the Second Rescue continued to multiply and a collective memory developed around the events. One such story, as recounted by Lorimer, identified the dead pioneers as having an active presence in the events of this world. "Ephramine Wickland was assigned to a lady out on the reservation, Sister Hereford," he recalled. Hereford's home "burned to the ground two days after she was given the paper of Ephramine Wickland. When they went back into the house, there was a table that was completely charred, and on top of the table was a piece of paper. . . . That paper was so charred the fire marshal told us he didn't know how in the world it didn't explode." Lorimer recalled that something in the shape of sticks had been sitting on top of the paper. "And where those sticks were laying it's just pure white. The sticks were laying over the name of Ephramine Wickland, a little pioneer girl in the Willie Company who was two years old. Boy, I'll tell you, when you show that piece of paper to people it's tangible evidence that these people have been here. . . . I mean, that fire destroyed everything else, why didn't it destroy that piece of paper? That little girl wanted to make sure we didn't forget her again."[54] Here stake members imagined themselves working together with the dead toward a common goal of salvation.

Mary Hereford, the woman who received Ephramine's name, remembered her participation in the Second Rescue as a particularly significant and spiritual moment in her life. Her husband was not a member of the church, and with the fire, she felt as though everything was lost. Yet after finding the paper, she felt a greater drive to do the work for Ephramine. For her the paper clearly served as material evidence of the necessity of this work. She then "told [her] husband that [she] was to research this person and do her work"; she recalled: "he did not get mad or even say anything."[55] In both of these accounts, the materiality of the paper serves as confirmation that the Second Rescue effort was indeed a blessed occurrence. For Lorimer, it was a confirmation of the entire project. For Hereford, it was confirmation of a personal connection to Ephramine and also of her own position in the church.

When Hinckley gave a fireside talk at the Riverton stake in August 1992, he encapsulated the way the concept of rescue had been spiritualized in the late twentieth century to enable modern-day believers to participate imaginatively and ritualistically in the nineteenth-century pioneer journey. "I hope and pray that for as long as you live you will feel within yourselves a sense of having done something worthwhile. To rescue those in distress," Hinckley claimed, "it has been just as real and efficacious as was the effort of those who came to find in the snow and the howling wind of these high plains those who were in distress there."[56] Hinckley affirmed the movement between the two types of rescuers and their work as equally important by emphasizing imagination in thinking about the pioneers' trek: "I have in my imagination felt something of the cold that chilled them to the very bone. . . . I think I tasted the thin gruel . . . that they made and survived on when their rations were reduced. . . . I think I have walked through the snow along that miserable trail. . . . I have seen those who have dropped there and died there."[57] Much as is done in spiritual exercises, Hinckley imaginatively placed himself in the landscape and under the conditions the pioneers faced in order to affirm that both types of rescue were "real" and "efficacious" for his audience.

In 1996, Hinckley continued to affirm this understanding of rescue: "now I am grateful that today none of our people are stranded on the Wyoming highlands. But I know that all about us there are many who are in need of help and who are deserving of rescue. . . . If we are to build that Zion of which the prophets have spoken and of which the lord has given mighty promise, we must set aside our consuming selfishness. We must rise above our love of comfort and ease, and in the very process of effort and struggle, even in our extremity, we shall become better acquainted with our God."[58] Whereas the surviving nineteenth-century pioneers achieved their Zion as the rescuers helped them arrive in Salt Lake City, modern-day Mormons were told that Zion was a future principle that rested on their ability to imagine that they were still needed. Their role as rescuers was not yet complete; Zion relied on them. And it was an active and physical set of tasks that lay ahead.

Rock Creek Hollow

Though the pioneer journey and the concept of rescue were spiritualized in the Second Rescue movement, that understanding was then reinstated on the landscape and made physical and literal once again. The land had never lacked importance, but once the second and spiritual rescue was complete, it gained a new kind of significance. The land, it seemed, had been doubly blessed: first, by the lives lost there, and second, by the rescue of those lives from historical forgottenness. The Second Rescue made those lost pioneers important figures in Mormon collective memory. The members of the Riverton stake then turned to the purchase of land that was tied to the narratives of the pioneers and the construction of three monuments to remember the handcart companies. The space affirmed the collective memory, and the community then wrote those memories on the landscape in their monuments and through the rituals performed in that space.

That the space was unadulterated became an important part of their narrative. Members of the Riverton stake described it as lands that remained "as they were when the pioneers made their westward migration."[59] Thus, the experiential narratives of those visiting these sites could claim to be authentic—it was just as Bodil had seen it, they declared. And it was Bodil's suffering, along with the suffering of the others in the Willie and Martin handcart companies, that made the land significant and that told them "Rock Creek Hollow was the scene of some of the most profound and inspiring acts of sacrifice and courage on the Mormon Trail."[60]

Further experiences enhanced visitors' sense that the land was special. Much imaginative work was at play—viewing the landscape and picturing the weather conditions the Willie and Martin companies faced gave modern-day Mormons a sense that they physically *knew* what had happened. Susan Arrington Madsen begins her book celebrating the Second Rescue with a story of her experiences at the site when she and her husband briefly felt lost and the weather became cold: "mile after mile [the pioneers] comforted their little ones along the treacherous, snowy path. Death was constantly knocking at their door. As we drove through the darkness back to Riverton, President Lorimer apologized for the inconvenience on Rocky Ridge. I expressed to him, however, my deep gratitude for those few brief moments of isolation and fear. Because of those moments, I understand the strength and faith of the pioneers better now, and I love them even more."[61] Here Madsen asserts that she came to know the pioneers in a new way precisely because she had visited the site and experienced some of its dramatic landscapes and weather patterns. Her narrative was not much different from that of Scott Lorimer, who recalled that when he went to Rock Creek he suddenly felt "a very strong spirit there."[62]

As part of members' renewed dedication to the land itself and after the church acquired the land in 1992, the stake organized the construction of several monuments. Lorimer recalled that the process of organizing monument building was similar to the process of beginning the Second Rescue. He told stake members that it was "really wrong . . . [that there is nothing], absolutely nothing, to commemorate the people that died there."[63] Stake members felt persuaded, and believed, that they were righting a historical injustice—they were fighting against historical forgetfulness and thus affirming the collective memory and identity of the group. At one spot, now called Veil Crossing, to refer to the theological sense that the living and the dead passed especially close to one another in this space, stake members placed a stone monument. It was meant to be a reminder of "a time when we entered into a covenant with the Lord regarding those who had passed here many years ago, and that because of that covenant we were in a very literal sense, allowed to reach across the veil and touch each other."[64] Here we see the intersections of the spatial and the temporal at work. Lorimer suggested in this speech that the space itself enabled church members from different eras to touch one another in profound ways; thus the space allowed time to collapse, promoted the efficacy of the rituals, and sacralized the human activities that took place there.

Finally, a monument stone was placed at Rock Creek Hollow, which Lorimer referred to as "the birthplace of the Second Rescue." The monument itself was created to remember current events, much like the sesquicentennial monument described in chapter 6. According to Lorimer, the monument was meant as a reminder to the people who participated in the Second Rescue "to not become puffed up" so that they might "live forever with *our families*, in the presence of God, and become as he is."[65] The inscription on the six-foot granite marker monument reads:

> To the People of
> The Second Rescue
> REMEMBER
> Gordon B. Hinckley
> August 15, 1992
> Thomas S. Monson
> July 15, 1997
> James E. Faust
> July 25, 1992
> Helaman 10:4–5

Helaman 10:4–5, found in the Book of Mormon, reads:

> Blessed art thou, Nephi, for those things which thou hast done; for I have beheld how thou hast with unwearyingness declared the word, which I have given unto thee, unto this people. And thou has not feared them, and hast not sought thine own life, but hast sought my will and to keep my commandments. And now, because thou hast done this with such unwearyingness, behold, I will bless thee forever; and I will make thee mighty in word and in deed, in faith and in works; yea, even that all things shall be done unto thee according to thy work, for thou shalt not ask that which is contrary to my will.

The list of the church presidency members and the dates are reminders of when those men visited the stake, blessed the sites as collective sacred spaces, and gave blessings to the people of the stake. The passage from Helaman serves to reiterate the significance of the activities of the Second Rescue and the spiritual blessings anticipated because of what had been done for the place and for the people. And, of course, the monument commands its viewers to *remember* the narrative of their spiritual ancestors, suggesting that remembering in and of itself is a religious act.

On July 23, 1994, Gordon B. Hinckley visited and dedicated the Rock Creek Hollow site. He called the place a "Sacred and Hallowed ground." To describe its sacred status, and in an analogous process to American leaders who have declared famous battlegrounds as sacred space, he explained that the entire trail was sanctified by the pioneers' sacrifices, sufferings, and deaths, but he also noted: "they were on their way to Zion."[66] In his speech, he recalled the difficulties the church had faced in attempting to acquire the land. He then declared that the church had been able to purchase the land and "it is now the property of the Church . . . where title belongs." In his dedicatory prayer, he thanked God for persuading the owners of the land to sell it so that it could "be preserved as a sacred place, a sanctuary . . . to which future generations may come and here renew their faith in remembrance of those who have gone before." He declared the ground sanctified and representative of "the long trail that these people traveled in their effort to reach their Zion."

A decade later in 2004, when Hinckley visited Copenhagen to dedicate a new temple, he returned again to the sacrifices of Bodil Mortensen and the people with whom she traveled. Suggesting that she was an ancestor for all Mormons, particularly those in Denmark, Hinckley described Rock Creek Hollow: "there she froze to death. There she was buried in a lonely grave. I can never forget Bodil Mortensen—all those who were with her who paid such a terrible price for their faith in God and in this great latter-day work."[67] Hinckley valued the sacrifices of all of the pioneers but also suggested that *she would not be forgotten,* claiming for the collective memory of the Mormon people that this martyr's sacrifice had been worthwhile.

In designating the site as sacred space and in acknowledging the ritual work that had gone into making it sacred—the historical research, the temple rites, and the monument building—Hinckley also affirmed that Zion was the point of reference for the journeys of both the nineteenth-century pioneers and their twentieth-century rescuers. This slippage allowed Zion to be understood as both a historical, literal fact, a place one could point to on a map—and a future principle toward which church members in the twenty-first century could strive.

Figure 6.1 *Angels Are Near Us,* This Is The Place Park.

6

Sesquicentennial Spectacular!

Physicalizing the Pioneer Story

In 1997 the Sons of the Utah Pioneers erected a monument in TITP Park that celebrates the sesquicentennial reenactment of the original trek across the Mormon Trail (see Figure 6.1). Participants, or "trekkers," as they are often called, began their April 1997 journey in Florence, Nebraska, and spent the next three months reenacting the thousand-mile migration of Mormon pioneers 150 years earlier. Titled *Angels Are Near Us*, the monument's bronze bas-relief depicts wagons moving across the land, silhouetted against the western sky. The bas-relief is fixed to a large, boulder-like, rough-hewn stone. "The stone's natural shape appears like one of the Wasatch Mountain peaks, which we viewed heading westward from hundreds of miles away," one participant recalled at the dedication ceremony.[1] The majority of the monument is covered in text, stating: "the trek was a commemoration of sacrifices, joys and was a testament to the honor and greatness of those who went before." It recounts an apostolic blessing that was made before the journey began and describes how the people on the trek in 1997 felt a "spiritual kinship with those who made the trek 150 years ago."

When the 1997 trekkers arrived at TITP Park, their final destination, LDS president Gordon B. Hinckley greeted them with these words, which became part of the monument's text:

> Your wheels again cut deep into the sandy soil of Nebraska. The silhouette of wagons against the Wyoming sky created a picture of unique and wondrous beauty. You looked at the starry heavens at night, in lonely desolate places, and contemplated the wondrous things of God. You marveled at the sunrise and sunsets which marked the passing of each day. . . . You have reached the end of the trail of which tens of thousands before dreamed in the long ago. . . . You will now go your separate ways, but you will never forget this remarkable experience, nor will we. . . . You will tell your children and your

Pioneers in the Attic. Sara M. Patterson, Oxford University Press (2020). © Oxford University Press.
DOI: 10.1093/oso/9780190933869.001.0001

grandchildren and your great-grandchildren about the year of 1997, when you made the journey west following the tracks of the pioneers of 150 years earlier.

The final text of the monument declares that the trekkers' "spirits transcended time and beckoned us to trace their journey for the trail never ends."

How do we make sense of the creation of a monument to memorialize people who have reenacted a historical event? Why would reenactors merit their own monument? What kind of community honors historical reenactors in such a monumental fashion?

The year 1997 served as an important historical moment for the LDS Church as it was shifting, attempting to create a sense of shared identity for an increasingly diverse membership. While in the late twentieth century the church did begin to emphasize the Book of Mormon as one shared story for group members, the 1997 anniversary permitted the church to retell and reinterpret the story of the nineteenth-century pioneers for a community ready to enter the twenty-first century.[2]

The 1997 sesquicentennial events allowed the church community to celebrate its pioneer heritage while working to "pioneerify" its increasingly international community who had no blood connections to that story.[3] Thus the story of the pioneers was unmoored from the more literal, historical understanding of generations past. At the same time, the theological concepts of Zion and gathering were divorced from place and physical proximity to other church members. Thus, Zion, gathering, and pioneer identity were spiritualized in new ways.

Even so, 1997 served as a moment to reconcretize those same concepts. Rituals like trekking, parades, and theatrical productions physicalized those concepts so that believers might touch and feel them. These new physical and spatial methods of imagining pioneers, Zion, and gathering were then celebrated as interpretations whose *legitimacy was equal to* those of the nineteenth century. Building a monument to the 1997 historical reenactors represents one such example. This monument declares that the *you* of the twentieth and twenty-first centuries is just as worthy of a monument as the nineteenth-century pioneers celebrated in the 1947 monument. It declares to an increasingly diverse set of members that the ritual reenactments in which they participate are just as meaningful and spiritually significant as the nineteenth-century trek to Zion. It sacralizes the present, a time that may not feel as rife with meaning as the pioneer stories seem to be. It celebrates the ritual activities that concretize and make meaning out of the same theological concepts that once drove the pioneers west.

Sesquicentennial Spectacular

Working with Utah government officials, Mormon leaders planned several events celebrating the pioneers' 1847 entry into the Salt Lake Valley. After all, the sesquicentennial was both a state and a religious celebration. Plans for the entire year included all sorts of activities: the Mormon Tabernacle Choir went on a tour; the church held a Faith in Every Footstep Sesquicentennial Concert in Temple Square; the Museum of Church History and Art hosted an international art competition; Promised Valley Productions put on a play especially written and produced for the sesquicentennial; Brigham Young University set up a Sesquicentennial Spectacular (with all sorts of family frontier activities and fireworks); and the church celebrated and supported a trek that followed the pioneers' footsteps across the western landscape. Latter-day Saints also proposed celebrating the sesquicentennial through service projects. Church leaders suggested that the pioneers had committed their lives to service and that part of church members' expression of their pioneer heritage ought to take the form of providing service to their communities. July 19, 1997, was designated Worldwide Pioneer Heritage Service Day, and about 20,000 church groups dedicated that day (and therefore about three million hours) to some form of service in their local communities.[4]

It wasn't just the church, though, that recognized the significance of these events. The New-York Historical Society and the National Museum of American History also sponsored exhibits commemorating the sesquicentennial.[5] For many Latter-day Saints, the acknowledgment of the significance of the Mormon exodus and pioneer trek by national public institutions was evidence that their church had finally come of age within American culture.

One must also remember that the sesquicentennial was a state affair, and the Utah Pioneer Sesquicentennial Celebration Coordinating Council was designed to make sure of that. In the first group newsletter of the *Sesquicentennial Star*, the council noted: "during 1996 we celebrate the 100th birthday of statehood for Utah. The State, in reality, had its birth when the Utah Pioneers made the trek from Nauvoo to Salt Lake Valley in 1847."[6]

The council dated Utah's origins to the arrival of the Mormon pioneers in their promised land and emphasized 1847 over and above the date of Utah's statehood. First, the newsletter declared: "we know there were Native Americans, trappers, and explorers who visited these valleys before the Utah Pioneers came. But we must never forget the purpose of the original trek. It has been referred to as a 'Glorious emergency.' The pioneers came 'because they were compelled to—because they were driven.' They were determined to preserve a heritage for their children through fostering faith in God, devotion to family, loyalty to country, freedom of conscience, commitment to work, service to others, courage in adversity, personal integrity, and unyielding determination."[7] These claims reveal much about the council's understanding of Utah's history. The values that were tied to Utahan identity were drawn not from statehood or even from the first inhabitants of and visitors to the state but instead from the Mormon pioneers. It should be noted that in this passage Native Americans are placed in the same category with trappers and explorers as transient "visitors" to the valley, thus dismissing and erasing any indigenous claims to territory and permanence. Instead, the council readily embraced a narrative that rooted state values in one religious group and saw the Mormon pioneers as the progenitors of Utahan identity.

Sesquicentennial celebrations in Utah encompassed all sorts of artistic commemorations. Church celebrations often included a new hymn written for the events, "Faith in Every Footstep." The hymn recalls the pioneers as people "who gave all their heart, mind, and strength to the Lord with wisdom and virtue so clear." The hymn also taught that late twentieth-century Latter-day Saints were themselves called to the work of building up Zion. While the pioneers remained "examples of virtue and faith," later generations of church members should "assist in this work and thrust in [their] sickle with might."

A musical produced by the church's Promised Valley Productions, titled *Barefoot to Zion*, was originally authored by Kevin and Khaliel Kelly and then turned into a musical by Orson Scott Card and his brother. It was designed in honor of the sesquicentennial.[8] The musical portrays a group of English converts to Mormonism on a journey toward faith and toward Utah. The notes accompanying the play's script made several things explicit to would-be directors. First, they were told that the musical was to communicate and honor the spirit of gathering, a concept that Mormons in the nineteenth century understood literally as a call to gather together and build Zion in the Great Basin. However, the play's notes made a distinction between 1847 and 1997: "the foundation laid by the pioneers is still strong, but the spirit of gathering in the Church is different now. Church members are taught to remain in their homelands, to build up the Church wherever they live. When the characters in *Barefoot to Zion* talk with fervor about the need to go to America to build up Zion, they are being obedient to the Lord's instructions in their day. It is the faithfulness and courage of the pioneers, not the destination of their journey that Church members should emulate."[9] The notes recognized that what had once been understood literally must now be understood metaphorically. The journey of faith, not the geographic destination, was paramount.

The notes also emphasized that persons of all backgrounds should envision themselves as pioneers. The instructions explained: "race should not be a factor in casting. . . . The skin color or ancestral homeland of the actors should have no importance in casting this play. Characters may be played by persons of any ancestry, and no attempt should be made to use makeup to change an actor's skin color. Nor should there be any explanation to the audience if persons of different races play members of the same family."[10] Here we see members of the church trying to reconcile the increasingly diverse nature of the contemporary community with the primarily white ancestry of their nineteenth-century predecessors. In attempting to allay racial explanations and to allow for a multiracial cast, the church navigated a narrow path. The church wanted to celebrate its historical roots while also ensuring that contemporary audiences saw themselves as descendants of those pioneers. As mentioned earlier, Eric Eliason has called this phenomenon the "pioneerification" of new Mormon converts and suggests that the process is a redeployment of what was a powerful symbol in the LDS community in a way that speaks to current situations.[11]

In order to "pioneerify" the modern Mormon community, church leaders often repeated the claim that all church members were inheritors of the church's pioneer history. Materials produced by the state of Utah for the sesquicentennial made the same claim for all Utahans. The Utah Pioneer Sesquicentennial Celebration Coordinating council published a handbook of "97 ways in '97 to Celebrate the Sesquicentennial" for classrooms throughout Utah. In that handbook, teachers were instructed that "everyone can be a 'pioneer.'" Alongside activities that served to teach children about the Utah pioneers was material encouraging children to learn about "modern pioneers" and to celebrate their stories as well.[12] Thus both non-Mormon and Mormon Utahans were encouraged to view the Mormon exodus as their shared heritage.

The sense that pioneer identity had expanded was accompanied by a message that it was the values of the American West that present Latter-day Saints should share with their ancestors. In this way, church members celebrated the European-American narrative of western progress—they viewed the West as a place that defined individuals and made them Americans. The western narrative embraced here was a simple, nationalist narrative of the West as the space that transformed Europeans into Americans and made Americans unique. Freedom, independence, hope, and courage were celebrated as values that were and are part of *both* Latter-day Saint and American character. No critical analysis of that westward expansion and its effects was offered to audiences at the events.

Church-created sesquicentennial publications offered an often-repeated version of the Mormons' nineteenth-century past. The narrative began in Nauvoo, "once home and haven but now menacing and unsafe."[13] The pioneers were portrayed as innocents driven out of their homeland and searching for refuge and the freedom to practice their religion. They had been "expatriated from their town (Nauvoo), from their state (Illinois) and from their country (the United States), after suffering physical and emotional harassment and the loss of their property."[14] Persecuted and without a place, the pioneers began their journey.

That narrative then turned from oppression to a celebration of the pioneers' character: "they came because they believed that people could create Zion on earth where pure hearts could find rest and happiness." Over the prairies and western landscapes the people came, "but thousands would die before their journey's end," the storytellers explain.[15] Nonetheless, the pioneers persevered in the face of great odds. Listeners and readers were told to "imagine facing this ridge in a wagon. Then imagine pulling a handcart." They were taught that they ought to imagine the hardships the pioneers had faced in order to symbolically retrace those footsteps in their own life journeys. "In the heroic effort of the pioneers we learn an eternal truth," Gordon B. Hinckley declared in a sesquicentennial film; "we all must pass through a refiner's fire."[16]

Virtually every sesquicentennial historical narrative of the nineteenth century concluded with a lesson for Mormons today: "we are all pioneers still. With those who have gone before, we journey together, step by faithful step, to arrive at a promised valley and find 'it is the right place.' "[17]

Creating Trekkers

Since 1849, Latter-day Saints have celebrated July 24 as "Pioneer Day" in remembrance of the day on which Brigham Young saw the valley and declared
that it was the "right place." These celebrations of the Saints' movement into
the West quickly became elaborate festivals and parades. During the Jubilee
celebration in 1897, a four-day event honored the surviving pioneers, fêted
as state-makers, faith founders, and people of character. Utahans tended
to view pioneer life stories as the stories of a state's citizens and of a chosen
people. That 1897 celebration of the pioneers helped mark July 24, 1847, as
the significant day in Utah's founding, rather than its 1896 statehood (which
represented, in part, all that the Latter-day Saints had had to give up in order
to achieve reconciliation with the U.S. government).[18]

The 1947 centennial celebration was a particularly intriguing attempt to
reenact the pioneers' entry into the valley. Put on by the Sons of the Utah
Pioneers, a group that frequently funded a number of the memorials and
monuments throughout the state of Utah, the main centennial events were
also made exclusive by that same group. In order to be as "authentic" as
possible, the group chose only descendants of Utah pioneers as the central
participants. At that time, both the Sons and Daughters of the Utah Pioneers
defined "pioneer" as someone "who came to the geographic area covered by
the State of Deseret/Utah Territory; died crossing the plains; or was born in
the Utah Territory/State of Deseret before May 19, 1869, the coming of the
railroad."[19] Interestingly, the definition of "pioneer" provided in 1947 was not
the first one offered by the Daughters of the Utah Pioneers. At its founding
in 1903, the group defined "pioneer" as anyone who came to Utah before
January 1850. Not too long after that, the group extended the time frame for
the pioneers to 1853. It was in 1910 that it finally decided on May 10, 1869, as
the final date for the pioneer era, choosing the day that the transcontinental
railroads met in Promontory, Utah.[20]

During the 1947 trek, the decision to include only pioneer descendants
demonstrated a significant social distinction in the LDS community.
Those who were descendants of the pioneers claimed a special, privileged
status (often accompanied by socioeconomic status) in Utah, much as the
descendants of those who came to America on the *Mayflower* or those who
fought in the American Revolution have claimed a privileged, special status
in the nation as a whole. The commemorative program for the event listed
all of the participants and every way they were related to nineteenth-century

pioneers. Their ancestry celebrated, the participants were described as "un-usual" people who "had to have a vision. Without it, [they] couldn't have understood the grand purpose of the reenactment. [They] had to have a love of heritage, a respect for those who had given so much so that others would be happier."[21]

Continuing their claims to authenticity, the centennial reenactors traveled in seventy-two automobiles in order to represent the seventy-two covered wagons that had traveled with Brigham Young. Those cars were decked out with covered wagon tops, and participants dressed in pioneer clothes and camped out "frontier-style" at night.[22] "Simulated oxen," apparently crafted out of plywood, also accompanied the 143 men, three women, and two boys "representing President Young's first company."[23] These 1947 trekkers arrived in the valley in time to participate in a parade down Main Street that ended with ceremonies at Temple Square's Brigham Young Monument. That the procession used "simulated oxen" pasted to cars points to the ritualization of an imagined western landscape. In an era when Utah still had a strong ag-ricultural and farming economy, it would have been easy enough to use real oxen for the event. Yet the ritual's pilgrims chose to reenact with cars and fake oxen, demonstrating the celebration of their western past *and* the celebration of how far they had come in "civilizing" that western landscape.

Fifty years later, the 1997 sesquicentennial celebration also attempted to ritualize and reenact the 1847 trek. This time, however, the attempts to achieve authenticity looked different. In 1997, authenticity meant that those journeying on the trail would actually walk, push handcarts, or ride in cov-ered wagons. Some trekkers wore pioneer clothes all the time, some just for the cameras, and some wore their modern-day clothing and attempted au-thenticity in other ways. While only a select number of church members participated in the trek, church leaders encouraged all Latter-day Saints to visit the trail: "there is no equivalent to experiencing firsthand the Mormon Pioneer Trail." However, they counseled that church members did not need to "retrace the entire trek from Nauvoo to Salt Lake City to experience the spirit of being on the trail." Rather they should "do only that which is most meaningful to you."[24] Here one sees an impulse that would rise again and again as the ritual of the trek developed and became popularized in the LDS community. Church authorities asserted that the experience of the trail could be distilled into particularly significant moments and that Mormons need not undertake the entire journey in order to learn what the spirit had to teach them.

The planners for the church-supported trek ensured that portable toilets and water trucks followed the participants along the way. Even so, some of the leaders of the trek did not like being called reenactors because they were "dealing with many of the same trials and hardships of the original pioneers."[25] Part of the 1997 trek was called the "authentic camp." Even though participants in this camp lived in dwellings designed after nineteenth-century tents, often wore pioneer-style clothing, and ate food the pioneers ate, they had access to water and toilets and could walk into towns and enjoy treats at a local restaurant. One authentic camper described the space as looking "like a small community . . . or a small village. The kitchen is the center area. . . . This is where all of the action takes place. Not only does all of the cooking (a wonderful major part) but the washing of dishes, clothes and all sorts of things. We mend our clothes most of the time near this wondrous place."[26]

The 1997 trek began on April 19. Over 10,000 people participated in the trek at one point or another; some church members committed to the entire trek, while others walked for a day or a weekend.[27] During the trek, the website following the trekkers received 300,000 hits each week, and trek leaders claimed that about 300 million people had seen a story about the trek in the media.[28] Some trekkers walked, and some rode in wagons. Handcarts, though, had become *the* symbol of Mormon trekking. Why? After all, handcarts were not the only or even the most common mode of transportation for Mormons journeying west in the nineteenth century. Perhaps the handcart as a symbol has become so popular because handcarts can be claimed as a distinctively Mormon symbol, while covered wagons have come to symbolize westward movement more generally. No doubt handcarts represent, much more than covered wagons, precisely what believers wish to emphasize as they trek: the values of industry, commitment, and faith. The physical labor that accompanies pushing and pulling handcarts allows believers to access those traits in ways that riding in a covered wagon cannot. Handcarts symbolize the values Mormons wish to claim as they reenact the journey west.

The trekkers weren't the only ones on this journey. Together, the press, news crews, and movie companies constituted a significant element of the movement. They followed the trekkers throughout the journey, often asking them to reenact specific moments for news or film footage. One trekker recalled a particular day when "much of our day was dictated by the CBS news crew. They wanted pretty pictures of us pulling our handcarts over some steep sandhills. . . . We followed the original wagon ruts and it was really hard pulling in some places. But we were not just there for our own enjoyment—the TV cameras would film us as we went a few hundred yards, then we would have to stop in our tracks while they repositioned the cameras. So, a distance that would normally only take 15 minutes to cross took us almost 45 minutes."[29] That staged press coverage helped bring the church into the national spotlight in a positive way. And so trek reenactors were reminded that they had multiple audiences observing their journey. There were fellow Mormons who saw the trek as an opportunity for vicarious pilgrimage, participating through online coverage and through the journals kept by trek participants. Yet trekkers were also being tracked by outsiders, and in this instance the trekkers had much control over the narrative being told about them and their religious community. News media outlets writing about the events associated Mormons with the hard work and stick-to-itiveness of the American West. The sesquicentennial trek was a public relations boon for the church, as non-Mormons celebrated the Latter-day Saints as the epitome of American values.

Fifty years after an exclusive centennial celebration that had included only individuals with pioneer ancestors, the definition of a "pioneer" had changed and expanded. That change reflected church leaders' awareness and celebration of Mormonism's growing geographic diffusion and diversity. The 1997 sesquicentennial trek was open to anyone, and believers were taught that they were "pioneers in many ways today in the things we learn and how we conduct our lives."[30] One member of the Quorum of the Twelve Apostles gave a fireside talk that articulated the church's attempt to expand the definition of "pioneer" for those celebrating the sesquicentennial: "when we speak of the great events of our collective past, it is all *our* history. Occasionally I have heard a new convert and someone in another land say, 'My ancestors did not cross the plains or settle Utah. . . . I do not feel part of that great legacy of the Church.' . . . No matter how new you may be to the Church, this is our collective past—we are adopted into all of this history and heritage, if you will, and we have equal claim upon all of its blessings and promises."[31] Church leaders emphasized a spiritual inheritance, a collective identity, and a past to which any Mormon could lay claim. In a similar vein, Gordon B. Hinckley said in a sesquicentennial interview that all members of the church could "draw strength from our pioneer forebears and meet the challenges of today in the same way. . . . Every member of this Church, whether of pioneer ancestry or baptized yesterday, has a great legacy for which to be thankful. We're all beneficiaries of that tremendous legacy—the faith, the integrity and the vision of our pioneer forebears. They laid the foundations of this community."[32]

By creating a series of lesson plans to be incorporated into the curriculum of the LDS seminaries and Institutes of Religion called "Faith in Every Footstep," the institutional church promoted the idea that *all* church members, no matter where they lived, had something to learn from the pioneers—all members were church heroes even on the cusp of the twenty-first century. That the material was standardized, meaning it was taught to every believer who was teenaged or college-aged, is important. The material was designed to encourage students to understand the pioneers as spiritual kin and to "see the pioneers and themselves as important participants in the gathering of Israel and the establishment of Zion."[33] At the end of the twentieth and beginning of the twenty-first centuries, that message was taught to an increasingly place-less population of church members. By focusing on youth, the church could rehearse and ritualize its stories for young members. Doing so would mean that by adulthood those stories would be second nature, having the potential to be sustaining spiritual stories for adult believers.

By creating a sense of community, the trek tied contemporary believers to one another. One 1997 trekker even felt resentment toward folks just stopping by: "have had several visitors the past two days. It is good to see them and nice of them to drop by, but actually I would prefer not seeing any of them until after we reach the Salt Lake Valley. Not a nice comment to make. The reality is, however, that I just want to enjoy the company of the folks on the Wagon Train until it is over."[34] Here we see the power of the ritual reenactment: a member of the trek saw friends and family members as outsiders, feeling that even familiar faces would be an intrusion on his trek experience and preferring the company of the stranger-trekkers who had been with him over the previous weeks. In that moment, his identity as trekker became his primary social identity and the one to which he clung.[35]

The trekkers experienced a sense of community through shared experiences. During the trek, three couples got engaged, and a baby was born. Along the way, the group visited the grave of a Mormon child and dedicated it. "It reminded us of all the children . . . who died and were buried . . . and it became so much more real," recalled one trekker. "I think that was one of the spiritual moments for us. To really feel, at least partially, what it would be like to lose someone."[36]

Trekker Ted Moore vowed to walk from Nauvoo all the way to Salt Lake City. Along the way, one of the friends he had made became sick and had to spend a few days in the hospital. Ted stayed with his friend while he was in the hospital, but in order not to miss the trail, "he went back to the point at which he had left off and then he went back to where he stopped . . . and walked 40 miles a day . . . until he caught up." When his friend returned to the trek, Ted pushed him in a handcart until he was able to walk for himself.[37]

In later interviews and reminiscences, many 1997 trekkers suggested that the trek strengthened and concretized their faith in God. Several saw a divine plan at work in their participation. Echoing Brigham Young's words, trekker Wendy Westergard wrote "to think that we were adding our own legacy of faith to the trail made us speechless. . . . It only made everything worth every moment. I know I was born at the right time at the right place. I used to not believe that, but now I have a surety of being born at the right time."[38] Many other trekkers echoed this idea, that God actively intervened in the world to fulfill divine plans for individuals and for the church. As Brian Hill recalled, "God was watching over us. . . . It was as if we were under a protecting blanket." For many trekkers, their reenactment of the pioneers' journey reaffirmed their sense of God's providence. It also affirmed that they, too, were a special people, divinely called to participate. Their activity indicated to them that 1997 was a sacred time and the Mormon Trail was a sacred place. God did indeed work in the world as they had believed.

Many trekkers also repeated the claim that the "veil" between this world and the spirit world was thin—that they could feel the original pioneers traversing the territory with them. They imagined both God and the nineteenth-century pioneers pulling for them, sometimes sensing that they were not the only ones moving their handcarts through particularly difficult stretches of terrain.[39] When the trekkers reached Martin's Cove, they decided to have a testimony meeting. One woman named Jane recounted that as she was walking, she "felt a presence" and eventually said "Grandmother, is that you?" and felt a conviction that it was, in fact, her grandmother, who had laughed at Jane when she converted to Mormonism.[40] For her, the experience affirmed the presence of those who had died, as part of the community. Later, a trekker named Margaret talked about how she felt: "the spirit . . . moves with the wagon train" when she recalled hearing a voice that told her to go purchase candy bars and find the handcart companies. Margaret "just knew" that the companies were in trouble and traveled to find them and provide them with the sustenance they needed to arrive at the next campsite.[41] Thus the trekkers stories were full of accounts of the spirits of ancestors trekking with them, of the collapse of time between historical and present events, and a special, physical awareness of that spiritual knowledge that made it feel even more real.

The 1997 trekkers' accounts suggest that they came to know theological and religious claims in a more experiential way than they had previously in their lives. In fact, one of the trek leaders, Brian Hill, took umbrage at the accusation that the 1997 experience wasn't "authentic." He recounted that the weather was similar, that at times they had a hard time getting fed, and that they had to deal with sick animals. "The trail conditions were more real than you imagine," he recalled, "so we knew something of suffering." In his account of the trek, he went on to say about the pioneers: "in a sense I've read their journals better than the way they could write it."[42] Here Hill claimed an experiential authority to speak about the history of the pioneers. He drew that authority from his trek. He knew them, he said, because he had walked in their footsteps.

Wendy Westergard noted that she and her fellow trekkers created a "moving community." That movement—through time, but also through space—is significant to modern-day LDS interpretations of what is taking place. She imagined that as the pioneers moved forward "the West was opened," and she celebrated the understanding that God manifested promises in a spatial way. Westergard commented that her dream for the trek was one of "doing 'the West,' " which meant, for her, traveling some of the time in a covered wagon.[43] At this time, Mormons were encouraged to see the landscape itself as sacred but also as untouched, emphasizing its significance to the modern gaze. Visitors were told that much of the trail was "pristine" and that they could view the trail and surrounding landscape as "almost unchanged from that viewed by the Mormon pioneers 150 years ago."[44]

"People want to gather," recalled Brian Hill as he tried to answer the question of why the wagon train was so popular. He wondered why until he *experienced* the trek. He then believed that he "understood that gathering to Zion . . . is not something that people do just because it is an idle thought or because they are commanded. It is because of the feeling that Zion has." He recalled that it was "like a magnet," not something participants willed but something they felt. It was a bond he considered akin to familial ties and to a truer sense of community than he had felt elsewhere. Zion was a place where "you provide for [people's] needs."[45] And so Hill and others came to know the concepts of gathering and Zion as spiritual concepts, but those idea became most real when they were felt and physically manifested in a specific community.

Perhaps one 1997 trekker's phrase best describes what Latter-day Saints imagine happening as they trek, if only for a few hours and if only over a local hill; she described the trek community as a "traveling Zion." She declared that she would "always treasure my small glimpse of an understanding of what Zion is all about." For this trekker, and for many others, the destination Zion—a physical, geographical space one could locate on a map—was not as important as the "traveling Zion" that developed as people physically labored to push and pull handcarts and moved through space together. Recall the director's notes for the 1997 musical *Barefoot to Zion*: "it is the faithfulness and courage of the pioneers, not the destination of their journey, that Church members should emulate." So it seems that as the notion of the gathering was spiritualized, so, too, were the concepts of Zion and the West. Once spiritualized, they were reconcretized through community formation and ritual activity. At one and the same time, Zion was a physical place, the end of their journey in the Salt Lake Valley, a spiritual concept driving their actions, and an idea manifested through ritual activity.

The Trail's End

When the 1997 trekkers completed their journey, they did so at the site of a gift from Utahans of 1947: TITP Park, next to the 1947 monument *This Is the Place* sculpted by Mahonri M. Young. Over 51,000 people greeted the trekkers at the end of their journey, and much pomp surrounded the event. Greeters stood on the two sides of the final mile of the trek, clapping and cheering for the trekkers. As they entered the park, the trekkers passed by several handcarts that had been painted white and a group of people dressed in white standing silently and waving white handkerchiefs. These individuals represented the pioneers who had died during the 1847 journey, and for some, seeing these representatives was "a very spiritual moment. The spirits of those earlier handcart pioneers were definitely present."[46] Their loved ones, as well as many others who had followed their journey online, greeted the trekkers. Experiencing the end of the journey was a coming home of sorts. One of the most well-known trekkers, Larry "Turbo" Stewart, was baptized when the train reached TITP Park, a sign that the trek had, for him, made the spiritual beliefs professed by Mormons seem really real.

After many joyful reunions, everyone gathered around the 1947 monument at the center of the park. Rather than in the Salt Lake Valley itself, the 1997 trek ended when participants reached the point where Brigham Young, their Moses, is thought to have looked out over that valley and known that it was their promised land. Why?

In contemporary Mormonism, it is the site of prophetic vision that remains most significant. For Latter-day Saints, the belief that Brigham Young stood in this spot and proclaimed that the Salt Lake Valley would be the church's place of refuge and new place of gathering marks the spot as sacred. In an age when Latter-day Saints still affirm ongoing revelation but official revelations are fewer and farther between, the site itself confirms church members' sense of prophetic vision. Visitors can look out over the Salt Lake Valley and the landscape itself—including the neatly defined roads, the Great Salt Lake, and the buildings of Temple Square marking the skyline as a Mormon skyline— to confirm the truthfulness of Brigham Young's vision. As Brian Hill remembered, he initially wondered what it would be like to see the valley, but when he arrived at TITP Park, he believed he had realized what the pioneers must have felt: "I was overcome . . . and the emotion that I felt as I stood there and cried was gratitude. . . . I was grateful to God."[47]

As modern trekkers along with their welcomers gathered around the monument, a choir encouraged participants to sing "High on a Mountaintop." Soon thereafter, president Gordon B. Hinckley got up and remarked that the trekkers had done something extraordinary and had caught the imagination of everyone. He argued that the trekkers in 1997 were more authentic than their 1947 counterparts who rode in cars and congratulated them on reaching "the end of the trail." He also made an interesting set of connections in this space. First, he declared that the "desert has truly blossomed," calling to mind the fulfillment of the prophetic vision Brigham Young had of the valley. He noted that Young had "recognized the reality of prophetic vision when he declared 'This is the right place.'" And Hinckley, a full participant in the Smithification process, declared that Young had known that it was the same place that Joseph Smith had also seen in a vision. In so doing, Hinckley connected the western landscape with the prophetic visions of Joseph Smith, suggesting that all that happened to the church from 1830 onwards was part of a divine plan for the Latter-day Saints. Trekkers and their welcomers were invited to see the space that confirmed the truthfulness of it all.[48]

It may seem odd to memorialize a fairly recent reenactment as a significant historical event in its own right, yet the connections to sacred space help make sense of it. The monument to the 1997 reenactors represents both place and movement. Trekkers had reached the end of the trail—they could look out over the valley just as Brigham Young had 150 years earlier. They could see the geography and city that served as evidence of his prophetic vision.

At the same time, the monument declares that the trail never ends and the values and the spaces of the West will continue even as the people are scattered. The final text of the monument declares that the trekkers' "spirits transcended time and beckoned us to trace their journey for the trail never ends." Indeed, since 1997 trek reenactments have continued to gain in popularity. As of 2004, reservations for the 300 church-supplied handcarts at the Mormon Handcart Historic Sites in Wyoming were being taken three years in advance.[49] More than sixty missionary couples help manage the throngs of people coming to reenact treks during the summer months.[50]

By 1997, most Latter-day Saints lived outside the United States, and most American Mormons lived outside Utah. Only a small minority were descendants of the mid-nineteenth-century Mormon pioneers. Nevertheless, the church's collective memory of the experiences of exodus and gathering retained their importance, especially as the ritual of trekking grew in popularity in other parts of the world. In 1997, the church found that its pioneer roots helped cast contemporary Mormonism in the positive glow of shared American values. Commemoration and reenactment, moreover, connect contemporary Latter-day Saints with each other, their faith, and the pioneers who continue to be celebrated as exemplars for church members no longer gathering to a place of refuge but still dedicated to building communities of Zion.

Figure 7.1 Row of handcarts, This Is The Place Park.

7

Traveling Zions

Pilgrimage in Modern Mormonism

The website for TITP Park guarantees that visitors will have an authentic experience: They will get "the West . . . just as it was!" and have "a true experience of life as it was in the early days of the West." The park also offers day-long treks, claiming that that experience is the best way to learn history. During those treks, young trekkers are promised that anyone "who pushes and pulls a pioneer-era hand cart up a dusty mountainside will learn teamwork, cooperation and friendship" as well as having a "greater appreciation for the sacrifices of those ancestors who came before" (see Figure 7.1). These treks are guided by a trail boss wearing period clothing. Participants also wear pioneer outfits and meet up with historical figures, including Brigham Young, John Taylor, Mary Goble Pay, and a Pony Express rider.[1] Female participants share in their own experience of "the arduous women-only handcart pull over Rocky Ridge," which is expected to promote an independent spirit in young women. In creating these daily treks, the park attempts to consolidate the experiences of a several months' journey into one day, distilling the lessons down to their simplest forms.

Such distillations happen all along the Mormon Trail. Recall that at the Winter Quarters visitors' center, visitors can dress as pioneers (donning bonnets, shawls, skirts, vests, and hats from a large chest full of all sizes of pioneer clothes) and push a handcart across a large room. Knowing that it is fairly easy to pull an empty handcart across a carpeted floor the first time, and wanting visitors to take away the *right* lesson, missionaries then place rocks underneath the wheels of the handcart and visitors are asked to again pull it across the room. Since the 1997 sesquicentennial trek, the popularity of trekking has grown exponentially in many manifestations and distillations, particularly for Mormons in the American West. Yet those treks have taken on a distinctly different flavor. They are no longer four-month ritual reenactments. Instead, they are shortened versions, chock-full of what are supposed to be the highlights of historical lessons and spiritual moments.

Pioneers in the Attic. Sara M. Patterson, Oxford University Press (2020). © Oxford University Press.
DOI: 10.1093/oso/9780190933869.001.0001

Thousands of miles from the place where the pioneers actually trod, sometimes halfway around the world, Latter-day Saints also reenact the Mormon trek westward. These international Saints, some having never visited the American West, can be found from Italy to Sierra Leone, Mongolia to Scandinavia, and many places in between.[2] They, too, use handcarts, often building their own, which has become a type of ritual activity in its own right. All of the preparation—building handcarts, sewing bonnets, reading about the pioneers—helps mark the time spent pulling the handcarts and trekking as sacred, special time. But to think of this preparation only as an attempt to enter sacred time would be to miss part of what these believers are attempting to achieve. They are also participating in a ritual that engages sacred space. In fact, the contemporary ritual of trekking points to the messiness of the relationship between space, history, and religious experience.

What exactly are these trekkers getting from their treks? Their starting points and their ending points have no direct correlation to the 1847 pioneers' entry into the Salt Lake Valley. Yet their insistence on pushing a handcart across land, preferably over some geographical obstacles like rocks, hills, or mountains, demonstrates the spatial significance of their ritual activities. In pushing a handcart over a hill, they are ritualizing the settlers' experience of the American West, the nineteenth-century Mormon pioneers' exodus, and in so doing claiming a stake as the spiritual descendants of the Mormon pioneers. Because of the increasing globalization of the church, the Mormon leadership has attempted to root the belief system in place even as fewer and fewer members are living in the places that are central to church historical narratives.[3] As discussed in other chapters, historical spaces have become increasingly important in the lives of some church members and to the institutional church. Yet the ritual of trek points to something new and indicates that the spatial sense of rootedness, a connection to the LDS chain of memory that *feels* three-dimensional in that it is rooted not just in time but in place, has taken on a different look in the twenty-first century. At the same time that church members are visiting historical sites at higher and higher rates, they are also participating in ritual activities that engage space in a new way.

A second important component of that ritualization of space is the kinesthetic and material connection to the past fostered in community with other trekkers.[4] What I will show is that the institutional church deploys the ritual of trekking to foster the historical lessons and spiritual moments that enforce the theological claims made by the church. As historical reenactment, trekking is shaped to inspire participants, particularly the teenaged participants around whom the church now focuses the trek ritual, to feel that the theological messages are *really real*. At the same time, I will show that not all participants experience what the church wants them to experience, especially when those trekkers are wily, independent teenagers.[5]

Reenacting Zion

When talking about trekking, Latter-day Saints, both the trekkers and the institutional church, choose to use the term "historical reenactment" rather than "pilgrimage" to describe what they are doing. What exactly is historical reenactment? Several anthropologists who study the phenomenon and its popularity in contemporary culture note that historical reenactors feel as though they are encountering the actual past as it was lived, much as the TITP website promises. This sense of "the actual past" is created in part because reenactment opens "a performative space where a strict divide between past and present can be collapsed."[6] Reenactment "indulges the twin passions of work and play, which are generally divorced from each other. It licenses dressing up, pretending and improvising, casting oneself as the protagonist of one's own research, and getting others to play along."[7] And so reenactment has a component of fun to it, of moving out of the ordinary and the everyday to step into another world.

As reenactors step into that world, though, they are not often historically accurate in their choices. Instead they make choices based on current notions of authenticity, pinpoint aspects of the history that they want to highlight, and creatively employ what they imagine might be accurate about that past. They do so in a move toward the felt life: reenactment "is less concerned with events, processes or structures than with the individual's physical and psychological experience." That personal embodied experience, then, becomes evidence of how the reenactors understand the historical peoples and narratives they reenact.[8] Their bodies become the primary source of historical knowledge. Because modern-day reenactors often choose moving historical narratives of suffering and persistence, suffering also often plays a critical role in how they come to understand the past.

Reenactment can tell us a lot about the modern-day reenactors but often much less about the historical figures they are recalling. Because reenactment privileges embodied experiences, reenactors view their activities as apolitical, as simply factual, and as a way to bring to light what was. Yet much work goes into choosing the narratives they tell and how they recount them. Anthropologist Vanessa Agnew, who studies historical reenactments of many types, suggests that there is a dominant narrative to reenactment, and it is not the historical narrative the reenactors tell. Instead, it is "one of conversion from ignorance to knowledge, individualism to sociability. . . . These conversion experiences take the form of testimonials: reenactors attest to profound experiences that are markers on the hard road to knowledge. They begin as novices . . . undergo trials, acquire skills and experience, and are finally inducted into a community of dedicated reenactors."[9] These narratives function within the community as forms of membership and help to solidify identity. Thus, the reenactors congregate around a particular historical narrative, yet the narrative of innocence to knowledge is key in their understanding of themselves as a community.

The community of reenactors selects the past it wishes to enact. Yet in an interesting twist, "it is the very ahistoricity of reenactment that is the precondition for its engagement with historical subject matter." Reenactment therefore allows the group to address a conflicted sense of identity in the present while focusing on a specific past.[10] The collapse of present and past enables the present community to creatively play through conflicts in current identity.

What conflicts of identity might Mormon reenactors be addressing through reenactment? A few that have already been mentioned include the shift between being a community bound to a place and an *anywhere* community, the unmooring of key theological concepts from the physical world, and moving from a persecuted minority to a recognized mainstream religious community. Through reenacting, Mormons can reassert their commitment to place and a narrative of persecution while also attempting to reconcile that past truth with current identities and memberships.[11] While reenacting reinforces the centrality of persecution to LDS identity, it also reminds reenactors of their safe distance from those events.

Reenactment, while playing all of these roles for many reenactors, may be doing something distinct within Mormonism because of the nature of Mormon theology. Reenactment becomes its own form of theological activity. Because Mormon history-telling is so closely tied to theology, reenactment reinforces theological claims, making them feel embodied and factual. It emphasizes the felt nature of Mormon theology.

Then, too, the role of reenactment can function to enforce the theological understanding of how the spirit works. Passages from the Book of Mormon describe to Mormons just how the spirit works and form the core of a Mormon epistemology. Moroni 10:4 counsels: "and when ye shall receive these things, I would exhort you that ye would ask God, the Eternal Father, in the name of Christ, if these things are not true; and if ye shall ask with a sincere heart, with real intent, having faith in Christ, he will manifest the truth of it unto you, by the power of the Holy Ghost." Over and over again, Mormons hear this epistemological framework on testimony Sundays and throughout their religious communities. As Hildi Mitchell argues, "the Mormon narrative form par excellence is the testimony."[12] The repetition of structure and truth claims helps bind the community together: *this is how we as believers know the truth.*

Yet bodies must be trained to recognize the spirit, to understand its function within a Mormon worldview, and to narrate it for others in testimony. As E. Marshall Brooks has noted, Mormon testimonies conflate cognition and emotion, thus promoting the sense that "depth of feeling" and "depth of knowing" are the same; thus, participants are "led to believe that [they know] something in some empirically verifiable way."[13] Even though Moroni 10:4 suggests that the spirit does the work for willing individuals, for Mormons to sense and to feel the spirit may well require some training. For this reason, an emphasis on teenage trekking can serve the important function of beginning the process of training young bodies to feel the spirit.[14] "Feeling the spirit" has to be practiced but, at the same time, "is effective in bolstering one's testimony in the church only inasmuch as it is experienced as involuntary."[15] And so the practice of reenactment allows Mormons to do theological work and train their bodies to "feel the spirit" within the frame of historical accuracy. This framework can then promote an understanding of the felt nature of the spirit being *really real.*

Although reenactment can play an important role in Mormon theological formation, using the term "reenactment" may serve a secular purpose as well. Many of the trekking rituals done today are carried out, in part, on lands owned by state or federal agencies. While "pilgrimage" may sound decisively religious, "reenactment" does not. And so Mormon youth can do trek activities at TITP Park alongside their non-Mormon classmates without the question being raised of whether or not they are participating in a religious ritual. Mormons doing the religious work of trekking can also do so on public lands, with some of the aura conjured by the term "reenactment" suggesting history rather than religion, fact rather than spirit.

Are trekking Mormons who claim they are reenacting really participating in a form of pilgrimage? Even though they are not always traveling through space to visit a particular historical site, in this case the place where Brigham Young stood, looked out over the valley, and knew that it was the place, they are still participating in a movement through space that dovetails with the narratives about the nineteenth-century exodus, physically moving with one another toward a theological conceptualization of Zion. As discussed in chapter 6, Zion has been unmoored from physical space in many Mormon sermons and theological discussions and therefore has become a metaphorical concept. Yet through the ritual of trekking Mormons reanchor Zion in physical space through their activities and movements, through their communal reenactments.

Though two participants in my survey called trekking "pilgrimage," most Mormons, including the institutional church, avoid the term. And so to use the language of pilgrimage is in some ways to impose an interpretive framework on the trek. As Douglas Davies has argued, "from the profanity and geographical distance of evil Babylon they crossed the liminal wastes before entering Zion. The moral power engendered by this pilgrim-migration resembles the power generated in many if not all pilgrimages even though it may be described in a variety of ways depending upon the dominant ideology or theology involved."[16] Whether or not individual Mormons take on the language of pilgrimage, their activities echo certain traits of other religious pilgrimages performed around the world.

There are still other reasons why Mormons might eschew the language of pilgrimage. Within institutional discourses there is an attempt to move away from ideas that any particular landscapes are spots that are uniquely sacred. At the same time, church members are encouraged to embrace the idea that particular places are special, are sacred to believers, because important events happened there.[17] In this way, church leaders' theological language supports the notion that the divine is at work in history rather than in space. The general use of the language of "reenactment" to discuss the treks also supports this notion. Using this terminology enables Mormons to emphasize their engagement with their history, deemphasizing any discussion of the spatial and spiritual components of what is taking place.

Why might the language of pilgrimage still be appropriate for analysis? Some understandings of pilgrimage emphasize the journey as much as the destination, the movement through space as key.[18] In the words of Paul Elie, "a pilgrimage is a journey undertaken in the light of a story. A great event has happened; the pilgrim hears the reports and goes in search of the evidence, aspiring to be an eyewitness. The pilgrim seeks not only to confirm the experience of others firsthand but to be changed by the experience."[19] A pilgrim, then, engages the stories of the group while actively moving through space. At the same time the pilgrim experiences the material culture of religion.[20] The pilgrim engages the objects of belief with all of the senses, making the pilgrimage a physical encounter with the sacred and the holy. During the pilgrimage, participants also claim new identities, a process I will describe later. They take on the status of pilgrims, thus unifying the group. Even though pilgrims take on a new status as pilgrims, it does not mean that their social status in life does not affect the ways they experience the pilgrimage.

In order to accurately use the language of pilgrimage to analyze the rituals of religious people, one must begin with an understanding of the group's theology of place. Because Mormons have chosen a model of God who works historically and in human events, they shy away from language about particular landscapes being *more sacred* than others. Yet the approach of Mormons to particular spaces and to spatial conceptions of the sacred shows a determination to think about spaces and spatial concepts as sacred. And so members of the Mormon hierarchy can make claims that appear on the surface to be contradictory. They can say that no space, aside from the temple, is any more sacred than any other for Mormons, while thousands of Mormons visit the historical sites of their church every year. They can emphasize a God who works in history even as they are discussing and celebrating the spaces where they claim God has worked in the world. Ritual reenactment allows such truths to be held in tension with one another.

The Institutional Message about Trekking

Over the course of two years, I conducted a qualitative survey of current and past Latter-day Saints who had participated in trekking. The survey respondents came from two different sources. First, I asked Latter-day Saints I knew or had been connected with through my social networks to participate. Second, the *Juvenile Instructor* announced and provided a link to the survey to its readership. The answers to this qualitative study, and therefore a small sample, are the basis of some of the analysis that follows. While these narratives do show that many Mormons experience the trek as the institutional church dictates, they also demonstrate a diversity of experiences of trekking, an important reminder that the institutional church cannot ultimately control people's experiences, even while it can shape the ritual toward achieving a standard outcome.

Because history carries the weight of theology in the LDS community, the institutional church has a significant interest in how that history gets told and interpreted. In her study of British Mormons' visits to church historical sites, Hildi Mitchell found that the experiences of British visitors were surprisingly similar. She attributed these similarities to the church's emphasis on controlling the narratives told at the sites and shaping the sites to engender particular responses. She notes that the institutional church "controls the dissemination and interpretation of history through claiming it as theology." Further, she argues that "to look at a religion such as Mormonism without recognising the immense influence of its organisational and hierarchical structures is a mistake."[21] In response to the argument of religion scholars Eade and Sallnow that pilgrims tend to have heterogeneous experiences of pilgrimage sites, Mitchell's research is an important reminder. In Mormonism there is an emphasis on experiential unity, and the institutional church claims considerable control over theological discussions and interpretations. Mitchell argues that this is precisely because the line between history and theology is blurred.[22] Her arguments are affirmed by Michael Madsen in his study of Mormon historic sites. He asserts that Mormon sacred spaces are in the process of "becoming *sanctified* from the 'top down'" and that the church hierarchy is "currently engineering the creation of 'sacred space.'"[23] And so to truly engage pilgrimage in the Mormon context, one must examine how the intentions of the institutional church, laid out in the literature proscribing the way treks should work, compare to the experiences described by actual trek participants. One must explore the relationships between these theological and institutional expectations and the actual lived experiences of trekkers.

Throughout church materials about the trek, one can see an impulse to regularize and standardize the ritual and to ensure a particular type of experience for participants, especially teenagers. In this move to routinize and standardize, the church has come to portray trekking as a meaningful experience for youth. According to one trek leader, the youth will "go out and have these incredible spiritual experiences. . . . They go out and pretend to be pioneers and they pull handcarts. And they eat trail food and experience hardship. . . . And it's supposed to be really wonderful."[24] The treks are billed as a positive summer activity for church members all over the world, who can learn "how suffering and sacrifice brings one close to the Savior." Church authorities encourage participants to see themselves as following in the footsteps of the pioneers, enabling "empathy for those who heeded the call to gather to Zion."[25] In so doing, the trek taps into the theology of suffering discussed in chapters 4 and 5 and cements a tie between suffering, sacrifice, and virtue all through the embodied activity of reenactment.

A series of church-produced videos titled "Tracy's Trek" follows one teenager's trek experience from her preparation to her description of the lessons learned. Tracy, the star of the show, narrates a version of what the trek experience should be like for all teens. "If done safely," the church website explains, "trek reenactments can help today's youth learn to persevere, turn to God in their times of trial and gain a testimony that He will help bear their burdens." That set of messages forms the core of the attempts to standardize the trek experience as well as avoid any overzealous church members who might, in the eyes of the institution, take the experience too far. Or, in the institution's words, "you do not need to suffer through these same trials to gain an appreciation for the sacrifices of the handcart pioneers."[26]

In her preparation for the trek, Tracy discusses the way the leaders of her trek invited participants to find pioneer ancestors so that they could think about them while they trekked. The purpose of walking for a pioneer is to connect participants to a nineteenth-century pioneer's individual experience. They are encouraged to research that person and "try to do the things that he or she would have done on the journey to Zion."[27] Tracy notes that she has figured out that "people just like us did what we are going to do." The video follows Tracy as she and a friend choose Emma and Sarah James as their pioneer women identities. Tracy and her cohort prepare pioneer clothing to match their pioneer identities (except for the website's encouragement to bring modern, practical footwear). The institutional church asserts that the pioneer-style clothing "helps participants immerse themselves in the trek experience" by creating an aura of authenticity. In addition, the church says that the pioneer clothes "can also foster a sense of unity among the youth and help remove social barriers that may exist."[28] Sounding much like an attempt to create the experience of a pilgrimage, where participants shed their identities and social locations and share the identity of *pilgrims*, or in this case *trekkers*, the making and wearing of the clothing is given great weight— so much so that those who do not wish to make their own pioneer clothing (patterns for which can be found online) can order clothing from Zions

Mercantile and Deseret Books, where trekkers can purchase "bonnets, skirts, shirts, aprons, bandanas, hats, and satchels." At the same shop, trek leaders can find certificates for those who complete treks, journals, and dinnerware for "an immersive pioneer experience."[29] In the video, Tracy explains that the clothing "creates an atmosphere, an ambience." While encouraging clothing that promotes an aura of authenticity, the church also dictates what not to wear: "the wearing of white clothing to represent deceased persons or angels from the other side of the veil is not to be included as part of treks"[30] (see Figures 7.2 and 7.3).

Along their route, the trek participants discuss miracles that were recorded by nineteenth-century Mormons. In the evenings they square dance. Tracy claims that the dancing was "cool" and made the pioneers seem "more real." And so the same impulse to make the visitors' centers along the Mormon Trail portray a history that *feels authentic* appears in Latter-day Saint ritual life as well. An aura of ritual authenticity can promote a sense of connection to the past and a heightened religious experience.

During the trek, Tracy's friend Miranda did not drink enough water, became dehydrated, needed treatment, and missed out on the fun and activity of the last portion of the trek. Having not made that mistake, Tracy got to participate in a number of common trek activities. She participated in a Women's Pull, where only the women push the carts up to the top of a hill. The church describes this activity as one that can be important for young women, who learn they can rely on "their own strength and their faith in the Lord," and for young men, who "will long remember the effort and strength of the young women." Prior to the Pull itself, the young men and women are separated. "As guided by the Spirit," leaders are told to discuss topics "such as sacrifice, honoring the priesthood [held by men], respecting women, preparing for motherhood and fatherhood, morality, or missionary service." During the Pull, the women "pull the loaded handcarts over a difficult part of the trail" while "the young men watch silently and respectfully, either from a distance or beside the trail."[31] In her video remembrance, Tracy learns along the way that she can "do the hard thing" during the Women's Pull. While supporting the Pull as a key part of the trek, the church manuals admonish trek leaders that they cannot suggest "the absence of the young men by calling them to serve in the Mormon Battalion . . . [because] the Battalion occurred 10 years before handcart travel." Providing this particular narrative "is historically inaccurate and is therefore inappropriate."[32] This is an interesting assertion, as the Women's Pull itself is also not grounded in any

Figure 7.2 Pioneer Trek certificate.

Figure 7.3 Trek supplies.

historical events. Here one sees the interplay between attempting to manage the narrative being told and allowing for creativity in the ritual aspects of the trek.

Later, Tracy enjoys both a testimony meeting and the experience of splitting off from the group for some "Solo Time," when she and her peers are able to reflect on what they have learned "and how we are going to apply it to our lives." Church manuals for trek leaders suggest that this Solo Time be used to prepare the youth for a spiritual experience. The manuals encourage parents of the trekkers to write letters to their children that "express their love, testimony, and other thoughts and feelings with their son or daughter." Before the teens receive the letters, a bishop or stake president discusses "personal revelation and listening for the promptings of the Holy Ghost." Leaders might describe the Holy Ghost as a guide, helping people make important decisions in their lives. The youth are then sent off on their own for Solo Time, to find a rock or a peaceful place to sit, read the letter from their parents, and reflect. Solo Time is portrayed as the place and time when you can have intense religious experiences and spiritual lessons.[33] And this time is the focus of all of the other activities. After all, the bishop has told the teens about his personal revelations and the movings of the spirit, they have read letters from parents describing their own testimonies (often articulated as being prompted by the spirit), and finally they are left alone to listen for that same voice. This time is shaped to promote that experience of feeling the spirit.

When Tracy returns home, she continues to be moved by the experience and reflect on the pioneers. She ends the video series with a few key lessons: "I learned that I can do hard things," that "you have to stay on the trail, metaphorically speaking," and, finally, that "it's a good thing to listen to those who have been down the trail before." Thus, Tracy's experience includes an experiential living out of lessons to work hard, trust authority, and follow the institutional church wherever it may lead. An article written by an independent source as a guide to treks tells the story about a nineteen-year-old Philip Millett, who asked to go on trek again, after doing it four years before. On his second trek, a storm came in and temperatures dropped, bringing rain and sleet. Some of the trekkers began to suffer from hypothermia and were bussed to safety. Millett stayed behind and loaded the trekkers' belongings into vehicles. At a testimony meeting after the intense ordeal, Millett, who described himself as a "tough guy," cried and announced to his church members that he had a "spiritual confirmation" that weekend that "the Church was true."[34] He had felt the spirit as the institutional church would want. These types of trek stories create high expectations for all trek participants. Leaders are told that they are responsible for helping to set the scene in which such experiences can happen, and teens are told that these are normal experiences for average trekkers around the world.

Guidelines for adult leaders of the trek emphasize several lessons the institutional church would like participants to take home with them: faith, obedience ("in gathering to the American West, the pioneers were obeying the call of a prophet, Brigham Young"), charity, sacrifice, and perseverance through adversity. Leaders are told that the purpose of the trek should not just be to have fun or to enjoy recreation but to "strengthen testimonies and foster personal growth." Over the course of the trek, each teen is assigned to be part of a family, with a Ma and Pa who oversee the youth in their assigned family. The website counsels Mas and Pas to "prepare themselves spiritually and seek the Spirit in all they do and say" and expects them to see themselves as the key to ensuring that the youth take spiritual lessons from the trek.[35] While the goal of the trek involves spiritual lessons and experiences, history is also central to the journey. As I have discussed, the two are not often easily separable. The official guide for leaders dictates that they are responsible for ensuring that "any stories that are told and reenacted during the trek are historically accurate."[36]

Experiencing the Trek

The institutional expectations for treks, as laid out in the church guides created by the church hierarchy and certainly reflected in some independently sponsored descriptions, can be measured against participants' actual experiences of trek. As mentioned, in her discussion of British Mormons, Griffith notes that while visiting American landmarks of the faith, pilgrims often have very similar understandings of their experiences. She attributes this to Mormonism being a religion "where corporate control is paramount, and where branded religiohistorical experience is part of the problem of homogeneity."[37] In what follows, I will share some responses from more than eighty anonymous survey respondents about their trek experiences and measure them against the institutional descriptions provided in the video series "Tracy's Trek" and in church manuals. It is important to note here that my analysis will focus primarily on Latter-day Saints in the United States because virtually all my survey participants were Americans.[38] Again, while these surveys are not a representative sample, what they do show is a diverse set of experiences of trekking, even while many participants have precisely the outcomes the church would desire.

The first question to examine is *why* Latter-day Saints participate in the trek. For Mas and Pas and other trek leaders, the primary answer is *call*. Asked by bishops or stake presidents to lead the trek, these individuals commit their extra time to leading youth on treks in hopes of having fun and inspiring the spiritual experiences and connections to history outlined in the church guides. They are not specially trained but operate as lay leaders.

The answer for teens is both more and less complex. Quite often, the answer is along the lines of "my parents decided I would go" or "my siblings had done it and it was my turn." In the words of one adult looking back at her trek time: "it was a stake activity and my parents wanted me to. I also wanted to since all of my friends were doing it, and it seemed like it would be kind of a cool experience."[39] For most survey respondents, enthusiasm for the trek did not surface until they were on the trek, if at all. As one male participant explained: "it would have been difficult not to participate . . . [because of] parental expectations"; another recalled: "my mom made me."[40] Some participants anticipated that the trek might offer new experiences; one saw an opportunity to "experience a little taste of pioneer life"; another thought that it would be a "spiritually strengthening experience." Others recognized the social pressure and the role of the ritual in LDS expectations. One respondent who was representative of this position claimed: "it was a 'thing' to do as an LDS teen."[41] Others felt as though they might be ostracized or deemed a "bad" Mormon if they didn't participate.

And so, at least from a teenage perspective, trekking is often something one does out of obligation and a sense of social pressure, a desire to be included. Yet in some instances, enthusiasm for the objects that might offer authenticity to the experience— bonnets, pioneer clothing, and the like—offered a sense of the unusual, of stepping out of the daily world and into a different, special, and more sacred space. After all, "without the clothes, we would've just been a group of kids hiking through the desert."[42] This response, then, reflects the intention the institution sets for pioneer garb. The move toward supposed authenticity, here, should raise questions: what aspects of trek are being lifted up as important to authenticity? Why? What is being excluded from understandings of authenticity and why?

How, then, did the pioneer clothes function in the experiences of the trekkers themselves? The bonnets and long skirts for women, along with the trousers for men, served to mark the time on the trek as different, somehow "farther from the world for a few days." The clothing enabled them to see the difference between simply going on a hike and trekking.[43] It made them "feel different" and drew them "into the spirit" by removing them "from our comfort zones."[44] Another respondent suggested that the clothing and the activities created a sense that they were far away from the everyday world and that what they were doing was somehow unique. She explained that she "never felt we were replicating the pioneer experience. But we were creating our own."[45] Here she seemed aware that the trek, while utterly different from the nineteenth-century migration it reenacted, was its own special ritual that the trekkers created together. One declared that the clothing "contributed to an element of being in a different space."[46] Another allowed that the clothing helped the teens "get in character for the trip, much like a scout in a uniform or a deacon in a tie."[47] Rather than automatically sensing a world set apart, the participants seemed to understand that the clothes helped them *feel* as though they were characters in a scene of pioneers, with the clothing marking them as separate and different from their everyday selves. For another participant it was not just the pioneer clothing but being "organized into families, eating mush . . . pulling handcarts all day." For her, the activities "made it feel authentic to me as a youth (although it probably wasn't really very authentic at all)." As an adult she saw that "being out of normal paradigms fostered strong bonds with my trek family."[48]

A majority of respondents felt that the greatest nod toward authenticity was pulling the handcarts themselves. What stood out in their minds was the physicality of the labor that pulling and pushing the handcarts over hills and across streams required. For them, there was a kinesthetic lesson about the ideals of sacrifice, faith, and hard work. One respondent felt that the clothing and other "outward forms" did not shape his experience or help him feel a closer connection to the pioneers. Rather it was pushing the handcart, walking and talking as they went, that made the experience a profound one.[49] The nods at authenticity through physicality "made it worthwhile and a one-of-a-kind type of experience."[50] Thus the church's attempts to make pioneer character traits *real* through active, embodied living out of the ritual of trekking seems to have been successful for many young trekkers.

Some survey respondents remembered eating pioneer food and having food limited so that they, as trekkers, would experience what it would have been like to have food rationed at the same time one was participating in arduous physical labor. Although this practice is not endorsed by the institutional church—in fact it is prohibited—it can and did happen at the local level. It functions to mark the time as separate and to physically teach a lesson of privation. Six participants recalled being fed a "pioneer diet" of some sort. It is not surprising that these practices have appeared and at times continue to appear on local treks. Of historical reenactments, anthropologist Vanessa Agnew notes that in television reenactments "participants were subject to new and ever more challenging situations so that their surprise, incompetence and sense of dislocation could be registered by the viewer."[51] While Mormon trekking is not usually filmed by the media, that same sense of dislocation, surprise, and a feeling of incompetence may well be imagined by trek leaders as moments where the *feeling* of trek might be most intense, the feeling of facticity and truth.

Still other attempts at authenticity included "bandits who confiscated our belongings . . . pioneer storekeepers, pioneer games . . . sitting on hay." The respondent who recalled these nods toward an aura of authenticity connected the activities to a lesson about "how different people respond to trials."[52] Some trekkers carried sacks of flour or sand to represent babies that needed constant care and supervision. For one trekker, these aspects "admirably recreated the experience of the early pioneers."[53] Those flour-sack babies sometimes died, and trek families would stop to dig a shallow grave, hold a brief memorial, and move on. The popular 2018 film *Trek* , which tells the story of a Mormon trek, has a similar storyline. In this film, one young woman on the trek carries a doll with her to represent a pioneer child. Over the course of the trek, she finds out that the infant has died, and the group stops to bury the doll, placing stones over it in its grave to protect the "corpse" from the wolves. For some, this type of experience can be incredibly moving as they seek to imagine themselves as pioneers leaving behind a baby in a grave to which they will never return. Yet others found it insulting to the pioneers: it seemed to minimize a real death and the loss of a child in nowhere kind of place.

The strategies of authenticity are designed to inspire a sense that one is simply reliving past events and to provide a sense that reenactors have stepped out of the normal, everyday modern world. However, not everyone enjoyed the attempts at authenticity. One respondent recalled: "during our journey, some white leaders appeared dressed as Native Americans on horses, and 'kidnapped' and 'killed' random members." As an adult she viewed the experience as very misguided: "I didn't think much of the Native American portrayal, but now [I] see it as very problematic."[54] This practice, too, while it may happen on the local level, is not part of the institutional plan and, again, is strictly prohibited by the institution. The respondent saw what occurred as an instance of what historian Philip Deloria has called "playing Indian."[55] Playing Indian includes the practices white Americans have employed through the centuries that stereotype Native Americans and present them as an obstacle to a westward-moving, white, civilization project.

Since 1997, especially, the institutional church has worked to standardize the trek experience, both to prevent certain popular practices like those described here (the "pioneer diets," the "surprise attacks," etc.) that have been deemed undesirable and to routinize the religious experiences of the people involved. Nonetheless, popular attempts at "authenticity" like these still occur and reinforce stereotypes about race and empire. Take, for example, a 2005 trek in Gilbert, Arizona. On the second day, leaders dressed up in bandana masks and blackface and demanded that the trekkers hand over Joseph Smith. Following a script, one trekker stepped forward in Smith's place to receive a tarring (with chocolate pudding) and feathering. The other trekkers jumped into the scene and came to the prophet's defense, attacking the mob with poles and other objects, actually injuring some of the leaders playing the mob.[56] In this instance, the trekkers became so involved in the narrative of the reenactment that they fought for the release of Joseph Smith. Yet what they didn't address is more telling. First, Joseph Smith was never part of the nineteenth-century trek westward; he had died before the Mormons went to Utah. Second, the use of blackface reinforces the idea that the story of the pioneer movement west is a story of whiteness, much as the reenactments that include "attacks" by "Indian" bands. Both narratives end up celebrating the whiteness of the pioneers as a key portion of the story, thus reinforcing a triumphalist narrative of white empire. They include, in the words of Vanessa Agnew, "casting oneself as the protagonist," without much consideration of who in the narrative becomes the backdrop for the protagonist's story.

These narratives of race that often linger in the unspoken background of a few trek experiences are a reminder that stories about the pioneers serve to highlight and erase certain aspects of history, foregrounding pieces of the story that the group wishes to remember and downplaying or outright forgetting others. The foregoing examples are certainly aberrations of regular trek practices, yet even the treks that follow the institutional scripts show a similar type of forgetting. This is best shown in the words of Elise Boxer, a

Dakota Mormon who narrates these hidden and erased narratives found in the folds of the pioneer trek celebrations. She remembers:

> one specific activity that many LDS youth participate in is a recreation of the "pioneer" experience. For example, we had to dress in period clothing, long skirts and bonnets for girls, and push a handcart. This is an experience that many young men and women, ages 12–17, participate in annually. The purpose of this recreation is for young men and women to have an understanding and appreciation for the "pioneers" who made the long trek west due to religious persecution. It is also intended to be a religious experience for the individuals who participate. Young men and women who participate recall the spiritual aspects of this reenactment; it reaffirms their faith in the truthfulness of the LDS Church but also the affirmation of these Mormon "pioneers" whose trek west was sanctioned by God.
>
> I did not participate in these reenactments because I knew they were part of the religious colonization process. I would not buy into this narrative because it conflicts with my Dakota identity. As a Dakota young woman, I made sense of this day on my own terms. I believed this event to be hypocritical at best. How could we celebrate the Mormon move west to escape religious persecution yet remove Indigenous peoples from their traditional lands because they were not Mormon? How could I celebrate a church holiday that did little to acknowledge Indigenous peoples as an integral role in the Mormon historical narrative? Indigenous peoples were not included in any historical narrative and I knew if we included Indigenous peoples, there would have to be an acknowledgement that Mormons settled on Indigenous lands. Furthermore, not only did they claim land as their own, but from the Mormon perspective, this land was open and free for colonization. However, this was never the case. Utes, Paiutes, Shoshones, Goshutes, and Navajos lived within these boundaries of what we now know as Utah. While they did not clearly demarcate their land as Ute, Paiute, Shoshone, or Goshute the way Mormon settlers did, they had made this land their own long before Mormon "pioneers" arrived. They were knowledgeable and intimately connected to the land. Instead, Indigenous peoples remain invisible not only in the historical narrative, but their lived experiences remain invisible to the larger LDS community.[57]

Boxer's reminiscence serves as an important reminder of the high stakes in the erasures that take place during the trek experience. Enforcing a theology that the Mormon settlement of the West was "sanctioned by God" and the seizure of indigenous lands was part of that same divine plan, Mormon youth are taught to see God as sanctioning colonialism. They are taught to see the pioneers as examples of faith and righteousness without any questions being raised about the colonial project in which they participated. Boxer understood the stakes all to well—that the ritual of trekking was also a ritual erasure, in which her own identity and the identity of the Utes, Paiutes, Shoshone, Goshute, and Navajo who were displaced and erased would not be narrated but ritually forgotten. And it is in the midst of these narratives of white colonial triumphalism that trekkers are encouraged to have profound spiritual experiences, their testimonies are then framed by these broader narrative erasures and celebrations of whiteness.

The Women's Pull

The Women's Pull, mentioned earlier, originated out of a historical inaccuracy that was repeated again and again as people passed the practice from ward to ward. The story told, before institutional manuals demanded its disuse, was that in the nineteenth century, as the handcart pioneers were crossing the plains, most Mormon men were called away to be part of the Mormon Battalion and to take up arms in the Mexican-American War. Because of this narrative, trek leaders told young women that they would have to push and pull the handcarts over a hill, often the highest one in the area, on their own, seemingly replicating the actions of women who did not have men with them on their pioneer journey westward. The ritual that formed around this inaccuracy asked young women's male peers to stand to the side and watch as the women went about their work.

The Women's Pull is now a staple of treks, even though official church guidelines advise trek leaders not to present the false narrative about the Mormon Battalion. Rather, the women are told that there were women along the trail who had to push and pull their own carts because they were widowed, had sick spouses, or shared a handcart with other singles. And so the Pull remains, transformed into a set of messages and lessons about gender roles. Many survey respondents marked the Pull as a time of great emotion for participants. As I will show, the emotional responses vary dramatically, and the messages and lessons are received in different ways.

Prior to the actual Pull, Mas and Pas separate male and female participants and teach each group different lessons. Young men receive lessons about holding the priesthood, while young women learn about their roles as women and as mothers. Ultimately, both genders are taught the importance of dual gender complementarity—that the genders rely on each other to form two halves of a complete whole. Men are to act a certain way, the lesson goes, and their natural inclinations to protect and provide are complemented by women's natural inclinations to nurture and care.

In the survey, those trekkers who found the Pull to be a positive event were mostly women, and they cited their experience of feeling empowered—that they could do anything they set their minds to—as the key takeaway from the Pull, much as Tracy recounts in the church's video. One such participant noted the difficulty of the Pull and concluded: "we realized the strength we have as sisters."[58] In a similar vein, several respondents noted a message about working as a group, working together to make it "over rocky terrain."[59] One female participant recalled the Pull as "very meaningful" and appreciated "having the boys encourage the girls but doing the really hard work . . . as just females. Very empowering."[60] Another trekker took it one step further and appreciated that men were learning that women could "do just fine without them" and that women were taught "that they didn't need the men."[61] Still another declared: "it was the hardest thing I've ever done."[62]

One Ma recalled: "before we left, the leaders were involved in the planning. The Women's Pull was not 'Mormon Battalion' or 'dead men' on the trail. We decided it would show synergy. When men or women are not involved with something . . . things are harder. My girls really were amazing. We said a prayer and took our strength. We made it to the top and my girls immediately ran down to help the next groups. It taught synergy . . . but it also taught 'we can do hard things'—it taught love for each other and love for the men in our lives."[63] While the lessons here were clearly crafted in a particular way by the leadership of the trek, several themes echo with other participants: hard work, stick-to-it-ive-ness, and care for the group. Ultimately, this particular Ma saw a lesson about gender roles as well—that men and women need each other to do hard things. She found no contradiction in the lessons that men and women are both needed to get things done, a lesson in complementarity, and a lesson that the young women could do hard things independently. Another respondent recalled: "we came to a very steep & tall hill. . . . They made the men stand to the side, while the women pulled the cart by themselves. It was extremely difficult. I remember it being very emotional to the men to watch us struggle so much & not be allowed to help. The men were allowed to encourage us, but not allowed to help. Once we came to the top of the hill, we saw that there was another, and then another. It was very difficult and emotional at the time."[64] One male participant said he felt weird "just standing aside and watching women under significant strain."[65] Here he confirmed that he had learned the lesson that men step in to help, especially in times of physical difficulty. Another male participant remembered getting "the message that women were capable and persevering."[66]

One trekker was "dubious" at first, but then "the dudes left and we had a devotion . . . on being a strong independent woman. . . . Many of the girls commented that they liked it better, without the boys to be loud or distracting or whatever. There were some tough spots, but doing it made the girls super proud that they could accomplish it on their own."[67] The feeling of accomplishment, of doing something hard, trumped any initial doubts about the Pull.

A few trekkers told about "angels" appearing to help the women with the Pull. These angels were male leaders. As they recalled this aspect of the Pull; some recognized a spiritual message about those on the "other side of the veil" pushing alongside the living. Yet others believed the angels reinforced the idea that ultimately women did need men. Indeed there is an interesting double message—men appearing as heavenly beings who help out women when things are too difficult to do on their own. One trekker who had trekked five times commented that the Pull was always one of the most meaningful moments, one that was remembered in testimony meetings and "revisited for years and years afterward." She recounted another view of help from angels. On the last trek she made as a Ma, she recalled: "our cart didn't have enough women to pull up the three-quarter-mile steep hill. I had two injured girls and one other and myself. . . . We began with a prayer, and I asked for angels to be dispatched to aid us all. We began to pull and the steep hillside soon became too much for us. The doctor pulled us aside and asked us all to jump onto other carts to help others. As we reached the top—the men all lined the road with their hats off—tears streaming. The women ran back to help others when they reached the top. To me . . . it was very visual—that angels WERE dispatched. The lord asked us all to be earthly angels to others. Very powerful!"[68] A trekker with a similar experience of feeling "rescued" by women who had already climbed the hill declared it "the most spiritual part of the trek." Here the Pull served both a community-building and a spiritual function, confirming physically theological messages they simply had heard in the past.

Trekkers who did not appreciate the Pull cited a number of reasons that can be clustered around a few themes. First, there were those who deemed the Pull inauthentic, declaring: "it was not true to the pioneer experience."[69] Some found it "much ado about nothing" and claimed it was a distraction from the more meaningful portions of the trek. The largest number of critiques of the Pull centered around finding the messages about gender problematic. One male commented that the Pull made him uncomfortable and reflected: "most of these women [participants] were probably pulling much harder loads in their family life." He believed that the women should have some time to discuss their own burdens and loads rather than reenacting nineteenth-century ones.[70] Another participant noted that it seemed to reinforce, rather than challenge, the idea that women need men to help them, naming the contradiction others had glossed over in their accounts noted above. One critic found numerous problematic messages about gender, declaring the Pull "contrived and false" and "a misguided, sexist, and historically false" practice. This trek Ma recalled: "the women were told to appreciate the men. Some of the youth testified that angels helped pull the cart up the hill. The boys were encouraged to cry. Some of the boys teased the girls. Some of the young women felt insulted that it was assumed they would not make it up the hill without the men cheering them on."[71] In this instance, the trek leader felt as though young adults felt pressured to have particular emotional responses, ones that enforced rigid gender norms.

The forced emotionalism of the event also felt off-putting to some participants. Ten years after her trek, one respondent did not know how she felt about it: "in a lot of ways it felt oversensationalized, with girls crying about how hard it was and the value of the priesthood, and boys exclaiming how hard it was to watch. . . . I disliked that trek[king] split us up according to gender. I tried to take it seriously and empathize with my women pioneer ancestors, but as a teenager I mostly rolled my eyes at the whole experience."[72] Here she described a situation where men felt encouraged to feel helpless. That helplessness was expected to engender a sense of protectiveness and a desire to provide for others, basically reinforcing an exaggerated sense of masculinity.

This trekker's comments, along with the other critiques, raise another important question: how is the Women's Pull also (and perhaps equally important) a ritual of masculinity? What if one was to pay just as much attention to what the men are doing during that experience as to what the women are doing? In a church that embraces a complementary gender model—where women and men are seen to occupy two halves of one whole—scholars of religion and gender always need to be watching what is happening to both halves to better understand how gender is being ritualized. This trekker described a situation where the outcome was men feeling an exaggerated sense of masculine protectiveness, a "benevolent patriarchy," in the words of one female trekker, rather than women feeling a sense of independence. While the ritual appears to be about women doing things on their own, those same women were encouraged to see the importance of having a male figure in their lives, a message they might well receive in other church settings.

The Pioneerification Project

As I have shown in previous chapters, the institutional church made and continues to make a concerted effort to render the narrative of the nineteenth-century exodus to the American West a meaningful one to the members of a global, twenty-first-century church. What Eric Eliason has called the "pioneerification" of Mormonism is one name for this process. With more and more Mormons living outside the United States and fewer believers having ever visited the Intermountain West, the story of the pioneers, so central to church identity in the twentieth century, has the potential to wear thin. It is a story of a place and a people that may be fraying at the edges as a narrative of cohesiveness when many believers have not seen the place and don't have biological connections to the concept of peoplehood.[73] What, then, has the church done to enhance the connections and build a robust narrative with which many global members can connect? One of the functions of trekking as a ritual is to connect teenagers, at a critical moment in their lives when identity formation is taking place, to the stories of the pioneers. A key goal of trekking is to help teens connect to the history of the pioneers, to give them a sense that *these are my people and this is my story.* In addition, the goal is for teens to come to value traits such as hard work and sacrifice, with the ritual reinforcing these values kinesthetically for them.

It seems that the pioneerification process, of which trekking is a primary ritual, may well be operating at different levels of effectiveness for trekkers. For some of my survey participants, the connection is strong, and trekking offers a way of connecting the history through the pioneer clothing and the physical connection to the land. As with Tracy in the trek video created by the church, many trekkers were assigned the task of researching the history and lives of ancestors beforehand so that they would have specific individuals with whom they might feel a special connection. One trekker perhaps evidenced pioneerification the best when she listed three pioneers by name and then said: "these pioneers all gave of themselves, served unselfishly and had such incredible faith. I have paintings of them hanging in my living room with a mirror right next to them. I teach my family to look at themselves and the painting to see if they are reflecting those same characteristics."[74] Here, in an interesting example of material religion, the respondent, who had participated in numerous treks as both a trekker and a trek leader, saw the significance of connecting to the pioneer story *to the degree* that her family could see themselves reflected in those same stories through the character traits the pioneers exemplified.

Some trekkers walked in honor of an ancestor and felt a new form of connection to their familial roots or, in the words of one trekker, "an added layer of meaning." That same trekker wondered whether the same type of meaning would occur for trekkers who were not biologically related to the pioneers: "I have pioneer ancestors, and because of that I think the trek was more meaningful."[75] Many respondents listed the names of their ancestors who crossed the plains and recalled reading journal entries and studying the lives of these relatives before heading out on the trek, prompting a sense of a "special connection" with the stories of their ancestors.[76] Much like the 1997 trekkers, some even related that they "took" their ancestors with them on their own treks. The connection felt, though, is often recalled in terms of blood ties: "they are my ancestors and I look up to their faith, dedication, and sacrifice."[77] In these examples, values are connected to bloodlines, definitely connecting the trekker to the story *these are my people and this is my history*, but in a familial way rather than through a ritual process of adoption into the narrative. The connection could be stated as *I trek as they once trekked*, creating a larger sense of people through common activity, connecting their link to a pioneer chain of memory.

Even though trekkers with an ancestral tie to the pioneers seemed to find the stories more meaningful, those ties do not ensure it. One woman recalled that she had "a big pioneer heritage" but added that she identifies more "with amazing Grandmothers who endured difficult lives but were not crossing the plains."[78] Another listed her ancestral connections but then claimed that she "feel[s] no real connection to any pioneers."[79] Yet another wrote that her mother liked to recount stories about pioneer ancestors, "but I'm not sure that I feel a strong connection."[80] Still another critiqued the trek's lack of authenticity. He spoke of his great-great-grandfather, who crossed the plains and endured hardships, as someone whose "life experiences and hardships are mocked by trekking." This trekker forbade his children from participating in trekking when their ward decided to go. He felt that the process of trekking was "meaningless" and that his ancestors would be "disrespect[ed] . . . with kitsch."[81] With no such guarantees of biological descendants connecting to the story, the process of pioneerification may not always be functioning as the institutional church would prefer.

It seems, though, that the trekkers in my survey who were not *biologically* connected to the pioneers, who could not claim that direct connection, did not always connect to the pioneers with the same intensity but rather continued to feel disconnected from the story. As one respondent put it, "no pioneers in my lineage and no one ever really bothered to make pioneers 'real' to me."[82] Another simply remarked: "my parents are converts" as an explanation of why he did not feel connected to the pioneers, nor did he recognize the pioneers as a significant aspect of the trek experience. From this handful of experiences, it appears that the attempt to pioneerify may still encounter some stumbling blocks in this arena. Outside trekking and in regular church life, believers are taught to research their ancestry and take part in the ritual of baptism for the dead on their behalf. These same people, they are taught, can enjoy eternity together as a family if they reach exaltation. The messages of the church are very family-centric. These general messages—along with the privileging of the heritage of many central church figures who can claim ancestral ties to the pioneers and even further back—can make and keep pioneer identity a point of *disidentification* for some believers. They do not always sense that the stories and narratives are theirs to lay claim to in the same way members with biological ties can.

Lessons

What exactly do trekkers take away from their trek experiences? Is it along the lines of the institutional church's goals for their experience or is it something else? What is the most meaningful aspect of trekking for participants in this relatively new ritual?

To begin, it is important to note that nine of the respondents simply did not find the trek very meaningful; several of those same respondents just enjoyed themselves. One even declared that he "despised everything about it, except for the scenery."[83] Another felt as though the leaders were " 'making it hard' simply for the sake of making it hard." "I spent the entire trek feeling punished, rather than uplifted . . . I spent all of trek thinking that I wasn't spiritually mature enough for the experience." Later in life, conversations with others who did not enjoy trekking made this participant feel better; she changed her understanding, seeing the ritual itself as the problem rather than her own lack of maturity.[84]

Yet many others found something of significance in the trek ritual, whether or not that meaning aligned with institutional expectations. One trekker connected each meaningful component of the trek to the physical activity, recalling that he "built stronger friendships with other youth by working with them on a physical challenge. I felt more personally confident that I could accomplish something difficult. I felt more connected to or aware of pioneer lives and work."[85] Clearly for this trekker, the bonds between trekkers were significant, stronger than bonds that might be created outside the ritual world of trekking. Those bonds extended back in time as well, building a connection between the trekker and the stories of the pioneers. At the same time, individual growth was possible because of the physicality of the activity.

Other trekkers connected what they found meaningful about the trek to material objects, both the presence of historical objects (or versions of historical objects) and the absence of modern-day objects. One woman recalled "going without things" as the most significant part of trekking: "very little clothing, make-up, technology. Walking into a mall right after the trek was a shock. We have so much stuff to purchase."[86] Not only going without stores but also going without technology surfaced in several accounts as setting the trek time apart. "Being offline" allowed better and stronger relationships to form.

Echoes of the emphasis on relationships rang throughout trekker accounts. Because of the setting, participating in a ritual together far from the normal routine, intense relationships often formed in a short time. One trek Ma remembered that she "felt like these 'kids' of mine changed my life. Trek to me was the idea that you can be thrown together with people you did not know and learn to love them in a very short time."[87] Those relationships felt very special to another Ma, who claimed that the most meaningful part of trekking was "connecting with the youth during the walking, seeing how much they wanted to recreate something true (by singing hymns and having relevant conversation)."[88] It was outside the church building, several trekkers noted, that more "real" relationships happened. Conversations could be had that couldn't be had during Sunday ward services, such that participants felt more open to discussions about trials they faced in their lives. For one young woman, it was connections formed, specifically with female leaders, through "physically working together . . . [and] working hard," that was a meaningful experience.[89] It allowed her to appreciate female leadership in the church in a new and more profound way.

The bonds formed out of a shared activity, out of physical movement toward a shared goal, really solidified those relationships. One trekker explained that his "trek 'family' actually bonded really well and [he was] able to forge that connection with what was a group of strangers through hard work and shared trial." He believed that the hard work and shared experiences were "a better microcosm of Zion than any quorum, ward, or stake I've ever been a part of."[90] For this trekker, the physicality of the labor reinforced particular character traits the group needed. It also made the theological concept of Zion, so central in Mormon theology yet often abstract, a more concrete reality. Zion existed in a separate place, as group members labored toward a shared goal and felt connections to one another. Or, in the words of a sesquicentennial trekker, a "traveling Zion" was created and sustained through shared physical movement through space.

It is clear in the survey responses that the bond with other trekkers played the most significant role in the trek experience. The physical and material aspects of the trek helped create those relational bonds with one another. Some trekkers understood that shared communal identity as a feeling of the spirit, while others understood it as a powerful experience of intense social connection. Not only were the physical activities of the trek important, but the *place* of it was. By this I do not mean that all trekker respondents experienced the ritual along the Mormon Trail or even in the American West. Rather, they experienced the site of trekking as a place set apart, marked by the ritual activities that occurred there. One trekker noticed that it was this not-so-usual space that made it "clear that we all had our own struggles and unique traits or ways of dealing with trials that helped us along. Some became more introverted, others became more extroverted. . . . I also found that thinking about my own family history helped me clarify for myself what I looked for in a spiritual experience, and what was really important to me."[91] And so the place-set-apart aspect of trekking still functioned in a meaningful way even when the location of the trek is not particularly significant. Thus, concepts like Zion could be felt on the trek without reference to location. It was a movement through space as a community that could conjure up a "better microcosm of Zion."

Figure 8.1 Re-creation of original stone cairn, Mountain Meadows Massacre Grave Site Memorial.

8

Anxious Landscapes

Expressing Regret in an Age of Apologies

On April 7, 2004, government officials from the state of Illinois arrived in Utah to meet with Governor Olene S. Walker and leaders of the LDS Church. The officials from the Midwest were there to present the LDS leadership with a copy of House Resolution 793, passed on March 24, which stated: "biases and prejudices of a less-enlightened age in the history of the state of Illinois caused untold hardship and trauma for the community of Latter-day Saints by the distrust, violence and inhospitable actions of a dark time in our past." It went on to describe the Latter-day Saints as a faithful people who had worked hard as they settled in the city of Nauvoo. The resolution called the anti-Mormon sentiment in nineteenth-century Illinois "misguided" and expressed "official regret" for what had happened to the Mormons in Illinois. At the meeting in Utah of both Mormon and Illinoisan leaders, Illinois state representative Daniel J. Burke said: "the murder of Joseph Smith and the expulsions of the members of the Church of Jesus Christ of Latter-day Saints was a time we are not proud of." And so it appeared that 160 years later, Illinois was sorry for the death of Joseph Smith Jr. and his brother Hyrum and for the general mistreatment of Mormons that led to the migration of over 20,000 Mormons from the state of Illinois. Illinois lieutenant governor Pat Quinn declared: "it wasn't right. We acknowledge it was wrong and express our regrets and look forward to the future."

Intriguingly, the meeting of the delegates from the state of Illinois, the government leaders of Utah, and members of the LDS Church hierarchy happened in the church administration building in the heart of downtown Salt Lake City. The room where the meeting was held had "towering columns, marble walls and gilded molding."[1] Why is the *place* where the expression of regret occurred (note that it was not an official "apology") important? In part, the place mitigated the expression of regret. It allowed the expression of regret to be received with welcome and smiling faces precisely because the place where the meeting happened indicated that the Mormons

Pioneers in the Attic. Sara M. Patterson, Oxford University Press (2020). © Oxford University Press.
DOI: 10.1093/oso/9780190933869.001.0001

had survived the turmoil in Illinois; in fact, it suggested that they had thrived after their ejection from the "Gentile" Midwest. Their Moses had led them to their promised land. They had done just fine. The narrative of the past offered and implied at the meeting of government and church officials—through the lens of a prospering twenty-first-century people—tells us quite a bit. The ceremonial presentation of the expression of regret is multifaceted: on one level it affirms Mormon identity as a "peculiar people" on the American terrain. After all, it recalls that at one time Mormons were so intolerable that many in Illinois decided that they could not be neighbors with them. On another, it suggests that despite their outsiderhood and their enemies, the Saints triumphed and lived into their future—the gilded molding served as evidence that the Saints had not, in the end, been held back. Perhaps this was the first time historically that the Saints could willingly accept such an apology and the state of Illinois could willingly offer it.

Why would this time and this place be an opportune moment for an apologetic act? Political scientist Brian Weiner explains that an individual's sense of membership in a group, the development of a sense of "us," requires that the individual (and therefore the group) have a sense of self situated in both time and space.[2] Identity is established by an understanding of boundaries between self and other; those boundaries are both geographical and temporal. For Mormons the church's presence in Utah, the ability of visitors to stand where Brigham Young once (presumably) stood as he looked out over the Salt Lake Valley and knew "this is the place," enables them to confirm both a sense of peculiarity (after all, they had been driven out of eastern and midwestern states) while also allowing them to accept an apology from others—an acknowledgment of their status as part of American identity. Indeed, Illinois's apology suggested that the state's ancestors had unfairly created a "them" out of a group that was, in fact, a part of an American "us." The expression of regret implied that Illinois's ancestors had been wrong and implied the seeking of a new type of relationship in the future—a mended one, such that Illinoisans and Mormons could be considered a "we."

The degree to which Mormons have been incorporated into the American "us" by the late twentieth and early twenty-first centuries has allowed them to participate in a set of apologetic acts. While they have often been the recipients of apologies, in other instances groups have looked to the Mormons to apologize for oppressive historical acts and take responsibility for historical injustices they perpetrated in the American West. As a group accused of past atrocities, the Mormons became part of an American "us," those who had lived out Manifest Destiny—a destiny often posited in history books as a regretted but violent and unchangeable reality.

As I will show, for decades the LDS Church avoided taking any responsibility for participation in the event known as the Mountain Meadows Massacre. For some time the church told alternative, false narratives about that time. It has only been in the twenty-first century that the Mormons have addressed their church's participation in, at least at a local level, the Mountain Meadows Massacre and acknowledged that the Paiutes, an indigenous Utahan group, took the blame for these historical injustices for far too long. While participating in all of these apologies, as recipients and as givers, Mormons have been negotiating their religious and national identities. They have been participating in shaping collective memory on both a Mormon and national level, as having been complicit in all that was included and excluded in the narratives that were told.

Anthropologist James Bielo reminds us that in the process of history-telling, "selected realities are removed because they have the potential to undermine, contradict, or simply co-exist uneasily with the version of history being promoted."[3] What I will show in these examples of apologies is the role of forgetting in the formation of collective memory. I will show how groups choose to forget historical events and situations that do not gel with their members' sense of identity. Just as members of the LDS Church have come to celebrate Bodil Mortensen as a martyr, so, too, have they participated in forgetting the role members of their faith played in the massacre at Mountain Meadows. That forgetting may have been active, actively promoting a particular narrative while being aware of other counter-narratives supported by historical evidence. And it may well also have been passive, accepting as truth the version of history taught by members of an institution with a particular stake in the narrative. And so this chapter continues an exploration of collective memory. It turns to a place a few hundred miles from TITP Park in order to explore the intersections of place and collective forgetfulness. It asks how people shape historical sites to support particular narratives of the past. I will investigate the slippages in Mormon memory work between the historical and the spatial, and how storytelling gets played out on landscapes. I will ask why the descendants of the victims of the Mountain Meadows Massacre could not "close the book" on the history of Mountain Meadows when the LDS Church refused to acknowledge their narratives of this site of tragedy. This chapter explores an anxious landscape of the American West.

An Age of Apologies

The Illinois resolution and the speeches that attended its presentation to its Utahan recipients was an expression of "official regret." Earlier drafts of the resolution asked for forgiveness, but some in the Illinois government did not want to ask to be forgiven for sentiments and actions in which they themselves had not participated.[4] It was their state's early residents, after all, not they, who had treated the Mormons poorly. The disagreements over how to word the resolution, the careful discussion over what kind of responsibility would be taken for historical deeds, exemplified a common theme in recent debates over such apologies, expressions of regret, and reparations. Were the apologies the Latter-day Saints participated in unique? Not really. Though the circumstances and contours of these apologies may be distinctly Mormon, the fact that apologies for historical injustices are happening is not.

These apologetic acts have happened in the midst of what some scholars and journalists have deemed the "age of apologies," which began not long after World War II. This "age" is defined by the frequency of macrolevel apologies for historical injustices and violations of human rights. Religious organizations; local, state, and national governments; educational institutions; and private firms have all entered into the activities of apologizing. Victims of historical injustices now often demand apologies from those who have mistreated them, and some ask for reparations. The U.S. government has apologized for the internment of Japanese Americans during World War II and for the loss of property of indigenous groups in Alaska. President Bill Clinton apologized for the role of the nation in the international slave trade, apologized to native Hawaiians, and apologized to African American survivors of the Tuskegee Institute syphilis experiment.[5] All of these national-level apologies (and international-level apologies, such as Queen Elizabeth's apology to the Maori people of New Zealand), have inspired other smaller-scale but still group-level apologies.

What exactly is an apology? It is an act of contrition for past events that allows the parties involved to form a different understanding of one another for the present and the future. Between two individuals, an apology enables an injured party to feel that a wrong (which would cause the injured party to feel hurt, disrespected, resentful) has been acknowledged by the injurer. An apology is a recognition of fault by the injurer that opens the way for new forms of understanding and relationship.

Philosopher Charles Griswold has written much about apologies and even more about the related process of forgiveness. About forgiveness, he writes that it aspires "to something impossible: knowingly to undo what has been done."[6] He argues that forgiveness requires the parties involved to imagine themselves in one another's shoes. The injurer to some degree accepts the narrative of the injured, takes responsibility for the wrong done, expresses regret for the action, and hopes for a different relational future with the injured.[7] The injured to some degree gives up the moral anger at the acts done and relinquishes "revenge and resentment, all the while holding the offender responsible." In this way, forgiveness does not become condonation of the act or an excuse for the choices of the injurer.[8] Both these positions require that the two parties be in active relationship to one another and that they imagine the possibility of a different kind of relationship in the future.

Narrative is crucial in the activity of apology and forgiveness. Memories of past wrongs are precisely the reason that they shape present and future relationships. The narrative of what has happened, "claims to represent, in some sense, how things are (or were)." Griswold notes that the narratives are both recollective (in the sense that they are about the past) and projective (because they imagine a different relationship in the future).[9] Thus the stories told about how the wrong happened and why, how the injurer came to do the wrong (without suggesting that it is constitutive of the injurer), how the injurer came to know or understand the wrong done, and how the people involved will move forward in the future are all key in the process of resolution.

Narrative and memory play central roles not just in individual acts of apology and forgiveness but also in the exchanges between groups. How are forgiveness and apology negotiated at a group level? In what ways are group apologies different from and similar to individual apologies? One of the most important similarities is the significance of narratives and the importance of memory and truth-telling as part of the construction of narratives as two parties attempt to reconcile with one another after past wrongs.[10] Some level of agreement on the narrative of the past must occur for the participants to move forward into the future. Perhaps the importance of truth-telling and narrative formation is even heightened at the level of group apologies, because more collective work goes into the process of remembering and forgetting, for the narrative can have higher stakes. This is a key point to which I will return.

The primary difference between apologetic acts between individuals and those between groups has to do with identity and narrative. In group apologies, the act of apology is often offered by proxy. The apology is made by an individual or individuals who did not participate in the wrongdoing. At the same time, the apology is often about historical acts, so the recipients are often also not the actual injured party (though they may well still experience the ramifications of the past acts). Thus group apologies are tied to the notion of representation: "the notion that X acts in the name of . . . Y."[11] Here is the point at which narrative is important. As I've shown in earlier chapters, individuals not only understand their identities in relation to individual stories but also shape their sense of identity in relation to collective memory. Individuals understand who they are as they come to hear and accept who "we" are in the narratives provided by the group. Thus the apology is offered and accepted by one party on behalf of another party, making it symbolic in nature. Griswold points out that the language of forgiveness often does not work in these political macrocircumstances: the language of forgiveness can become metaphorical, "as when we speak of 'the nation' being angered, or proud, or what have you. All this makes it very doubtful that the close connection between the moderation and the forswearing of resentment and interpersonal forgiveness is reproducible at the political level." Thus, phrases "such as 'we regret' or 'we apologize' when uttered in a political context are not reports of sentiments—at least not necessarily—but are speech acts aiming at some different purpose."[12]

What is that purpose? The answer is complex. The speech acts are quite often part of a formal ritual in which the parties have come together, such as the Illinois expression of regret. In that instance, the speaker often serves as a proxy for the collective and offers a narrative that accepts the wrongdoing and includes some portion of truth-telling. Yet the narrative offered is different in this situation; it rarely provides an account of how the injurer came to do the wrong. Rather, it is "much more centrally concerned than is forgiveness with putting truth 'on the record.' The publicness of the act is of its essence. And a public record is not served by a lengthy discourse . . . clarity, brevity, intelligibility, and accessibility . . . [are] crucial." A second significant difference between interpersonal and group apologies is audience. In interpersonal relationships, the audience is obviously the other party. In group apologies, the audience is what Griswold calls the "moral community." That means that unlike the interpersonal apology, the group apology "does not depend on the true motives of the abstract agent in question." Instead, the apology seeks to affirm "the moral spectator's norms, as well as the appropriate actions that demonstrate publicly the reliability of that reaffirmation.

It re-establishes trust, and shows that the responsible entity or agent can be counted on to act . . . in a way that is consistent with the established norms."[13] Thus the apology is targeted at the community that is witnessing the apology and has a different aim. The party representing the injurer offers the narrative account of the apology in order to stake a claim as part of the moral community to which it speaks.[14] Its act of "truth-telling" serves as its entry fee into the moral community.

In every act of apology, it is important to investigate how power plays a role. This is especially true in group apologies. Who gets to narrate the past—who gets to decide what is remembered and what is forgotten—is very much a question of power. If a dominant group decides that a particular memory or set of memories is not part of their narrative, it becomes very difficult for minority groups to gain any traction in offering counter-narratives. Thus the refusal to apologize for a past act is also a power move. To avoid apology or to refuse to accept a narrative offered by an injured party is a refusal to accept the narrative tied to the injured party's identity and thus a refusal of that identity. The question of who is responsible and what the truth of the past might be is not explored by the parties involved.[15] To refuse that exploration of the historical narrative is to accept a strained relationship and draw a firm boundary between the "us" who refuse to engage a counter-narrative and the "them" who are offering that narrative as a component of their identity. In other words, to refuse to apologize is to reject the identity narratives of the injured parties.

Apologies that happen on a macrolevel can be a way of ameliorating the past and opening the way for reconciliation and new relationship in the future.[16] Just because an apology is offered does not mean that the past is erased. Rather, it indicates that the apologizer is willing to recognize the identity claims of the injured party and is hoping that a new relationship can be developed without historical injustice being the defining act of the relationship. When apologies happen at the macrolevel, their ability to move people relies on the extent to which individuals identify with the groups involved and feel the effects of and the importance of an apology for historical injustices.[17]

As political scientist Melissa Nobles has noted, apologies "publicly ratify certain reinterpretations of history" and "morally judge, assign responsibility, and introduce expectations about what acknowledgment of that history requires." Further, apologies "help to bring history into conversation . . . focus on a neglected past and demand that moral reflection be brought to bear and that some attempt at remedy be undertaken."[18] Because of the role of history in apologies and in the formation of individual and group identities, it is important to note that those who offer apologies or expressions of regret believe that they can do so on behalf of historical actors. In so doing, they are recognizing that they claim membership in a group that has failed to achieve its present-day, ideal vision of itself. They must accept that past members of the group acted in an unethical manner.[19] Through the act of apologizing, the current ethics of the group can be confirmed, and individuals in the group can affirm their sense of value.

And so when Anne Burke, an appellate justice in Illinois, returned home from a ski trip to Utah with new knowledge of Mormon history in her state, she felt as though she had to do something to address the wrongs that had been perpetrated by citizens of her state on its nineteenth-century Mormon citizens. She discussed what she had learned with her husband, Alderman Edward Burke, in Chicago who did some legal research on the issue, and her brother-in-law, Daniel J. Burke, a state representative who ended up supporting the resolution. In Utah, Anne had met Myron Walker, the husband of Olene Walker, the governor of Utah, who told her the story of his great-grandfather and the persecution he had faced in Illinois. " 'I could not get over that this kind of religious persecution happened and this was not so long ago,' " Burke recalled. Of the dinner where the two met, she remembered that the guests "all spoke of their ancestors' history just like it was yesterday.' "[20] In this recollection Burke acknowledges that the Mormons with whom she dined had a clear tie to their history and that their sense of who they were was bound to who their ancestors were and the narrative of what had happened to them in Illinois. She was embarrassed that she had known nothing of what happened at Nauvoo; here she expressed a sense of failing to know the history of her own group. She claimed that she felt as though "no. 1, the people of Illinois ought to know more about their own history and, no. 2, it's a travesty that's gone on for too many years.' "[21] She addressed both an "us" (Illinoisans) who had neglected history—an act she found unethical in and of itself—and a "them" (Mormons) who might not be able to move past that history because it still held open wounds.

Some have accused Burke and other Illinois legislators of having developed a ploy to encourage more Mormon tourism, more than was already happening with visits to historic sites, to the state and masked it in the aura of regret and apology. Just how much tourism played a role in this apology has been a question raised several times; it is impossible to answer. Intriguingly, tourism to one state (for Utah skiing) inspired regrets that might well have encouraged tourism back to the other. Thousands of Mormons travel to Illinois each summer to visit the site where their prophet was murdered and to see the temple in Nauvoo.

This issue seems particularly important in terms of the Illinois apology, which, though recognized and discussed, did not receive a lot of attention in Utah's media or church publications. Though Latter-day Saints internally identify with their past history of oppression, as Myron Walker's story demonstrates, the narratives they tell do not usually point a finger at fellow American offenders. Rather, official church accounts often employ the passive voice, a strategy that allows Mormons to self-identify as an oppressed group without pointing a finger at or naming a specific oppressor or group of oppressors. Why? To do so would be to acknowledge just how outside mainstream American culture the Mormons were not that long ago. It would place them outside the American "us." Instead, Mormons' fashioning of their history celebrates their own religious ancestors as enduring oppression and hatred; the oppressors go unnamed. In so doing, Mormons can both affirm their identity as a people set apart, an identity very much tied to their understanding of themselves as part of God's people, *and* claim an unproblematic identity as Americans. To name their past oppressors as the ancestors of their fellow Americans would be to mark a divide Mormons would rather leave unmarked.

How the LDS Church responded to the expression of regret speaks to the role the regret played in the church's understanding of its identity. James Faust, a church leader, explained: "we view this resolution as an affirmation that Nauvoo is a place of peace and an affirmation that Latter-day Saints will always have a place in Illinois." Here the discussion emphasizes the relationship between history and place. Acknowledgment of past wrongs allows Mormons to move through space, to feel comfortable in space, and to feel that Illinois might be a "home" to which they can return.

Governor Walker, who spoke as a representative of Utah, understood the expression of regret as an apology and declared that it "was certainly a very generous gesture on their part to realize historically they had really driven a whole group of people out of their state. Now they're saying they're sorry it happened. I think it does bring a great deal of friendship and . . . warm feelings about Illinois."[22] Here we see the expression of regret functioning in the way it might ideally function for all parties. Because a past wrong was addressed, because a group took responsibility for that wrong, and because the group receiving the apology had overcome the hardships wrought by their oppression, the parties involved were able to imagine a different future with one another.

More Apologetic Acts

When the Latter-day Saints set up shop in Nauvoo, Illinois, during the winter of 1838–1839, they were fleeing the state of Missouri. Just as later Illinoisans would, Missourians considered the Mormons to be an intolerable peculiarity because of their religious, economic, and political practices. Missouri had been simply the next in a series of stops as Mormons continued to move, looking for safe space and freedom to practice their religion. They had begun in New York, the home state of Joseph Smith Jr., and moved to Kirtland, Ohio (where they stayed from 1831 to 1838). Many of those years in Kirtland over-lapped with the time when even more followers began to settle in Missouri. There they stayed approximately eight years before moving on to Illinois, where their prophet was murdered in 1844.

Why did the Saints leave Missouri to head to Illinois after they had been settling there for eight years? Why would they leave their Zion? As discussed earlier, tensions with neighbors over political and religious disagreements had reached a climax. Latter-day Saint missionaries entered Missouri as early as 1831, but it was during the next few years that Mormon settlements re-ally developed. The Jackson County settlements saw the tensions between Mormons and their neighbors begin to move toward serious consequences. Missourians feared Mormons for many reasons, including reasons related to race and slavery. They were concerned that the Mormon settlers were prima-rily from New England, when Missourians were largely from southern states that supported slavery. In addition, the Mormons saw Native Americans as a target for missionary work.[23] Missourians saw Mormons as a group who would act as a political voting block and as an economic block, supporting Mormon-owned businesses over other businesses. They also saw Mormons as a dangerous religious group with odd practices that to the Missourians appeared non-Christian. For their part, the Mormons did not seek to make close connections with their neighbors. Their past history of abuse and their tightly knit sense of communal identity made them suspicious of their non-Mormon neighbors.

What is often called the "Mormon War" started in 1838 and resulted in property damage, physical assault, and the loss of life. The most dangerous event, the Hawn's Mill Massacre, occurred on October 30, when an angry mob attacked a Mormon settlement, which resulted in the loss of seventeen Mormon lives and many more injuries. At that point in time, Mormons had already been forced from county to county in Missouri out of intolerance and violent vigilantism.[24]

On October 27, 1838, then governor Lilburn W. Boggs signed what is often referred to as the "Extermination Order." It declared: "information of the most appalling character which entirely changes the face of things . . . places the Mormons in the attitude of an open and armed defiance of the laws and having made war upon the people of this state." It instructed: "the Mormons must be treated as enemies, and must be exterminated, or driven from the State, if necessary for the public peace." The order signaled that it was time for the Mormons to continue on their journey, and around 10,000 Mormons left their property and homes, left what they had called Zion, and moved to Illinois. In the Extermination Order, Boggs rhetorically created an "us" and a "them." The Mormon "them" was a threat to the peace and prosperity that Boggs suggested other Missourians held dear.

After settling in Nauvoo, Illinois, Joseph Smith and several others traveled to the nation's capital at the end of 1839. Their goal was to petition Congress for the return of their lands in Jackson County, Missouri, and to receive damages for what they had lost while in Missouri.[25] Their hopes for some kind of acknowledgment of the damage done to the group and to group members' property were never realized. And so the Extermination Order became the evidence of Mormons' historical narrative of the persecution of the faithful—another wrong in a long litany of wrongs. It was not for over another 140 years that the Extermination Order gained attention from another corner.

On June 25, 1976, Christopher S. Bond, then governor of Missouri, issued a second executive order that rescinded Bogg's Extermination Order and expressed regret on behalf of the state of Missouri for what the Mormons had endured within its borders. At a conference hosted by the COC, the group of Mormons who had stayed in the Midwest after Smith's murder, Bond offered his own executive order:

whereas, on October 27, 1838, the Governor of the State of Missouri, Lilburn W. Boggs, signed an order calling for the extermination or expulsion of Mormons from the State of Missouri; and WHEREAS . . . [that] order clearly contravened the rights to life, liberty, property and religious freedom . . . and WHEREAS, in this bicentennial year, as we reflect on our nation's heritage, the exercise of religious freedom is without question one of the basic tenets of our free democratic republic . . . I, CHRISTOPHER S. BOND, do hereby order as follows: Expressing on behalf of all Missourians our deep regret for the injustice and undue suffering which was caused by the 1838 order, I hereby rescind Executive Order Number 44.

The 1976 executive order focused its attention on the ways Boggs and other Missourians had failed to live up to the values of the nation and of the state of Missouri, implying that they had not been acting as Americans should. Thus Bond allowed a space for his audience to envision themselves as an American "us" who despised the actions of Boggs and others in the past. The act of judging the past, then, became a communal act, and present-day audience members could imagine a moral twentieth-century American "us" who could accept a narrative of past wrongs that exempted any modern-day people from responsibility.

How did the LDS Church respond to the 1976 executive order? Its response was primarily directed internally and for the church community. Church president Spencer W. Kimball wrote a letter to the president of the Kansas City, Missouri, stake, Christian F. Sanders, that explained that the church authorities had given the 1976 executive order "some publicity in the General Conference, feeling that the people generally should know of this change of attitude." Kimball continued that he hoped the statement given to church members was "factual and friendly and favorable to both the state and to ourselves."[26]

In 2006, thirty years after the second executive order and on the steps of the state Capitol, then senator Bond represented Missourians of the past and present when he further discussed the apology: "treatment of the people of the Mormon Church in Missouri during the late 1830s and beyond was barbaric. Women were raped and tortured. Men were killed by mobs or driven out of the state. Their property was stolen. The lucky ones were the ones who were left alive with nothing and were forced to make their way into a more hospitable state."[27] Here Bond again distanced the audience before him that day and all present-day Missourians (whom he represented in the speech act) from Missourians of the past by offering a moral judgment on what had been done in the nineteenth century. By declaring those acts barbaric, Bond affirmed the present-day community (both Mormon and non-Mormon alike) as a morally innocent community.

Bond went on to argue that "What makes it so difficult to understand is that this barbarism was state-sanctioned and even state-ordered. Gov. Lilburn Boggs issued the extermination order making it legal to kill anyone who belonged to The Church of Jesus Christ of Latter-day Saints. The governor claimed that his action was 'necessary' to curb Mormon outrages and keep the public peace."[28] In this passage, Bond widens the gap between those present at the apology and historical actors. He suggests that a state that would condone and even encourage such behavior in the interest of peace not only was unjust but was not operating as a state should. In his role as former governor, he particularly condemns the actions of Boggs.

According to Bond, how should an American state operate? With full support of religious freedom. In the end of his apologetic speech he shifted from judging past acts to "a brighter future and much higher hopes ahead." He ended his speech with a statement about the values of the moral community to whom he spoke: "God bless you in achieving the goals that we all seek of religious tolerance and freedom and celebration of our life as a multi-faceted free country *and* free state." Here he suggested that the audience—both Mormon and non-Mormon alike—shared the same God and that that God desired religious freedom for all. His statement also affirmed the idea that the values and morals of the audience were *shared*, thus creating a present-day "us," who were condemning past acts that separated Missourians.

The church did not make much of either the Illinois or Missouri apologies but rather quietly accepted them. In so doing, it allowed the narratives of the past oppression of its members to be acknowledged but also quietly passed by. After all, the church had blossomed in Utah (a place to which its members fled to *get away* from their fellow Americans) and because of that blossoming had participated in a concerted effort to stake a claim in American identity, to demand recognition that its members, too, were Americans. Mormons had spent decades claiming the stories that made Americans American as their own. They had told the stories of their pioneer ancestors as exemplars of American values. To make too much of the apologies would be to distance themselves from how far they had come. It would publicly recall a time when they were deemed too peculiar to be truly American.

The Mountain Meadows Massacre

In this "age of apologies," Mormons have not always been the oppressed "them" but have also played a role as oppressors, persecutors in their own right. About 300 miles south of TITP Park is another western space that has been marked by significant historical events and memorialized many times over. In fact, monument after monument has been built there over the years, as each generation has attempted to get the narrative right so that the people who know of the events can move on, forgive, and maybe even forget. At the site of the Mountain Meadows Massacre of 1857, a site of tragedy that carries the weight of historical wrongs and collective forgetfulness, one can see that just as collective memory has been written onto the landscape by Mormons, so has collective forgetfulness. That forgetfulness plays just as important a role in identity as memory and has been contested in that same landscape just as fiercely. Where TITP Park and other sites along the Mormon Trail serve as examples of the erasures of Native American history and spatial claims that have taken place in Mormon collective memory, Mountain Meadows offers an example of how the struggles over narrating spaces shape group identity.

Why end my story with such a site? Mountain Meadows highlights the intersections of historical memory and sacred spaces in a new way that puts the discussion of TITP Park in stark relief. Mountain Meadows is a site that witnessed historical events many would rather forget and some can't seem to forget. Since the massacre, the LDS community has spent a good deal of time and energy trying "to blot out the affair from [their] history." Juanita Brooks, a Mormon who wrote an important history of the massacre in 1950, recalled that in the Mormon community the massacre "must not be referred to, much less discussed openly."[29] It is no wonder that the LDS community would much rather allow the massacre to fall into historical forgottenness, that it might even will a type of historical amnesia. After all, the story of the massacre disrupts so many of the narratives that I've shown are crucial to the fabric of Mormon collective memory in the late twentieth and early twenty-first centuries—the story of rugged pioneer individualism *and* communalism, of a chosen people's exodus, and of martyrs who died for a cause because God was on their side. In the words of Juanita Brooks's biographer, Levi Peterson, "if good Mormons committed the massacre, if prayerful leaders ordered it, if apostles and a prophet knew about it and later sacrificed John D. Lee, then the sainthood of even the modern church seems tainted. Where is the moral superiority of Mormonism, where is the assurance that

God has made Mormons his new chosen people?"[30] Mountain Meadows has the ability to challenge each of these aspects of Mormon identity: of an oppressed people led by their God, following a path of moral fortitude, with a divinely inspired prophet at their center.

The Mountain Meadows Massacre teaches about nineteenth-century Utah and Mormon relations with other non-Mormon Americans. At the same time, it teaches about the significance of apologies by providing an instance where one group denied another an apology for many years. It offers a window into the ways modern Mormons remember their past and their role in Utah's history.

What happened at Mountain Meadows has been a very hotly debated topic. Scholars and lay historians debate the facts, wondering who was responsible for everything that happened in that valley. What no one debates is that on September 11, 1857, Mountain Meadows became the site of the murder of about 120 migrants who were heading from Arkansas to California. These members of what was called the Fancher-Baker wagon train, coming from Arkansas, became the victims of a brutal massacre perpetrated by local Mormon settlers. Tensions with the train mounted as it entered Utah and continued to pass through the territory despite opposition. So much anxiety about the train's presence led to one of only a few white-on-white massacres in nineteenth-century U.S. history. The murderers first killed the men, then the women, and finally the children, whom they deemed too old to be innocent yet old enough to remember the events. Only seventeen children survived, all of them under the age of six; those children were returned to Arkansas several weeks later. After they massacred the pioneers, the aggressors plundered their possessions and their clothing.[31]

Why were the Mormons so suspicious of the Arkansans moving through their territory? What created a climate where something like this event could happen? At the same time that Mormon pioneers were pouring westward, U.S. president Buchanan had determined that Utah was in a state of rebellion and that the federal government needed to take control. Politicians and residents in Utah ignored federal orders and began to act as though Utah was a sovereign territory. In March 1857, the territorial government proclaimed that it would decide which federal laws applied to Utah.[32] In response, Buchanan ordered troops to head to Utah to help quash the rebellion. At the same time that Mormons in Utah felt as though the federal government as a whole had it out for them, they also felt as though Arkansans, in particular, were an enemy. On May 13, 1857, Parley P. Pratt, a member of the Quorum of the Twelve, was murdered in Arkansas by a man named Hector McLean. Pratt had baptized McLean's sons and taken McLean's wife as his twelfth wife. In an act of revenge, McLean murdered Pratt; he was never prosecuted for the murder.[33] Mormons took great offense at these events and believed that the people of Arkansas were particularly to blame for not holding McLean accountable.

In response to the growing pressure from outside forces throughout the 1850s, Brigham Young had inaugurated an internal reformation of the church that required members to renew their loyalty to the institution and to cherish it above any other institution.[34] And so it is important to remember that what happened at Mountain Meadows was, in the words of Sarah Barringer Gordon and Jan Shipps, "a complex cocktail of religion, violence, and patriarchy, tangled up with westward expansion and the ongoing construction of an American empire."[35] One of the theological concepts that played a significant role in this context was the theology of blood atonement. Some today believe that it was a theological "rhetorical device," while other historians are convinced that in this nineteenth-century context, church members understood it literally. The theology focused on the idea that there were unpardonable sins and suggested that believers who committed them had to shed their own blood to atone for them.[36] The Fancher-Baker train was unfortunate enough to be one of the first wagon trains to move through Utah in this climate of anger, anxiety, and pressure. When they arrived in Salt Lake City, they were not greeted warmly but found a community that mistrusted them, saw them as enemies, responsible for Pratt's murder, and were at times reluctant to sell or trade provisions with them.[37] Forced to continue south without much rest, the train encountered ever greater hostilities in southern Utah, where theological fervor had reached a heightened frenzy. It was there that so many in the train were brutally massacred.

Was the prophet Brigham Young responsible for the massacre? After the massacre, federal authorities believed that he was directly responsible but could not provide enough evidence in support of that claim for a court.[38] Most historians today agree that he was not directly responsible and that responsibility lies with local leaders who were members of the church. In fact, Young had written a letter to Isaac Haight, a local church leader, stating: "in regard to emigration trains passing through our settlements we must not interfere with them until they are first notified to keep away. You must not meddle with them."[39] Haight received that letter too late, after the massacre had already happened. Even though he does not bear direct responsibility for the massacre, Young had contributed to the climate that allowed the massacre to happen, the heightened political and theological tensions that created a volatile climate throughout the territory. Once he understood what had happened, he recognized it as a disastrous event, contributing to even further tensions between his community, the federal government, and the broader culture.

After the massacre, local leaders instructed those involved to keep silent and sought to bury, at least metaphorically, what had happened at Mountain Meadows. From the very beginning people wondered how high up in the church hierarchy responsibility lay. No matter where that was, the massacre at Mountain Meadows injured already tense relationships between Mormons and other Americans. As courts began to search for those responsible and as the military moved further into the territory, church leaders continued to maintain that the massacre had been carried out by renegade Paiutes. Blaming the Paiutes for all that happened in the meadow has been a point of contention between the Paiutes and the LDS Church ever since. Historians now agree that any participation on their part happened at the behest of local Mormon leadership.[40] The Arkansas children who survived the massacre remembered that the people who killed their parents washed the war paint off of their faces after the massacre, suggesting that the perpetrators sought to appear to be Paiutes but were in fact white settlers.[41] Not long after the massacre, those same settlers began to tell stories that blamed the Paiute; some of those stories recounted that the Arkansas emigrants had poisoned the local creek and the Paiutes had massacred them as an act of revenge. All of the narratives pointed the finger of blame away from people who had orchestrated the events.

As the immediate pressure surrounding the massacre began to dissipate, it was clear that the church needed to provide an explanation for it. When it appeared that blaming the Paiutes would not be enough—that federal authorities hadn't bought the story—church leaders pointed a finger at John D. Lee, an adopted son of Brigham Young, respected church leader, and local leader in southern Utah. Lee had most certainly played a role in the massacre, but was not the sole actor on that bloody field. As part of their attempts to place blame on others, to point the finger away from the institution, the church excommunicated Lee and Isaac Haight, the local stake leader, in 1870.[42]

Even though a grand jury indicted nine men for the massacre, Lee was the only one who was tried by a jury. Several of the men, including Haight, went into hiding, while others were released for lack of evidence.[43] Lee underwent two trials for his responsibility in the massacre. In the first trial, church leaders protected him, working against the prosecution in the hope that no church member would be held accountable for the massacre. In the second trial, and under increasing political pressure, Young and his cohort decided to provide all of the necessary evidence to convict Lee—in return, the prosecutor did not charge Young or any other church leader with committing a crime.[44] At the end of the second trial, Judge Jacob Boreman sentenced Lee to death on October 10, 1876. Offered two possible methods of execution, Lee chose to be shot rather than beheaded. Some believe this choice was an attempt to thumb his nose at those who might deem him in need of blood atonement.[45] Lee's execution took place at the site of the massacre; a kind of spatial justice was imagined in this process. Once Lee was executed, concern for other issues allowed all the other perpetrators of the massacre to go free.

Remembering and Forgetting Mountain Meadows

In 1859 U.S. army soldiers interred the bodies of those who had been massacred and built a stone cairn to mark the spot at Mountain Meadows. They topped the cairn with a cedar cross; its inscription read: "vengeance is mine: I will repay, saith the Lord"—a quotation from the biblical epistle to the Romans. At the base of the cairn was a granite slab that read: "here 120 men, women, and children were massacred in cold blood early in September, 1857. They were from Arkansas."[46] This first grave marker and memorial used the passive voice and did not assign any blame for the massacre but simply respected the dead and marked Mountain Meadows as a site of tragedy. At the same time, the marker promised that divine judgment would hold those responsible accountable, if not in this life then in the next.

Not long after army soldiers built this first cairn, Brigham Young toured the region with a party of men in 1861. One member of the party recalled that Young gave a gesture and some of the men in his party disassembled the cairn. It may be the case that Young took offense that someone might have even obliquely pointed a finger of blame at members of his church and suggested that they might receive divine retribution for what had happened there.[47] A member of Young's party, Wilford Woodruff, recalled that Young claimed that the inscription should read "vengeance is mine and I have taken a little" —thus implying that perhaps the massacre was itself divine retribution: other Americans receiving just a mite of punishment for what had been done to Mormons in the past. If Young did say it, knowing the nineteenth-century history of movement from place to place to escape persecution that he had survived perhaps provides some insight into this comment. Just three years later the Second California Cavalry came to Mountain Meadows and rebuilt the cairn. Even so close to the events in time, it was clear that many Americans had the impulse to mark the site of the tragedy and that others, like Young, would have just as soon forgotten it.

In 1932 yet another group created a monument to memorialize the event: the UPTLA erected the first official monument at the site. The cairn that had been built in 1859 was only a pile of rocks; it suffered from dismantlement at Brigham Young's orders and (despite its rebuilding by the cavalry) was "in ruins" at the time of Lee's execution in 1870.[48] In 1932 members of the local stake believed that the site needed to be memorialized in a more permanent way and raised the money for the monument. The final version of the plaque that accompanied the stone wall that was built around the site of the massacre read: "in this vicinity, September 7–11, 1857 occurred one of the most lamentable tragedies in the annals of the west. A company of about 140 Arkansas and Missouri Emigrants led by Captain Charles Fancher, en route to California, was attacked by white men and Indians. All but 17, being small children, were killed. John D. Lee, who confessed participation as leader, was legally executed here March 23, 1877. Most of the Emigrants were buried in their own defense pits."[49] This final version avoided any explanation of motivations for the activities, though it certainly communicated the innocence of the Fancher party. Here one can see some of the complexities of the memory work surrounding the site. The monument does little to assign responsibility or provide explanation.

At the dedication ceremony William R. Palmer, the local stake president, brought up the issue of apologies before an audience of over 400 people when he said that there would be "nothing in these exercises today to satisfy or appeal to morbid curiosity. Neither will excuses or apologies be made for those who were active on this field seventy-five years ago today. With all of that we are not here concerned." He went on to remind the audience: "no living person is responsible in any way for what happened here and the controversial aspects of Mountain Meadows should now be closed."[50] Acknowledging that controversy surrounded the site, Palmer refused to offer an apology, the reason being that no one alive was responsible. It would appear from the speech that at this point no Mormons felt they could bear responsibility for what had happened that day and that the blame was assigned almost

exclusively to John D. Lee (the only actor named), who had been held responsible and paid with his life. At the same time, Palmer's speech acknowledged the power of historical memory. By attempting to "close" the narrative,
Palmer was, in effect, attempting to silence the historical narratives that
suggested that responsibility could not be Lee's alone, that somehow history
was more complex.

Even though Palmer may have wanted counter-narratives to be forgotten
and the official narrative to be embraced by all, descendants of those massacred, of the Paiutes who had been blamed for much of what happened,
and of John D. Lee still sensed that responsibility had not been appropriately
assigned. In fact, the Richard Fancher Society, a community of descendants
of those massacred, decided in 1955 to build a monument for the survivors
and victims. They agreed that the narratives etched in stone at the massacre
site were not the ones that should be remembered, and their identity was very
much tied to the counter-narratives they embraced. They placed their new
monument in Harrison, Arkansas. In 1956, the surrounding communities
organized a short wagon train reenactment to commemorate the doomed
Fancher party, embracing a narrative of innocence and being doubly
wronged: first by the massacre and second by the way it had been remembered.[51] Throughout the twentieth century the descendants of the victims
and the Paiutes continued to tell counter-narratives and to refuse to accept
the historical narrative offered by the LDS Church and the state of Utah.

During this time the church also contributed to anxiety about the
narratives being told about the massacre. Not only did the church hierarchy
maintain its story of the Paiutes' culpability but the institution also participated in actions that troubled many. In 1961 many of Lee's descendants were
excited to find out that for reasons never publicized, the church leadership
had met and decided to reinstate his membership and former blessings.
They saw it as a step toward institutional acknowledgment that Lee had been
scapegoated by the institution. Descendants of the victims may have seen it
as the church letting Lee off the hook. In May 1961, members of the church
performed proxy ordinances for Lee.[52] In this rite, living Mormons perform
the rite of baptism for non-Mormons who have already died. These rites do
not claim that the deceased then immediately becomes Mormon but that
they will have a chance to hear the truth in the afterlife and make up their
minds for themselves. After the request by one descendant, a church official
noted that though names could be removed from church records, there was
no way to undo the rites that had been performed.[53]

Juanita Brooks found out about the reinstatement and planned to publish the information in the next edition of her book. She "learned through the Lee family members that the new prophet, David O. McKay, did not want this confidential information to appear in her book. He threatened to rescind Lee's reinstatement if Brooks persisted in publicizing it."[54] Brooks chose to go ahead with including the information, and the reinstatement went forward anyway. For members of Lee's family, the reinstatement could serve as recognition that John D. Lee had somehow been unfairly scapegoated, that he alone wasn't at fault. For the descendants of the Fancher train and the Paiutes, such a decision may have felt like the institution's failure to accept even the smallest connection to the events. To seemingly absolve the one person who had been held responsible, even if reinstatement does not theologically mean the granting of forgiveness of sins, equaled another historical erasure.

In 1966 the owners of the massacre site, the Lytle family, donated the land on which the 1859 and 1932 monuments stand to the LDS Church. While the church did some sporadic upkeep, it also began to discourage people from visiting the site by removing signs that pointed the way and not keeping up the road that led to the memorials. Here one can see the intersections of collective memory and space at work. In its desire to allow the massacre to fall into historical forgottenness, the church attempted to shape the space in such a way that it was uninviting to visitors. Without the location, without the knowledge of precisely where the bodies were buried, the process of historical forgetfulness could continue. Negligence, especially by a church known for its ability to mobilize volunteer workers, was its own active attempt at forgetting.

Even though the church at the time would have rather put Mountain Meadows in closed history books, others very adamantly did not want that to happen. Scattered dissatisfaction with the public narratives of events led to a meeting of thirteen people on July 23, 1988. Participants included "four Mormons . . . eight outlanders with family ties to the Fancher party . . . [and an] unidentified Indian from Salt Lake. These folks met to see what was happening at the massacre site [and to] critique the narrative offered on the 1932 bronze plaque." At the meeting the group dialogued about the different accounts of the massacre. Participants decided that a new monument was necessary to help correct wrongs in the public narratives of the events.[55] To etch the corrections in stone would function as an active rejection of the process of forgetting.

The work begun in 1988 continued, and in 1990 members of Lee's family and descendants of the wagon train held a memorial service at the 1932 monument. They placed a memorial on top of the nearby Dan Sill Hill, on property owned by the U.S. Forest Service. The granite monument provided a list of many of the names of the people killed at Mountain Meadows. It also read: "In the valley below / Between September 7 and 11, 1857 / A company of more than 120 Arkansas Emigrants / Was Attacked While En Route to California / This Event Is Known In History As The/ Mountain Meadows Massacre."

The *Journal of the Mountain Meadows Association*, a publication begun by descendants of those involved in the events, wrote about the 1990 dedication that it was not the end of things, precisely because no finger had been pointed, no name had been named: "any accusation against anyone involved, or any attempted explanation of the underlying causes of the massacre has been purposely avoided. The meeting of the families and dedication was meant to be an occasion where all interested parties could come together in a spirit of cooperation, goodwill, and understanding, to especially memorialize those who lost their lives in the tragedy. We believe that this has now been done."[56] Having remembered the victims of the tragedy, having begun to name their names to remind everyone that they were real people, seemed like a giant act against forgetting.

Three years later a group of Lee's descendants met and performed temple rituals for the victims of the massacre. One of the descendants said that it "was very important for members of our family to do this work, but even among the Lees there has been some strong feelings and prejudice surrounding the Mountain Meadows Massacre. It's taken a lot to get us to this point, but what we've done here today has been good for us, and I think it represents closure for the whole church on this terrible tragedy."[57] What kind of closure did this ritual activity provide? It certainly allowed the victims of the massacre to progress further within a Mormon cosmology, if one accepted such a cosmology. However, it did not assign responsibility. It did not reconcile narratives. It did not imagine a different set of relationships in the future. And for some descendants of those massacred it may have felt like a further injustice, pulling victims who had been murdered by Mormons into a Mormon framework of life after death. Some descendants of those massacred asked the church to take their ancestors off the church lists, to undo what had been done. In response, church historian Marlin K. Jensen said: "under appropriate circumstances, we do grant requests to the extent that we no longer display those records in our public data bases. We have no way, as a church, of undoing ordinances that have been performed. . . . But out of courtesy, if there is a strong relationship demonstrated between the submitter and the party for whom ordinance work was done, in some limited instances we've limited the view of those names in our public data bases out of respect to those making the request and out of respect to the dead." Jensen acknowledged that one request by Scott Fancher had been made to remove a few names from the lists and that the church had granted that request.[58]

Even though these activities brought more attention to the site of the massacre in the early 1990s, it once again began to fall into disrepair. In 1998 President Hinckley visited Mountain Meadows and determined that yet another new monument needed to be built (see Figure 8.1). The church constructed a replica of the 1859 cairn, without the cedar cross that promised divine vengeance. In the midst of fixing up the area, people realized that the 1932 monument required new supports if it was going to continue standing. In the effort to provide supports, the remains of twenty-nine of the victims of the massacre were accidentally uncovered in August 1999.[59]

After examination by scientists at Brigham Young University, the remains were reinterred on September 10, 1999, and the new memorial was dedicated on September 11, 1999. At these events, Dennis B. Neuenschwander, an elder representing the church, called the site a "sacred and holy spot." He went on to pray for "a day of remembering, a day of forgiving, and also in its own way a day of putting behind us what is behind."[60] Even though no blame was assigned, Neuenschwander asserted that the past was behind those who had gathered for that day—he suggested that forgiveness ought to be offered, though no recipient or grantor of that forgivenness was named. Later in the ceremony Judge Roger V. Logan Jr., a descendant of victims of the massacre, spoke. He declared: "bitterness is destructive and it does none of us any good." He went on to argue: "no one now living, no matter whose church he goes to, no matter who he is descended from, or she, bears any blame for the awful crime that was committed in this valley so long ago. The people who were responsible for that have long since, in my belief, faced one whose unerring justice has already been done."[61] Interestingly, Logan, one whom many would feel would be right in demanding an apology, let the entire audience off the hook. In so doing he divorced the audience, and anyone currently living, from any sense of "us", of identification, with those who had lived in the past. His argument instead relied on an understanding of divine judgment—though no one alive could be held responsible, God would hold everyone accountable; Logan implied that God knew who was responsible even if no one ever took responsibility in this life. Finally, Logan recalled that the original cross at the site was inscribed with a statement that began "vengeance is mine." He went on to say: "there is no reason for that vengeance spirit to be here anymore." Logan, at least, had moved from bitterness to hope that "this old story . . . will no longer have to cause people—people of different heritage—to distrust and dislike one another."[62]

Later at that same ceremony Stewart L. Udall remembered what he had said to Gordon Hinckley in 1990: "the families cannot close the book, the church cannot close the book, but if we all work together we can close the book."[63] Here Udall suggested that history and its injustices can only be repaired with the hard work of people on both sides of the events that took place. He asserted that everyone must be involved in addressing the past and creating a narrative to which all parties can agree. Yet it was precisely because the parties did not agree to the narratives told about the place that the metaphorical book could not be closed. Instead the anxiety of conflicting narratives played out in monument making, each monument carrying the hope that *this time* the book could be closed. But it was precisely what the monuments *did not say,* the stories that were not reconciled, that held the book open.

At the 1999 ceremony president and prophet of the church Gordon Hinckley declared: "that which we have done here must never be construed as an acknowledgement on the part of the church of any complicity in the occurrences of that fateful day." He claimed for himself the status of "peacemaker" and further stated: "this is not a time for recrimination or the assigning of blame. No one can explain what happened in these meadows 142 years ago. We may speculate, but we do not know. We do not understand it. . . . We can only say that the past is long since gone. It cannot be recalled. It cannot be changed. It is time to leave the entire matter in the hands of God, who deals justly in all things. His is a wisdom far beyond our own."[64] Like Logan, Hinckley placed the responsibility for judgment, for pointing fingers, in the hands of God. In so doing he circumvented the question of who should take historical responsibility. In stating that the history cannot be directly recalled or changed, he implied that people needed to move on from recounting that past.

Noting, as he had in the past, that he sat in the same chair as Brigham Young, Hinckley affirmed that there was no question in his mind that Young had been opposed to what had happened. Hinckley stated that he had read much of the history and knew that if "there had been a faster means of communication, it never would have happened and history would have been different."

Later Hinckley went on to declare: "we have an obligation. We have a moral responsibility. We have a Christian duty to honor, to respect, and to do all feasible to recognize and remember those who died here." Finally, he, like Palmer, suggested that "the book of the past" should be closed.[65]

Rewriting the Landscape

What seems impossible, then, is that not ten years later, the church would "express regret" for what had happened in Mountain Meadows, even if not issuing an apology or asking for forgiveness. On September 11, 2007, at the sesquicentennial gathering marking the massacre, the LDS Church offered such a statement. Elder Henry B. Eyring of the Quorum of the Twelve read the church's statement, which placed blame for the massacre on local church leaders and church members who participated in the massacre of the un-armed emigrants. Eyring stated: "what was done here long ago by members of our church represents a terrible and inexcusable departure from Christian teaching and conduct."[66] Here he distanced the historical actors from the moral and, he implied, Christian community that was present on that day. He continued: "we express profound regret for the massacre carried out in this valley 150 years ago today, and for the undue and untold suffering experienced by the victims then and by their relatives to the present time." He went on to say: "a separate expression of regret is owed the Paiute people who have unjustly borne for too long the principal blame for what occurred during the massacre." Noting that historians debate the involvement of the Paiutes, he said: "it is believed they would not have participated without the direction and stimulus provided by local church leaders and members." Finally, Eyring affirmed what Hinckley had said earlier: that Brigham Young had not wanted anyone to interfere with the wagon train but that his message had arrived to the local church leaders too late. Research carried out by church historians and published a year later as *Massacre at Mountain Meadows: An American Tragedy* showed that "responsibility for the massacre lies with the local leaders of The Church of Jesus Christ of Latter-day Saints in the regions near Mountain Meadows who also held civic and military positions and with members of the church acting under their directions."[67] Eyring ended his speech by asking those present "to honor those who died here by extending to one another the pure love and spirit of forgiveness which his only begotten son personified."

Coming on the heels of a rising public awareness over the history-telling battles surrounding Mountain Meadows, this expression of regret is not much different from the statement made by Hinckley a few years prior. At the same time, it is distinct in a number of ways. First, it assigns blame to the Mormon settlers themselves rather than the Paiutes and recognizes that the Paiute were unjustly viewed as the perpetrators of the attacks because church officials pointed fingers in their direction. Second, it specifically acknowledges that the settlers who organized and carried out the massacre were local LDS church leaders. The name of the church appears in the same sentence as the perpetrators.

Richard Turley Jr., the managing director of family and church history in the LDS Church and coauthor of *Massacre at Mountain Meadows: An American Tragedy*, called the statement an apology.[68] Audience members, particularly those who were descendants of the emigrants, did not, however, miss the fact that the church chose not to issue an apology. "Simply saying 'I'm sorry' would go a long way," commented one of those descendants.

Why would the church move at this time toward nuancing its narrative and taking some responsibility at the local level for what happened at Mountain Meadows? Perhaps most important and immediate, Oxford University Press was about to publish *Massacre at Mountain Meadows: An American Tragedy*, the study to which Eyring had referred in his speech. What makes this text stand out from others on the same subject is that its three authors, Ronald W. Walker, Richard E. Turley Jr., and Glen M. Leonard, were all employees of the LDS Church who had been authorized to write a thorough and academically rigorous account of the events. The church had given the three historians free rein to write an honest history that would pass the standards of an academic press. The publication of the text itself indicates that the church was entering a new era in its reckoning with what had happened at Mountain Meadows.

Authorized in 2000 to write the book, and perhaps spurred internally by the 1999 ceremony, the church also knew that Mountain Meadows was receiving a lot of attention from the broader community. Since the 1999 ceremony alone, two films, *September Dawn* and a PBS documentary titled *The Mormons* had been released, both exploring the LDS Church's role in the massacre from different perspectives and both raising general public awareness about it. Historians were also paying more attention to it, and many were asking questions about the extent to which church leaders had known about and even authorized what happened there. In addition, descendants of the emigrants were pushing the church to hand ownership and maintenance of the site over to the federal government. "It's not right for the people who had complicity [in] the killings to be the grave owners," one said; "I asked [Jensen], 'How do you think the Kennedy family would feel if the Lee Harvey Oswald family had control of the Kennedy tomb?'" Finally, descendants were considering as a group what at least one individual had already done: requesting that the church remove from its records the ordinances performed for those who had been massacred.[69] No doubt a group request from the victims would have brought unwanted national attention to the church, its ritual practices, and historical events.

Descendants of the massacred group pushed to have the site declared a national historic landmark. In their push, they asked the help of the LDS Church as owner of part of the property. After the 2007 expression of regret, a new if partial peace was reached. Now that the church had in some ways recognized the complicity of its members in the massacre, descendants believed that perhaps they could have some overlapping goals for the site. One of the goals of such a move was to restrict what the church could choose to do with the land. The descendants also wanted to work toward creating another monument at the site.[70] In July 2011, their work came to fruition when the space was designated a national historic landmark, a status that did not change much about the daily operations there but does place limitations on what can be done with the area. The LDS Church still manages the portion of the land it owns, and the U.S. Forest Service cares for the rest.[71]

And so this contested western space continues to collect monuments as modern-day Mormons and non-Mormons attempt to negotiate a common narrative about what happened there. If nothing else, the monuments bear witness that this is indeed an anxious landscape. All call it "hallowed ground" because of historical events that happened there yet struggle to create a collective memory to which a modern-day "we" can agree. And the landscape itself bears the markers of this historical and contemporary anxiety.

What does Mountain Meadows look like after this historical tug of war of remembering and forgetting? How have the remembering and forgetting been written onto the landscape? Mountain Meadows bears the marks of historical forgetting and the anxiety that comes with that process. Viewing the space, full of markers and monuments, all purporting to remember the same set of events, one gets the sense that the historical narrative still is not quite right. Even after the expression of regret and the acknowledgments of some responsibility, this remains true. In 2011, after the expression of regret and the designation of the site as a national historic landmark, the LDS Church erected another memorial on land it had purchased not long before. Called the Men and Boys Monument, the monument bears a polished and engraved square memorial. At the base is a rock that was once part of the 1859 cairn. The text of this monument reads: "in memory of the emigrant men and boys from Arkansas massacred here in Mountain Meadows on September 11, 1857. Their lives were taken prematurely and wrongly by Mormon militiamen in one of the most tragic episodes in western American history. May we forever remember and honor those buried in this valley. May we never forget this tragedy but learn from the past." While certainly not addressing all of the narratives told about the site, the 2011 monument represents a new narrative being told about Mountain Meadows, one in which the LDS Church is more comfortable with accepting local church members' responsibility for what happened there (see Figure 8.2).

In addition to the memorials, the church published a "Gospel Topics" essay on its website that discusses the Mountain Meadows Massacre, contextualizing it within a broader nineteenth-century culture in which violence was committed against Latter-day Saints and Latter-day Saints participated in violence against others. The essay states: "despite these ideals [of peaceful interactions], early Latter-day Saints did not obtain peace easily. They were persecuted, often violently, for their beliefs. And, tragically, at some points in the 19th century, most notably in the Mountain Meadows Massacre, some Church members participated in deplorable violence against people they perceived to be their enemies. This essay explores both violence committed against the Latter-day Saints and violence committed by them. While historical context can help shed light on these acts of violence, it does not excuse them."[72] Here the church makes a moral judgment about the past, both in terms of its persecutors and those it persecuted. Interestingly, the church authors discuss both in the same essay, perhaps feeling as though the violence of being persecuted helped explain and contextualize the violence of church members. In the essay, relatively brief for easy consumption, the church begins the process of claiming a more complex identity today in relationship to its past. Even so, it has not gotten to the point where the pieces of persecution, colonialism, and conquest are all woven into one braided narrative. It has not yet embraced a narrative that Gordon and Shipps recount about that time: "once they arrived in the Great Basin, Mormons followed what was now a familiar American religious template; they, too, subdued their new Zion just as the

Figure 8.2 Boys and Men Monument, Mountain Meadows, Utah.

Israelites spread across Canaan—through conquest and settlement. The Mountain Meadows Massacre is part of that subjugation story."[73]

The compromises in the more recent monuments and in the Gospel Topics essay were in part generated by external pressures; the rising public awareness and criticism certainly encouraged the change, and perhaps a hope of returning to a new silence about Mountain Meadows. Yet the compromises also point to a significant internal shift as well; now more secure in their claim to their identity as Americans, perhaps Mormons can start to acknowledge

236 PIONEERS IN THE ATTIC

the tensions in their own collective memory. Perhaps this can also open the way for Mormons to celebrate their pioneer heritage *while also* acknowledging the imperial impulses of Manifest Destiny in which they participated.

The choices made in the new monuments can be seen in the assignation of responsibility to Mormon militamen alone as those responsible for the massacre. The monument also acknowledges that the actions taken were a moral wrong, allowing those viewing, whether Mormon or not, to distance themselves from the perpetrators of the massacre. Finally, the monument suggests that remembering and learning are the appropriate moral responses to visiting the site. In creating the monument in this way, in including an echo of memorials past (with the cairn stone) but also dramatically changing the historical narrative offered, the LDS Church may be moving into a new era in which it can remember itself as both oppressor and oppressed, as both morally right and morally wrong, and incorporate those anxious ambiguities into its identity in a way it could not in the twentieth century.

Epilogue

Zion

As second counselor to the First Presidency, James E. Faust wrote an article for the July 2002 issue of *Ensign* in which he heralded the "faithful pioneers in all of the countries of the world who have helped establish the Church in their lands." Although he recognized that first-generation members of the church anywhere "are indeed pioneers," he chose to focus on "the priceless legacy which belongs to the descendants of all pioneers, but especially to those who came into the Great Salt Lake and settled in Utah." He celebrated these pioneers as models of bravery, sobriety, determination, and faith.

Recalling a trip to Martin's Cove and Rock Creek Hollow he had taken several years earlier, Faust remembered a particular moment as his group walked over Rocky Ridge. While they were walking, "two square nails and an old-style button were picked up." Feeling as though the objects had fallen during the harrowing pull over the highest point on the Mormon Trail, he declared that his "soul was sobered to be in that historic spot." It seems that those objects gave him a sense of the gravity of the place, making it feel more real and authentic; they marked these places as landscapes of suffering. The nails and the button provided him with a link to the past and to the theological messages that had been shaped by his community.

As Faust recounted his journey through these sites of tragedy, he wondered if he had "sacrificed enough." He remembered the stories of Bodil Mortensen, James Kirkwood, and the rescuers who went to help the Martin and Willie handcart companies. For him they served as models of sacrificing for faith and as a legacy for all Mormons in the modern era. "I wonder what more I should have done, and should be doing," Faust wrote, "to further this work." His lesson was about suffering and redemptive sacrifice and about learning key lessons from the past. He believed that "these excruciating experiences developed in these pioneers an unshakable faith in God."

Pioneers in the Attic. Sara M. Patterson, Oxford University Press (2020). © Oxford University Press.
DOI: 10.1093/oso/9780190933869.001.0001

As he pondered the pioneer stories, he "wondered why these intrepid pioneers had to pay for their faith with such a terrible price in agony and suffering. Why were not the elements tempered to spare them from their profound agony?" In answer to his own questions, he said he believed that "their lives were consecrated to a higher purpose through their suffering," and that through their trials, they had "found reality and meaning in their lives."

Later in the article, the editors encouraged home teachers, young men assigned to visit ward members in their own homes and provide spiritual lessons, to use the article as a home lesson, asking the people they visited to "prayerfully consider [their] legacy of faith." One suggestion for teaching the lesson asked the home teachers to "give family members a taste of something that is sweet and satisfying, such as some fruit or candy." After having them experience the pleasure of that moment, they were told to ask family members "if they would like more" and "discuss why even the most difficult experiences in life can be sweet." Then the home teachers were told to read the testimony of Frances Webster, a nineteenth-century pioneer, whom Faust quotes as saying: "every one of us came through with the absolute knowledge that God lives for we became acquainted with him in our extremities."[1]

Recipients of this lesson were asked to *taste* the power of sweetness in their lives in order to think about how sorrow can ultimately end in what is "sweet" or good. They were asked to imagine the sweetness at the journey's end in the Salt Lake Valley. They were taught to think about the pioneers as exemplars who knew the sweetness amid their suffering. And they were asked to ponder what it might mean to know the divine in their extremities. It was a request to think about how to embody their faith more deeply, to know it in their bones.

Such lessons indicate the ways that ideas about Zion and gathering, even after having been unmoored from place in the twentieth century, continue to be concretized and pulled into the physical and embodied realm. The lesson plans demonstrate the enduring desire to touch, taste, and feel the theological concepts of gathering and Zion.

* * *

I was reminded of these desires when in the summer 2019 I visited TITP Park to take some photographs and wander around. As I was leaving the visitors' center, I saw a woman, probably in her late thirties, with three children under the age of ten. She was unfurling a map of the park as the kids buzzed around her, ready to move on. As she was looking at the map, she pointed at the 1947

This Is The Place monument and told them they were going to start there. "This," she said with excitement in her voice, "Is the place where Brigham Young entered the valley and saw that it was the place where Mormons would be safe and prosper!" The kids ignored her, chasing and trying to catch each other. "Stop! Stop!" she said angrily. "This is important. We've talked about Brigham Young. He was a prophet. And *this is where he stood when he knew we had arrived in the promised land.*" The children stopped and looked at her, for a moment, probably sensing the frustration and passion in her voice, and then started chasing each other again. She dropped her hand, with the map still in it, in a posture of exasperation. She seemed to feel that they did not understand the importance of where they stood. It was hallowed ground and, well, they were acting like children.

The mother led the children toward the monument, perhaps hoping that they would understand once they actually stood in the spot. Although I don't know what happened next, I saw in the scene evidence of what this book attempts to address. Perhaps that mother was beginning the training process of teaching the children how Latter-day Saints come to view a place as *the place*. Was she teaching them how physical objects—monuments, maps, and markers—and physical activities, such as rituals, group gatherings, and the creation of community, play a role? Was she showing them how those two elements come together to make Mormons *feel* their tradition in new ways? Perhaps there would come a day when they would come to know that legacy, the chain of memory, in their bones.

Notes

Prologue

1. The early significance of what is now remembered as the "First Vision" is debated by historians. In fact, Smith's account of the experience described here changed over time as it gained new meaning in different contexts. For detailed accounts of these aspects of his life, see: Milton V. Backman, *Joseph Smith's First Vision: The First Vision in Its Historical Context* (Salt Lake City: Bookcraft, 1971), Samuel Alonzo Dodge and Steve C. Harper, eds., *Exploring the First Vision* (Provo, UT: Brigham Young University Religious Studies Center, 2012), and Gregory A. Prince, "Joseph Smith's First Vision in Historical Context: How a Historical Narrative Became Theological," *Journal of Mormon History* 41 (October 2015): 74–94. See also Claudia Lauper Bushman and Richard Bushman, *Building the Kingdom: A History of Mormons in America* (New York: Oxford University Press, 2001).

Introduction

1. Doctrine and Covenants 57.
2. Richard Bushman, *Joseph Smith: Rough Stone Rolling* (New York: Knopf, 2005), 559.
3. Doctrine and Covenants 29:8.
4. Craig S. Campbell, *Images of the New Jerusalem: Latter Day Saint Faction Interpretations of Independence, Missouri* (Knoxville: University of Tennessee Press, 2004), xv.
5. Campbell, *Images of the New Jerusalem*, 63–65. See also W. Paul Reeve, *Religion of a Different Color: Race and the Mormon Struggle for Whiteness* (New York: Oxford University Press, 2015), 20–22.
6. Campbell, *Images of the New Jerusalem*, 64–65.
7. Ibid., 89.
8. In 2001, the Reorganized Latter Day Saints changed their name to Community of Christ. For the sake of consistency, I will refer to the group as the Community of Christ for the rest of this work.
9. For a discussion of a similar set of processes that occurs in Kirtland, Ohio, another site where the COC and the LDS Church share sacred space, see David J. Howlett, *Kirtland Temple: The Biography of a Shared Mormon Sacred Space* (Urbana: University of Illinois Press, 2014), 1–6.
10. *Journey of the Saints* (Herald Publishing House, 2009), DVD.
11. The schism formed a group of conservative members who disagreed with the new revelations. They called themselves the Remnant Church of Jesus Christ of Latter

Day Saints. Their mission statement declares that the church "has been called into renewal to preach the fullness of the gospel of Jesus Christ to all who will listen, and to prepare and gather a righteous people for the building up the Kingdom of God on earth, Zion." Their headquarters are located near the COC temple on West Lexington Avenue in Independence, Missouri. See Remnant Church of Jesus Christ of Latter Day Saints. www.theremnantchurch.com, accessed May 25, 2018.

12. Howlett, *Kirtland Temple*, 98.

13. *The Worshiper's Path* (n.p.: Community of Christ, n.d.).

14. Ibid.

15. David Howlett describes how the COC initially defined much of its identity over and against the Utah church. Yet they also needed a positive self-definition: "in the early twentieth century, they found this focus by embracing a syncretic combination of Protestant Social Gospel and Joseph Smith's revelations." See Howlett, *Kirtland Temple*, 50.

16. R. Jean Addams, "The Church of Christ (Temple Lot) and the Reorganized Church of Jesus Christ of Latter Day Saints: 130 Years of Crossroads and Controversies," *Journal of Mormon History* 36, no. 2 (2010): 54–58.

17. R. Jean Addams, *Upon the Temple Lot: The Church of Christ's Quest to Build the House of the Lord* (Independence, MO: John Whitmer Books, 2010), 13–16.

18. Addams, *Upon the Temple Lot*, 68–70.

19. Ibid., 29–31.

20. B. C. Flint, *History of the Church of Christ*, vols. 1 and 2 (Independence, MO: Church of Christ, 2012), 48–49.

21. Ibid., Vol. 1, 103.

22. Arthur M. Smith, *Temple Lot Deed: A Complete Record of All Legal Transfers of That Interesting Spot of Ground Known as the Temple Lot* (Independence, MO: Church of Christ, 1973), 4.

23. William A. Sheldon, *A Synopsis of the Church of Christ Beliefs and Practices as Compared to Other Latter Day Saint Churches* (Independence, MO: Church of Christ [Temple Lot], n.d.).

24. Addams, *Upon the Temple Lot*, 65.

25. *That Sacred Spot Is Definitely Located* (Independence, MO: Board of Publications of Church of Christ, July 2010).

26. I should note that during my 2018 visit to the LDS visitors' center, the missionaries, when guiding us through the site, and when asked, did confirm that Independence was Zion, adding that they did not like it when their fellow church members said that Salt Lake City was Zion and that Independence, along with Adam-Ondi-Ahman (discussed later) would be the first sites of the Second Coming of Christ.

27. The film shown during my visit in spring 2018 did not address the concept of Zion at all but focused on the multiculturalism and globalism of the Mormon movement, while assuming a metaphorical, spiritualized notion of the concepts discussed in this chapter.

28. Richard Lyman Bushman, *Making Space for the Mormons* (lecture), Leonard J. Arrington Mormon History Lecture Series, no. 2 (Logan, UT: Utah State University Press, Special Collections and Archives, 1997), 3–5.

29. J. Z. Smith, *Map Is Not Territory: Studies in the History of Religions* (Chicago: University of Chicago Press, 1978), 143–145. Richard Francaviglia notes that for Mormons "the concept of an actual place on Earth for the Second Coming enabled the Mormons to do something few Christian groups have ever done—mark its tangible location on maps rather than place in an abstract space. Because this earthly, yet heavenly, space would become *the* place, it had to be as perfect as possible" Richard Francaviglia, *The Mapmakers of New Zion: A Cartographic History of Mormonism* (Salt Lake City: University of Utah Press, 2015), 26.

30. For a discussion of how pioneers in the American West understood landscape in religious ways, see Amy DeRogatis, *Moral Geography: Maps, Missionaries, and the American Frontier* (New York: Columbia University Press, 2003), 1–9. See also Chris C. Park, *Sacred Worlds: An Introduction to Geography and Religion* (New York: Routledge, 1994).

31. Mircea Eliade, *The Sacred and the Profane: The Nature of Religion,* trans. Willard R. Trask (New York: Harvest Books, 1959), 26.

32. Mircea Eliade, *Patterns in Comparative Religion,* trans. Rosemary Sheed (New York: Meridian, 1958), 367–369.

33. Yi-Fu Tuan, *Topophilia: A Study of Environmental Perception, Attitudes, and Values* (New York: Columbia University Press, 1974), 31–32. See also Tim Cresswell, *Place: A Short Introduction* (New Jersey: Blackwell, 2004), 8–11, 102–103, and J. B. Jackson, *Landscape in Sight: Looking at America* (New Haven: Yale University Press, 1997).

34. David Chidester and Edward T. Linenthal, editors' introduction to *American Sacred Space* (Bloomington: Indiana University Press, 1995), 12–17.

35. Ibid., 17.

36. Belden C. Lane, *Landscapes of the Sacred: Geography and Narrative in American Spirituality* (Baltimore: Johns Hopkins University Press, 2001), 4.

37. Ibid., 4–7. See also Philip Sheldrake, *Spaces for the Sacred: Place, Memory, and Identity* (Baltimore: Johns Hopkins University Press, 2001).

38. David Morgan, *Visual Piety: A History and Theory of Popular Religious Images* (Berkeley: University of California Press, 1998), 182–183.

39. Colleen McDannell, *Material Christianity: Religion and Popular Culture in America* (New Haven: Yale University Press, 1995), 4–6.

40. David Morgan, ed., *Religion and Material Culture: The Matter of Belief* (Abingdon: Routledge, 2010), 70.

41. I am echoing here something that David Morgan argues about images that I think can be expanded to all objects. In his discussion of images, Morgan reminds us that the goal is not to describe what an image is but what it does. David Morgan, *The Embodied Eye: Religious Visual Culture and the Social Life of Feeling* (Berkeley: University of California Press, 2012), 69.

42. Terryl L. Givens, *Wrestling the Angel: The Foundations of Mormon Thought: Cosmos, God, Humanity* (New York: Oxford University Press, 2015), 95.

43. For a discussion of Smith's body theology, see Douglas J. Davies, *The Mormon Culture of Salvation* (Farnham: Ashgate, 2000), 107–124.

44. Givens, *Wrestling the Angel,* 210–211; 205.

45. For discussions of this emphasis in religion, see McDannell, *Material Christianity*, 6–14. See also David Morgan, *The Sacred Gaze: Religious Visual Culture in Theory and Practice* (Berkeley: University of California, 2005), 4–9.

46. David Morgan, editor's introduction to *Religion and Material Culture: The Matter of Belief* (Abingdon: Routledge, 2010), 2–9.

47. For a discussion of the auditory and visual aspects of early Mormonism, see Douglas J. Davies, *The Mormon Culture of Salvation* (Farnham: Ashgate, 2000), 114–115.

48. Morgan, *The Embodied Eye*, 166.

49. David Morgan, *The Lure of Images: A History of Religion and Visual Media in America* (New York: Routledge, 2007), 2, and Morgan, *The Embodied Eye*, 3–6.

50. Morgan, *The Sacred Gaze*, 105–107.

51. David Chidester, *Authentic Fakes: Religion and American Popular Culture* (Berkeley: University of California Press, 2005), 72–74. See also Sara M. Patterson, *Middle of Nowhere: Religion, Art and Pop Culture at Salvation Mountain* (Albuquerque: University of New Mexico Press, 2015).

52. For a discussion of the importance of touch in religious experience, see David Morgan, *The Lure of Images*, 2 and Patterson, *Middle of Nowhere*.

53. Hildi Mitchell, "'Being There': British Mormons and the History Trail," *Anthropology Today* 17 (April 2001): 9–15.

54. Mitchell, "'Being There,'" 14.

55. Danielle Hervieu-Leger, *Religion as a Chain of Memory* (New Brunswick: Rutgers University Press, 2000), 73.

56. Ibid., 76, 81.

57. Ibid., 87.

58. Ibid., 97, 123.

59. For a discussion of how collective memory operates at a particular Mormon site, see Matthew Kester, *Remembering Iosepa: History, Place, and Religion in the American West* (New York: Oxford University Press, 2013).

60. Eric Hobsbawm, "Introduction: Inventing Traditions," in Eric Hobsbawm and Terence Ranger, eds., *The Invention of Tradition* (Cambridge: Cambridge University Press, 1983), 1–12.

61. Davis Bitton, *The Ritualization of Mormon History and Other Essays* (Urbana: University of Illinois Press, 1994), 171.

62. Douglas J. Davies, "Mormon History, Identity, and Faith Community," *History and Ethnicity* (1989): 168–181. See also Mark Leone, *Roots of Modern Mormonism* (Cambridge, MA: Harvard University Press, 1979).

63. Davies, "Mormon History," 181. See also Hildi Mitchell, "Postcards from the Edge of History: Narrative and the Sacralisation of Mormon Historical Sites," *Journeys: The International Journal of Travel and Travel Writing* 3, no. 1 (2002): 141.

64. See Kathleen Flake, *The Politics of American Religious Identity: The Seating of Senator Reed Smoot, Mormon Apostle* (Chapel Hill: University of North Carolina Press, 2004).

65. Jared Farmer, *On Zion's Mount: Mormons, Indians, and the American Landscape* (Cambridge, MA: Harvard University Press, 2008), 370–372.

66. The Mormon Pioneer Trail: Church Pioneer Sesquicentennial (150th) Celebration, A Highway and Trail Etiquette Guide, pamphlet, University of Utah and Historic Ensign Peak Commemoration Program and Family Hike, July 26, 1993, Ensign Peak Foundation LDS Church Archives, Salt Lake City.

67. Thomas Carter argues that for nineteenth-century Mormons, Zion was "both a metaphysical proposition about human salvation and a literal place where this proposition would be built and tested." Carter, *Building Zion: The Material World of Mormon Settlement* (Minneapolis: University of Minnesota Press, 2015), xxiv.

68. Craig S. Campbell has noted that Salt Lake City was patterned after the early plans for the City of Zion. At the same time, it was not a matter of simply shifting the gaze from one Zion (Independence) to another (Salt Lake City). Campbell, *Images of the New Jerusalem*, 126–127. That process was one that took time. Salt Lake was a refuge in the hills, away from neighbors, and over time became central to an imagined Zion.

69. Claudia L. Bushman, *Contemporary Mormonism: Latter-Day Saints in Modern America* (Westport, CT: Praeger, 2006), 164.

70. Philip L. Barlow, "Shifting Ground and the Third Transformation of Mormonism," in Peter W. Williams, ed., *Perspectives on American Religion and Culture* (Hoboken, NJ: Blackwell, 1999), 148.

71. Jan Shipps notes that in the decades between 1890 and 1920 there was not much external growth in the LDS Church, yet "because the Saints continued to 'gather to Zion' from their homes in the 'mission field,' the LDS population in what is often described as the Mormon culture region (i.e., Utah, southern Idaho, western Wyoming, eastern Nevada, northern Arizona and eastern New Mexico) increased more rapidly than total church membership." Shipps, *The Scattering of the Gathered and the Gathering of the Scattered: The Mormon Diaspora in the Mid-twentieth century, Delivered at the St. George Tabernacle, 12 March 1987* (St. George, UT: Dixie College, 1991), 4.

72. See D. W. Meinig, "The Mormon Nation and the American Empire," in Dean L. May and Reid L. Neilson, eds., *The Mormon History Association's Tanner Lectures: The First Twenty Years* (Urbana: University of Illinois Press, 2006), 131–135; Shipps, *The Scattering of the Gathered*, 5–15; Richard O. Cowan, *The Latter-day Saint Century* (Salt Lake City: Bookcraft, 1999), 14; and Gregory A. Prince and Wm. Robert Wright, *David O. McKay and the Rise of Modern Mormonism* (Salt Lake City: University of Utah Press, 2005).

73. *Faith in Every Footstep: Instructor's Guide, 1847–1997*, prepared by the Church Educational System (Salt Lake City: Church of Jesus Christ of Latter-day Saints, 1996).

74. Eric Alden Eliason, "Celebrating Zion: Pioneers in Mormon Popular Historical Expression" (Ph.D. diss., University of Texas at Austin, 1998), 96–109. See also Eric A. Eliason, "Pioneers and Recapitulation in Mormon Popular Historical Expression," in Eric A. Eliason and Tom Mould, eds., *Latter-day Lore: Mormon Folklore Studies* (Salt Lake City: University of Utah Press, 2013), 174–211.

Chapter 1

1. The monument has two side pillars. The southern pillar portrays the Franciscan Escalante Expedition of 1776. The northern pillar memorializes the "Trapper Group," which was the first group to explore the Great Basin region: "in their quest for the valuable beaver, otter and other skins. . . . [the group] dominated the Western scene between 1820 and 1840." Along the long sides of the monument are three types of memorials. The first type depicts pioneer groups. The back of the main pylon, for example, is a memorial to the Donner-Reed party (a group who in 1846 lost several of their members as they tried and failed to enter the Salt Lake Valley on the way to California). The second type, on the back of the monument, recognizes significant individuals in the history of the state of Utah: Etienne Provot, for whom Provo is named; Father Desmet, S.J., who told the Mormons of his journeys in Utah; John Charles Fremont, whose maps of his expedition throughout the West gave Mormons a realistic sense of the lay of the land; Chief Washakie, remembered as an American Indian (of the Shoshone nation) who attempted to maintain peaceful relations with the Mormons; Peter Ogden, for whom Ogden, Utah, is named; and Captain Benjamin E. Bonneville. The third type consists of several bas-reliefs on the front side that illustrate the Mormons' entry into Salt Lake Valley; these include a wagon train portraying later Mormon pioneers. Thomas Edgar, *This Is the Place Monument Story and History* (pamphlet) (Salt Lake City: Church History Archives, 1995).
2. Victor Turner and Edith Turner, *Image and Pilgrimage in Christian Culture: Anthropological Perspectives* (New York: Columbia University Press, 1978), 33–36.
3. David Chidester and Edward T. Linenthal, editors' introduction to *American Sacred Space* (Bloomington: Indiana University Press), 6–20; Belden C. Lane, *Landscapes of the Sacred: Geography and Narrative in American Spirituality* (Baltimore: Johns Hopkins University Press, 2001), 15.
4. Richard E. Bennett, *We'll Find the Place: The Mormon Exodus, 1846–1848* (Salt Lake City: Deseret Book, 1997), 9–10; Ronald Esplin, "'A Place Prepared': Joseph, Brigham and the Quest for Promised Refuge in the West," *Journal of Mormon History* 9 (1982): 85–111; Lewis Clark Christian, "Mormon Foreknowledge of the West," *BYU Studies* 21 (Fall 1981): 403–415. Matthew J. Grow et al., eds., *The Joseph Smith Papers: Administrative Records, Council of Fifty, Minutes March 1844–January 1846* (Salt Lake City: Church Historian's Press, 2016).
5. Esplin, "'A Place Prepared,'" 105–107.
6. Bennett, *We'll Find the Place*, 233–234. American Indians occupied a unique place in Mormon theology. Because they were believed to be descendants of the tribes of Ephraim and Manasseh, and therefore children of Abraham (as the Mormons believed themselves to be), they were entitled to a particular type of treatment. There was an expectation in Mormon racial hierarchies that though sinfulness had degraded their status in the eyes of God, in fact, turned their skins and their characters "dark," they nonetheless had a special place in divine history. Therefore, Mormons believed that the gospel had to be preached to American Indians in order to bring about the millennial kingdom.

7. William Clayton, *William Clayton's Journal: A Daily Record of the Journey of the Original Company of "Mormon" Pioneers from Nauvoo, Illinois, to the Valley of the Great Salt Lake* (New York: Arno Press, 1973), 309.

8. Quoted in Will Bagley, ed., *The Pioneer Camp of the Saints: The 1846 and 1847 Mormon Trail of Thomas Bullock* (Spokane, WA: Arthur H. Clark, 1997), 232.

9. Erastus Snow Journal, 1835–1851, July 21, 1847. MS 1329, Selected Collections from the of The Church of Jesus Christ of Latter-day Saints. LDS Church Archives, Salt Lake City, Utah.

10. Howard Egan, *Pioneering the West 1846 to 1878* (Richmond, UT: Howard R. Egan Estate, 1917), 103.

11. Lorenzo Dow Young, "Diary of Lorenzo Dow Young: Written—Most of It by His Wife, Harriet Page Wheeler Decker Young, on Journey from Nauvoo to Salt Lake City, 1846–7–8," *Utah Historical Quarterly* 14 (1946): 163.

12. Will Bagley, ed., *Scoundrel's Tale: The Samuel Brannan Papers* (Spokane, WA: Arthur H. Clark, 1999), 208–214. See also W. W. Riter's account of seeing the valley in *In Honor of the Pioneers: Proceedings, Speeches and Oration at the Spot Where Brigham Young Stopped to View the Valley, and Where He Exclaimed "THIS IS THE PLACE"* (Salt Lake City: Bureau of Information, 1921).

13. Scott G. Kenney, ed., *Wilford Woodruff's Journal, 1833–1898*, vol. 3 (Midvale, UT: Signature Books, 1983), 233.

14. Ibid., 234.

15. For a description of similar processes in other groups see Amy DeRogatis, *Moral Geography: Maps, Missionaries, and the American Frontier* (New York: Columbia University Press, 2003), 2–8.

16. Brigham Young, "To the Saints of California" (draft), August 7, 1847, in Will Bagley, ed., *Scoundrel's Tale: the Samuel Brannan Papers* (Spokane, WA: Arthur H. Clark, 1999), 217; Brigham Young et al, *Journal of Discourses*, vol. 16 (Liverpool: F. D. Richards, 1874), 207. See also Erastus Snow, "Discourse on the Utah Pioneers," reported by Geo. F. Gibbs, July 25, 1880.

17. Bennett, *We'll Find the Place*, xiv–xv, 6–10.

18. Jan Shipps, *Mormonism: The Story of a New Religious Tradition* (Urbana: University of Illinois Press, 1985), 52; see her chapter 3 on this process.

19. Orson Pratt, "New Jerusalem; or, the Fulfilment of Modern Prophecy" (1849), in *The Essential Orson Pratt* (Salt Lake City: Signature Books, 1991), 114–118.

20. Clayton, *William Clayton's Journal,* 331.

21. Patricia Nelson Limerick, *Something in the Soil: Legacies and Reckonings in the New West* (New York: Norton, 2000), 248. Jan Shipps, *The Scattering of the Gathered and the Gathering of the Scattered: The Mormon Diaspora in the Mid-twentieth Century, Delivered at the St. George Tabernacle, March 12, 1987* (St. George, UT: Dixie College, 1991).

22. Shipps, *Mormonism,* 125.

23. D. W. Meinig, "The Mormon Nation and the American Empire," in Dean L. May and Reid L. Neilson, eds., *The Mormon History Association's Tanner Lectures: The First Twenty Years* (Urbana: University of Illinois Press, 2006), 130.

24. Shipps, *The Scattering of the Gathered*, 4.

25. Doctrine and Covenants 21:1.

26. John Giles to R.A. Hart, January 8, 1945. MSS 1353, box 5, folder 2, Utah Pioneer Trial & Landmark Association Letters, LDS Church Archives.

27. This small monument now stands about 100 yards behind the 1947 TITP monument.

28. *In Honor of the Pioneers*, 4–5.

29. Ibid., 18.

30. Mahonri M. Young, "The Title of the Monument is This is The Place," Mahonri M. Young Papers. MSS 4, box 7, folder 17, L. Tom Perry Special Collections, Harold B. Lee Library, Brigham Young University, Provo, Utah.

31. Ibid. Mahonri Young was interested in sculpting what was "symbolically true" in this monument. He later acknowledged that the three individuals atop the central pylon never stood together in the way he posed them, looking out over Zion, but asserted that the combination and their stance was "symbolically true." See Mahonri M. Young, "The Competition," Mahonri M. Young Papers. MSS 4, box 7, folder 17, L. Tom Perry Special Collections.

32. Mahonri M. Young, "The Unveiling," Mahonri M. Young Papers. MSS 4, box, 7, folder 17, L. Tom Perry Special Collections.

33. *Deseret News*, July 19, 1947.

34. See: Catherine Albanese, *America: Religions and Religion* (Belmont, CA: Wadsworth, 1999), 433; Conrad Cherry, introduction to *God's New Israel: Religious Interpretations of American Destiny* (Chapel Hill: University of North Carolina Press, 1998); and Robert Bellah, *Varieties of Civil Religion* (San Francisco: Harper and Row, 1980).

35. For a theoretical discussion of this type of process, see: Kenneth E. Foote, *Shadowed Ground: America's Landscapes of Violence and Tragedy* (Austin: University of Texas Press, 1997), 8–10; 253–264.

36. For a discussion of similar processes in the early twentieth century, see Kathleen Flake, *The Politics of American Religious Identity: The Seating of Senator Reed Smoot, Mormon Apostle* (Chapel Hill: University of North Carolina Press, 2004), 132.

37. For a parallel discussion see: Henri Lefebvre, *The Production of Space* (Malden, MA: Blackwell, 1973), 221–224.

38. Even in 1996 in preparation for the sesquicentennial and in a description of the 1947 monument, Washakie was still described using the noble savage trope: "when the Latter-day Saints came to this territory in 1847 various Indian tribes of the Shoshone nation occupied the northern valleys of these mountains. Washakie was a young Shoshone chief about 33 years of age in 1847, who was rapidly coming to be recognized as the head chief of the Shoshone nation. This young chief became intimately acquainted with the white people and was convinced of the futility of attempting to prevent their settlement within his domains. He became a firm friend of the white settlers and worked continuously through his long life to prevent bloodshed and promote peace between the red men and the white colonizers"; and later: "Washakie was a classic example of the idealized American Indian chief. Standing six feet tall, he was powerfully built, extremely strong, very courageous and controlled his followers through a wise mixture of love, bravery and wisdom." Edgar, *This Is the Place Monument Story and History*.

39. Elise Boxer, "'This Is the Place!': Disrupting Mormon Settler Colonialism," in Gina Colvin and Joanna Brooks, eds., *Decolonizing Mormonism: Approaching a Postcolonial Zion* (Salt Lake City: University of Utah, 2018), 87.

40. Ibid.

41. Boxer points out that the park's website highlights the historical record as follows: "'[w]ith several notable exceptions, relations between the Native Americans and the settlers were relatively cordial during the settlement era.' These 'notable exceptions' range from the Bear River massacre to the Blackhawk war. None of these 'notable exceptions' are mentioned at the park, including the Bear River massacre, especially the fact that unarmed Shoshone men, women, children, and elders were killed after settlers slowly claimed more land and resources." Ibid., 86.

42. Giles described Young's feelings about the bas-relief in this way: "[Young] gave it more attention than any other piece on the entire monument and said he was sorry to have to leave his studio, as it had become almost a part of his life. It certainly is a magnificent piece of sculpture and will undoubtedly be photographed by many thousands of people." See John D. Giles to Stanley W. Houghton, August 18, 1847, MSS 1353, box 5A, Utah Pioneer Trail & Landmark Association Letters.

43. Edward T. Linenthal explains the process whereby Jewish Holocaust memory was "Americanized." See Edward T. Linenthal, *Preserving Memory: The Struggle to Create America's Holocaust Museum* (New York: Viking, 1995).

44. See Flake, *The Politics of American Religious Identity*, 157 and 177.

45. John Eade and Michael J. Sallnow, editors' introduction to *Contesting the Sacred: The Anthropology of Christian Pilgrimage* (London: Routledge, 1991), 14–15.

46. Edgar, *This Is the Place Monument Story and History*.

47. Ibid.

48. J.J.R. no. 14, Cornerstone-Laying Ceremony, April 5, 1847 (audiotape), AV 102 segment 2, LDS Church Archives.

49. John D. Giles to R. A. Hart, January 8, 1945, MSS 1353, box 5A, folder 5, Utah Pioneer Trail & Landmark Association Letters.

50. John D. Giles to Noble Warren, editor, *Salt Lake Tribune*, MSS 1353, box 5a, folder 1, Utah Pioneer Trail & Landmark Association Letters.

51. Chidester and Linenthal, editors' introduction to *American Sacred Space*, 9.

52. *In Honor of the Pioneers*, 12.

53. Utah This Is The Place Monument Commission, *Preparing for 1947 "This Is the Place"* (pamphlet), 1945, LDS Church Archives.

54. Utah This Is The Place Monument Commission, *Preparing for 1947 "This Is the Place."*

55. *In Honor of the Pioneers*, 1931.

56. Y.M.M.I.A. Explorers Pioneer Trail Trek, *Instructions, Suggestions and Information for Explorers Planning to Participate in the YMMIA Explorers Pioneer Trail Trek* (pamphlet) ([Salt Lake City?], 1940), LDS Church Archives.

57. John D. Giles "Some Permanent Values from the Pioneer Celebration" *The Utah Magazine* (May 1946): 19.

58. "History," website of TITP Park, http://www.thisistheplace.org/info/parkhistory.html, accessed February 2015. Edgar, *This Is the Place Monument Story and History*.

Chapter 2

1. This monument, unveiled July 25, 1921, is called Pioneer View Monument and stands about 300 yards northeast of the TTIP monument. By the time the 1947 TITP monument was placed, Pioneer View Monument was obscured by underbrush and fairly forgotten: "a rather interesting thing from this vantage point, ladies and gentlemen, is the view of the traditional 'This is the Place' monument which is almost now obscured by brush, just about 200 yards north of the present site. For years, people have sought to find the place the pioneers came into the valley, looked up and said 'this is the place.' This little monument which has so faithfully guarded that spot, as I say, has now almost been obscured by the growing brush." Thomas Edgar, *This Is the Place Monument Story and History* (pamphlet) (Salt Lake City: Church History Archives, 1995), LDS Church Archives, Salt Lake City. Cornerstone-Laying Ceremony, April 5, 1847 (audiotape), AV 102 segment 2, L, Tom Perry Special Collections, Brigham Young University Archives, Provo, Utah.

2. John D. Giles to R. A. Hart, January 8, 1945, MSS 1353, box 5, folder 2, Utah Pioneer Trial & Landmark Association Letters, LDS Church Archives.

3. Utah This Is the Place Monument Commission, *Preparing for 1947 "This Is the Place,"* (pamphlet), 1945, LDS Church Archives.

4. John D. Giles to R. A. Hart, January 8, 1945, MSS 1353, box 5, folder 2, Utah Pioneer Trial & Landmark Association Letters, LDS Church Archives.

5. Ruby K. Smith, *John D. Giles: Modern Trail Blazer* (n.p.: written at request of Mrs. John D. Giles, 1961), 46.

6. Michael H. Madsen, "The Sanctification of Mormonism's Historical Geography," *Geographies of Religions and Belief Systems* 1, no. 1: 59. See also Barry Laga, "In Lieu of History: Mormon Monuments and the Shaping of Memory," *Dialogue* 43, no. 4 (Winter 2010): 131–153. .

7. Janet Donohoe, "The Betweenness of Monuments," in Forrest Clingerman, Brian Treanor, Martin Drenthen, and David Utsler, eds., *Interpreting Nature: The Emerging Field of Environmental Hermeneutics* (New York: Fordham University Press, 2014), 265–273.

8. Kathleen Flake, "Re-placing Memory: Latter-day Saint Use of Historical Monuments and Narrative in the Early Twentieth Century," *Religion and American Culture: A Journal of Interpretation* 13, no. 1 (Winter 2003): 69–109.

9. Armand L. Mauss, *The Angel and the Beehive: The Mormon Struggle with Assimilation* (Urbana: University of Illinois Press, 1994), 22.

10. The Kirtland Temple had been the site of meetings for many different factions of the church after the death of Joseph Smith Jr. It was in the 1860s that the Reorganized Latter Day Saints church (COC) began to meet regularly in the temple. See David J. Howlett, *Kirtland Temple: The Biography of a Shared Mormon Sacred Space* (Urbana: University of Illinois Press, 2014), 38–39.

11. See Howland, 43–47, and Madsen, "The Sanctification of Mormonism's Historical Geography," 56. Madsen also discusses the LDS Church's decision to not pursue a chance to purchase property in Nauvoo, Illinois, in 1909.

12. Keith A. Erekson, "From Missionary Resort to Memorial Farm: Commemoration and Capitalism at the Birthplace of Joseph Smith, 1905–1925," *Mormon Historical Studies* (2005): 71–73.

13. Michael H. Madsen, "Mormon Meccas: The Spiritual Transformation of Mormon Historical Sites from Points of Interest to Sacred Space" (Ph.D. diss., Syracuse University, 2003), 88.

14. Erekson, "From Missionary Resort to Memorial Farm," 69–70. Erekson notes: "church leaders did not embark on a mission-driven crusade to preserve cultural heritage. Instead, they acted cautiously, experimenting over the course of two decades with the site's purposes and functions" (70).

15. However important they are to marking Mormon identity as unique, temples do not dot the landscape enough to claim it as Mormon. The decision to create meetinghouses wherever groups of believers lived did. The standardized architecture of these meetinghouses meant that Latter-day Saints were visually present on the landscape. Religious Studies scholar Jan Shipps has called this a brilliant decision "from the standpoint of the maintenance of LDS identity in an altered situation." She argues that sprinkling the landscape with architectural structures that can clearly be defined as Mormon "cultivated among the Saints what might be called a zionic sense, making the very LDS meetinghouses themselves agents of assimilation and signals that wherever the Saints gather, there is Zion." The architectural standardization was accompanied by a standardization in church programming such that no matter where believers found themselves, the same feeling, in fact the same lessons, would be followed in a similar space. See Jan Shipps, "Emergence of Mormonism on the American Landscape (1950–1965)," in S. Kent Brown, Donald Q. Cannon, and Richard H. Jackson, eds., *Historical Atlas of Mormonism* (New York: Simon and Schuster, 1994), and Jan Shipps, "From Peoplehood to Church Membership: Mormonism's Trajectory since World War II," *Church History* 76 (June 2007): 11. Thomas Carter has argued that the creation of the temple and the meetinghouse shaped two sides of a Mormon architectural landscape; the temple offered an "*otherness* that staked out a distinctive and decidedly Mormon religious identity," while the meetinghouses offered an "*orthodoxy* that allowed them to fit rather seamlessly into mainstream American culture." Thomas Carter, *Building Zion: the Material World of Mormon Settlement* (Minneapolis: University of Minnesota Press, 2015), xii. See also Jan Shipps, *Sojourner in the Promised Land: Forty Years among the Mormons* (Urbana: University of Illinois Press, 2000), and Claudia L. Bushman, *Contemporary Mormonism: Latter-day Saints in Modern America* (Westport, CT: Praeger, 2006), 76–78.

16. See Cynthia Culber Prescott, "The All-American Eternal Family: Sacred and Secular Values in Western Pioneer Monuments," in *We Are What We Remember: The American Past through Commemoration,* Jeffrey Lee Meriwether and Laura Mattoon D'Amore, eds. (Newcastle Upon Tyne: Cambridge Scholars, 2012), 36–37 and Flake, "Re-placing Memory, 69–109.

17. *Constitution: Utah Pioneer Trails & Landmarks Association* (Salt Lake City, Utah 1930): University of Utah Archives.

18. Smith, *John D. Giles,* 46.
19. Ibid., 51.
20. Ibid., 51–55.
21. Utah Pioneer Trails & Landmarks Association, "Charting and Marking Pioneer Trails and Landmarks Outline of Campaign—July 1931," LDS Church Archives.
22. *Constitution: Utah Pioneer Trails & Landmarks Association.* Salt Lake City, Utah: University of Utah archives, 1930.
23. Utah Pioneer Trails and Landmarks Association, *Trail Blazer Bulletin*, no. 2, December 14, 1930, L. Tom Perry Special Collections, Harold B. Lee Library, Brigham Young University, Provo, Utah.
24. Davis Bitton, *The Ritualization of Mormon History and Other Essays* (Urbana: University of Illinois Press, 1994), 177–181.
25. Recollections of Melvin R. Baldwin, MSS 10231, folder 2, vol. 3, LDS Church Archives.
26. John D. Giles, "The M.I.A. Preserves History," February 1935, 10231, folder 2, v. 3, LDS Church Archives.
27. The text of the monument placed at the site says that it is dedicated to the "Survivors of Captain Edward Martin's Handcart Company of Mormon emigration from England to Utah," who "were rescued here in perishing condition about Nov. 12, 1856. Delayed in starting and hampered by inferior carts it was overtaken by an early winter. Among the company of 576, including aged people and children, the fatalities number 145. Insufficient food and clothing and severe weather caused many deaths. Toward the end every campground became a graveyard. Some of the survivors found shelter in a stockade and mail station near Devil's Gate where their property was stored for the winter. Earlier companies reached Utah in safety." The monument was dedicated by the UPTLA and "Citizens of Wyoming." Their hope was to mark a place of tragedy, a place of Mormon sorrow.
28. Giles, "The M.I.A. Preserves History."
29. Utah Pioneer Trails & Landmarks Association, *Trail Blazer Bulletin*, no. 2, December 14, 1930, L. Tom Perry Special Collections.
30. Utah Pioneer Trails & Landmarks Association, "Charting and Marking Pioneer Trails and Landmarks Outline of Campaign—July 1931," LDS Church Archives.
31. Ibid.
32. Utah Pioneer Trails & Landmarks Association, *Trail Blazer Bulletin*, no. 2, December 14, 1930. Utah Pioneer Trails and Landmarks Association. L. Tom Perry Special Collections.
33. Ibid.
34. *Trail News*, December 1996, LDS Church Archives.
35. The Mormon Trail "became a national historic site (Mormon Pioneer National Historic Trail) in 1978 and is maintained by the United States National Park Service." See Daniel H. Olsen, "Touring Sacred History: The Latter-day Saints and Their Historical Sites," in J. Michale Hunter, ed., *Mormons and Popular Culture: The Global Influence of an American Phenomenon*, vol. 2 (Santa Barbara, CA: Praeger, 2013), 227.

36. Stanley Kimball to Garn Hatch, February 17, 1993, Mormon Trails Association Papers, L. Tom Perry Special Collections.

37. National Park Service, Role and Function statement, Mormon Pioneer National Historic Trail, Mormon Trails Association Papers, MSS SC 2384. Mormon Trails Association. L. Tom Perry Special Collections.

38. R. Scott Lloyd, "Group Works to Preserve Mormon Trail," *Church News*, December 19, 1992.

39. Report of Mormon Pioneer Trail Planning Meeting, November 14, 1992, L. Tom Perry Special Collections.

40. "Trails Vision: The Mormon Pioneer National Historic Trail in 1997," Mormon Trails Association Papers.

41. Colleen McDannell, "Heritage Religion and the Mormons," in Ivan Gaskell and Sarah Ann Carter, eds., *Oxford Handbook of History and Materian Culture* (New York: Oxford University Press, forthcoming), 3–10.

42. See Madsen, "Mormon Meccas," 242–251; Madsen, "The Sanctification of Mormonism's Historical Geography," 51–52, and Barry Laga, "In Lieu of History: Mormon Monuments and the Shaping of Memory," *Dialogue* 43, no. 4 (Winter 2010): 134.

43. Madsen, "Mormon Meccas, 10.

44. Ibid., 7.

45. McDannell, "Heritage Religion and the Mormons," 9.

46. Richard Handler and Eric Gable, *The New History in an Old Museum: Creating the Past at Colonial Williamsburg* (Durham, NC: Duke University Press, 1997), 18.

47. Madsen, "The Sanctification of Mormonism's Historical Geography," 57.

48. Handler and Gable, *The New History in an Old Museum*, 3–7.

49. Ibid., 84.

50. Madsen, "Mormon Meccas," 156–164.

51. Erekson, "From Missionary Resort to Memorial Farm," 71.

52. Kent Ahrens, "Avard T. Fairbanks and the Winter Quarters Monument," *Nebraska History* 95, no. 3 (2014): 176–178. See also Conrey Bryson, *Winter Quarters* (Salt Lake City: Deseret Book, 2017).

53. Ahrens, "Avard T. Fairbanks and the Winter Quarters Monument," 180.

54. Prescott, "The All-American Eternal Family," 337–342. The sculpture representing hope, *Youth and New Frontiers*, was placed decades later in the LDS Conference Center in Salt Lake City.

55. Ahrens, "Avard T. Fairbanks and the Winter Quarters Monument," 80.

56. Ibid., 180.

57. John A. Widstoe, *Winter Quarters Is Immortalized in Stone Improvement Era* October 1936.

58. Eugene F. Fairbanks, *A Sculptor's Testimony in Bronze and Stone: The Sacred Sculpture of Avard T. Fairbanks* (Salt Lake City: Publishers Press, 1994), 82–84.

59. Winter Quarters description, website of Church of Jesus Christ of Latter-day Saints, www.lds.org, accessed June 21, 2017.

60. President Gordon Hinckley, Press Conference, April 18, 1997, Winter Quarters. www.youtu.be/ar2iGeQCAeA. Accessed June 2019.
61. Madsen, "The Sanctification of Mormonism's Historical Geography," 68.
62. Ahrens, "Avard T. Fairbanks and the Winter Quarters Monument," 185 n.
63. Scott Carlson, "Winter Quarters Visitors Center 2005," September 26, 2014. www.youtu.be/q090RTg4FUY, accessed June 21, 2017.
64. Prescott, "The All-American Eternal Family," 342.
65. Ahrens, "Avard T. Fairbanks and the Winter Quarters Monument," 182.

Chapter 3

1. A memorial sculpture at TITP Park also confirms the significance of Nauvoo. A bust of Israel Barlow sits atop a concrete stand and acknowledges him as "the first Mormon to contact Dr. Isaac Galland in the purchase of property at Commerce, Illinois (later to become the city of Nauvoo) Nov–Dec 1838." At first glance, the sculpture seems like an odd one in light of the others in the sculpture park and their symbolic significance to LDS narratives. Yet the memorial claims that Latter-day Saints were involved in the move to, purchase of land in, and construction of homes at Nauvoo. This claim's significance is clear in light of the identity politics taking place in Nauvoo that this chapter discusses.
2. Davis Bitton has argued that historical sites and shrines are part of the ritualization of Mormon history. He claims that they represent "the forms and symbols whose function is not primarily the communication of knowledge but rather the simplification of the past into forms that can be memorialized, celebrated, and emotionally appropriated." I would add to Bitton's argument that there is an important spatial component to the ritualization of that history as well. See Davis Bitton, *The Ritualization of Mormon History and Other Essays* (Urbana: University of Illinois Press, 1994), 170. See also Jan Shipps, *Mormonism: The Story of a New Religious Tradition* (Urbana: University of Illinois Press, 1987), 63–64.
3. For a discussion of the contested nature of sacred spaces, see David Chidester and Edward T. Linenthal, editors' introduction to *American Sacred Space* (Bloomington: Indiana University Press), 15–18.
4. In his dissertation, Michael Madsen addresses the role of Mormon historical sites in community-making. Madsen argues that the sites "serve to *reinforce* the official history that acts as a centripetal force that binds members to the Church through the construction of Mormon identity" while also allowing the church "to present a carefully constructed image of itself to the 'outside' world." See Michael H. Madsen, "Mormon Meccas: The Spiritual Transformation of Mormon Historical Sites from Points of Interest to Sacred Space" (Ph.D. diss., Syracuse University, 2003), 7.
5. J. Elliot Cameron, Mormon Trails Association Newsletter, *Trail News*, December 1996, LDS Church Archives.
6. Daniel H. Olsen, "Touring Sacred History: The Latter-day Saints and Their Historical Sites," in J. Michael Hunter, ed., *Mormons and Popular Culture: The Global Influence of an American Phenomenon*, vol. 2 (Santa Barbara, CA: Praeger, 2013), 234.

7. Elbert A. Smith, *Differences That Persist between the Reorganized Church of Jesus Christ of Latter Day Saints and the Utah Mormon Church* (Independence, MO: Herald House, 1943), 9.

8. Ibid., 52.

9. The narrative told by biographers and historians about Smith is more complex. Smith understood the danger brewing for the Mormon people when the *Nauvoo Expositor*'s first and only edition appeared, accusing him of heresy and adultery. The choice he and the council made to destroy the press was, in the words of one of his biographers, a "fatal mistake." After the destruction of the press and in an attempt to navigate rising tensions, he reluctantly turned himself in. Surely he knew his own death was one possible outcome, but as a savvy religious leader, one whose back was against a wall, he was no unsuspecting innocent. Rather his gamble to turn himself in seems an optimistic choice. He saw it as a means of protecting other Mormons (and, he hoped, himself) from dangerous mobs. Richard Bushman, *Rough Stone Rolling* (New York: Alfred A. Knopf, 2005), 537–548.

10. See www.utahartists.com/dee_jay_bawden.html, accessed August 2016.

11. Bushman, *Rough Stone Rolling*, 548–550.

12. Independence, Missouri, and Nauvoo, Illinois, are not the only places where the LDS and COC churches negotiate identities over historical sites. For an excellent discussion of the identity politics at work in Kirkland, Ohio, see David J. Howlett, *Kirtland Temple: The Biography of a Shared Mormon Sacred Space* (Urbana: University of Illinois Press, 2014).

13. Scott C. Esplin, "Competing for the City of Joseph: Interpretive Conflicts in Nauvoo's Restoration," *John Whitmer Historical Association Journal* 32 (Spring/Summer 2012): 48–56, and Benjamin C. Pykles, *Excavating Nauvoo: The Mormons and the Rise of Historical Archaeology in America* (Lincoln: University of Nebraska Press, 2010), 27. See also Scott C. Esplin, *Return to the City of Joseph: Modern Mormonism's Contest for the Soul of Nauvoo* (Urbana: University of Illinois Press, 2018).

14. Lee Wiles, "Monogamy Underground: The Burial of Mormon Plural Marriage in the Graves of Joseph and Emma Smith," *Journal of Mormon History* 39, no. 3 (Summer 2013): 12–14 and 29–41.

15. Stephen C. Taysom, "A Uniform and Common Recollection: Joseph Smith's Legacy, Polygamy, and the Creation of Mormon Public Memory, 1852–2002," *Dialogue* 35, no. 3 (2002): 113–144; Lee Wiles, "Monogamy Underground," 3, 45. For a biography of Emma Smith, see Linda King Newell and Valeen Timppetts Avery, *Mormon Enigma: Emma Hale Smith* (Urbana: University of Illinois Press, 1994).

16. Christopher James Blythe, "Emma's Willow: Historical Anxiety, Mormon Pilgrimage and Nauvoo's *Mater Dolorosa*," *Material Religion* 12, no. 4 (2016): 405–432.

17. Esplin, "Competing for the City of Joseph," 51.

18. Pykles, *Excavating Nauvoo*, 2.

19. Quoted in ibid., 87.

20. After a few decades of work, Nauvoo Restoration, Inc. shifted its goals to maintaining and operating the sites it had completed rather than taking on new projects. See Esplin, "Competing for the City of Joseph," 60. For an excellent discussion of the entire history and work of Nauvoo Restoration, Inc., see Pykles, *Excavating Nauvoo*.

21. Pykles argues that "because the Church's representation of its own history depicts the events of its past as part of a grand, divinely directed drama, the authentic reconstruction or restoration of the places where these events occurred becomes an essential component in perpetuating and legitimizing the LDS Church's theological tenets" (302). Those who work at COC sites are now "identified as professional museum personnel and professional historians." See Howlett, *Kirtland Temple*, 172–173.

22. *Faith in Every Footstep: Instructor's Guide, 1847–1997*, Prepared by the Church Educational System (Salt Lake City: Church of Jesus Christ of Latter-day Saints, 1996), iv.

23. "History, 1838–1856, volume D-1 (August 1, 1842–July 1, 1843]," p. 1362, *The Joseph Smith Papers*, (accessed March 1, 2020), https://www.josephsmithpapers.org/paper-summary/history-1838-1856-volume-d-1-1-august-1842-1-july-1843/5

24. Ibid., 4–5.

25. *The Journal of Anson Call* (Ogden, UT: Eborn Books, 2007), publisher's note.

26. Quoted in Barney, Gwen Marler Barney, *Anson Call and the Rocky Mountain Prophecy* (Salt Lake City: Call, 2002), 99.

27. *The Journal of Anson Call*, dedication to the original publisher.

28. Barney, *Anson Call and the Rocky Mountain Prophecy*, 97.

29. Ibid., 101.

30. R. Scott Lloyd, "'Eyes Westward' Tells Prophetic Vision" Church News July 25, 2008. www.thechurchnews.com/archive/2008-07-26/eyes-westward-tells-prophetic-vision-32046, accessed March 2019.

Chapter 4

1. For a discussion of the sanctification process, see Kenneth E. Foote, *Shadowed Ground: America's Landscapes of Violence and Tragedy* (Austin: University of Texas Press, 1997).

2. David Chidester and Edward T. Linenthal, editors' introduction to *American Sacred Space* (Bloomington: Indiana University Press), 15–18.

3. Kirk Johnson, "Along Public Trail, a Church Recounts Its History," *New York Times*, January 23, 2004.

4. Complaint, Western Land Exchange Project et al. v. Norton. (Salt Lake City, Utah: University of Utah library).

5. This is the title of one history of the Willie and Martin handcart pioneers; see Andrew D. Olsen, *The Price We Paid: The Extraordinary Story of the Willie and Martin Handcart Pioneers* (Salt Lake City: Deseret Books, 2006).

6. Tom Rea, *Devil's Gate: Owning the Land, Owning the Story* (Norman: University of Oklahoma Press, 2006), 9.

7. Paul H. Peterson, "They Came by Handcart," *Ensign*, August 1997.

8. Rea, *Devil's Gate*, 80–85. See also David Roberts, *Devil's Gate* (New York: Simon and Schuster, 2008), 88–94, and LeRoy Hafen, *Handcarts to Zion: The Story of a Unique Western Migration 1856–1860* (Glendale, CA: Arthur H. Clark, 1960), 24–43.

9. Rea, *Devil's Gate*, 87–89.

10. Howard Christy, "Weather, Disaster, and Responsibility: An Essay on the Willie and Martin Handcart Story," *BYU Studies* 37, no. 1 (1997–1998): 2–69.

11. For an extended discussion of the rescue mission, see Roberts, *Devil's Gate*, 225–258, and Rebecca Cornwall and Leonard J. Arrington, *Rescue of the 1856 Handcart Companies* (Provo, UT: Brigham Young University Press, 1981).

12. For more on this history, see Donald R. Moormna, *Camp Floyd and the Mormons* (Salt Lake City: University of Utah Press, 1992), Leonard J. Arrington, "Mormon Finance and the Utah War," *Utah Historical Quarterly* 20, no. 3 (1952): 219–238, and Richard D. Poll, "Thomas L. Kane and the Utah War," *Utah Historical Quarterly* 61, no. 2 (1993): 112–135.

13. Rea, *Devil's Gate*, 93–95.

14. Ibid., 95, 98.

15. Sierra Naumu, "Death in the Trek: A Study of Mormon Pioneer Mortality," *Deseret News*, July 14, 2014, news.byu.edu/archive14-jul-pioneer.aspx, accessed June 29, 2015.

16. "The Hijacking of the Mormon Trail Story by the Willie-Martin Disasters" (panel discussion), Mormon Historical Association Annual Meeting, June 5, 2015, Provo, Utah.

17. "Remembering the Rescue," *Ensign*, August 1997 www.churchofjesuschrist.org/study/ensign/1997/08-remembering-the-rescue.

18. Megan Sanborn Jones, "(Re)living the Pioneer Past: Handcarts, Heritage, and Mormon Youth Culture" *Theatre Topics* September (2006), 114.

19. *On the Trail of the Martin & Willie Handcart Pioneers: A Video Re-enactment of the Original Trek*. Thompson Productions, 200–?. University of Utah Archives.

20. Elder M. Russell Ballard, "Conquering the Wilderness," Pioneer Days Fireside, July 20, 1997. M273 B189p 1997. LDS Church Archives.

21. H.R. 36, H.R. 3858, and H.R. 4103, Legislative Hearing before the Subcommittee on National Parks, Recreation, and Public Lands of the Committee on Resources, U.S. House of Representatives, 107th Congress, Second Session, May 16, 2002, 29.

22. Jones, 115.

23. Margaret Clark Journals, May 1, 1997, Utah Education Network. Heritage.uen.org. Accessed June 15, 2013.

24. Wendy Westergard Journal, July 24, 1997, Utah Education Network. Heritage.uen.org. Accessed June 15, 2013.

25. Survey Respondent, 6. For a discussion of the survey, see Chapter 7.

26. Peter Fish, "The Cost of Salvation," *Sunset* 201 (1998) .

27. Quoted in ibid.

28. Christy, "Weather, Disaster, and Responsibility," 52.

29. Rea, *Devil's Gate*, 146–156; 238.

30. Kirk Johnson, "Along Public Trail, a Church Recounts Its History" *The New York Times* January 23, 2004.

31. Rea, *Devil's Gate*, 242.

32. Ibid., 242.

33. Ibid., 243.

34. Complaint, Western Land Exchange Project et al. v. Norton.
35. H.R. 36, H.R. 3858, and H.R. 4103, Legislative Hearing before the Subcommittee on National Parks, Recreation, and Public Lands of the Committee on Resources, U.S. House of Representatives, 107th Congress, Second Session, May 16, 2002, 29.
36. Holdsworth, "Why Martin's Cove Matters," 1004–1006.
37. Complaint, Western Land Exchange et al. v. Norton.
38. Quincy D. Newell, "Wyoming: A Westerner Encounters Open Range Religion," *Religion and Politics,* June 29, 2012.
39. H.R. 36, H.R. 3858, and H.R. 4103, Legislative Hearing before the Subcommittee on National Parks, Recreation, and Public Lands of the Committee on Resources, U.S. House of Representatives, 107th Congress, Second Session, May 16, 2002, 12.
40. H.R. 36, H.R. 3858, and H.R. 4103, Legislative Hearing before the Subcommittee on National Parks, Recreation, and Public Lands of the Committee on Resources, U.S. House of Representatives, 107th Congress, Second Session, May 16, 2002, 36.
41. H.R. 36, H.R. 3858, and H.R. 4103, Legislative Hearing before the Subcommittee on National Parks, Recreation, and Public Lands of the Committee on Resources, U.S. House of Representatives, 107th Congress, Second Session, May 16, 2002, 28–29.
42. Chad M. Orton, "The Martin Handcart Company at the Sweetwater: Another Look" *BYU Studies* v. 45, no. 3 (2006): 9, 35.
43. Survey Respondent 55.
44. Holdsworth, "Why Martin's Cove Matters," 1003.
45. Quoted in Christopher Smith, "Trouble at the Cove: Lawsuit Challenges LDS Church Lease of Handcart Site," *Salt Lake Tribune,* March 10, 2005.
46. H.R. 36, H.R. 3858, and H.R. 4103, Legislative Hearing before the Subcommittee on National Parks, Recreation, and Public Lands the Committee on Resources, U.S. House of Representatives, 107th Congress, Second Session, May 16, 2002.
47. Ibid., 8.
48. Ibid., 8.
49. Holdsworth, "Why Martin's Cove Matters," 1017.
50. For a discussion of the land controversies surrounding Devil's Tower, see *In the Light of Reverence,* produced and directed by Christopher McCleod, PBS, 2001.
51. Holdsworth, "Why Martin's Cove Matters," 1017–1018.
52. "Stop the Public Lands Transfer to the LDS Church!," American Atheists Legislative Action Alert, June 11, 2002, www.snotty_news.tripod.com/rb1105.html, accessed June 26, 2015.
53. American Civil Liberties Union, "Wyoming Residents, including Descendants of Mormon Pioneers, Sue to Block LDS Church Control of National Historic Site" (press release), March 9, 2005, and Complaint, Western Land Exchange Project et al. v. Norton. See also William Young, letter to the editor, *Casper Star-Tribune,* May 8, 2002.
54. American Civil Liberties Union, "Wyoming Residents, including Descendants of Mormon Pioneers, Sue to Block LDS Church Control of National Historic Site."
55. Complaint, Western Land Exchange Project et al. v. Norton.

56. H.R. 36, H.R. 3858, and H.R. 4103, Legislative Hearing before the Subcommittee on National Parks, Recreation, and Public Lands of the Committee on Resources U.S. House of Representatives, 107th Congress, Second Session, May 16, 2002, 44.
57. Holdsworth, "Why Martin's Cove Matters," 1004.
58. H.R. 36, H.R. 3858, and H.R. 4103, Legislative Hearing before the Subcommittee on National Parks, Recreation, and Public Lands of the Committee on Resources U.S. House of Representatives, 107th Congress, Second Session, May 16, 2002, 45.
59. Not every non-Mormon was against the lease. Other non–church members found themselves profiting from the new LDS interest in Martin's Cove. Alcova, the closest town to the cove, experienced an economic gain with the rise of visitors. In fact, the owners of the general store there began the construction of a small motel and even began to sell handcart-related souvenirs such as sun bonnets and handcart wheel t-shirts and jewelry. See Kirk Johnson, "Along Public Trail, a Church Recounts Its History," *New York Times*, January 23, 2004.
60. Carrie A. Moore, "ACLU, LDS Resolve Martin's Cove Dispute," *Deseret News,* June 8, 2006.
61. Holdsworth, "Why Martin's Cove Matters," 1007–1010.
62. Ibid., 1020.
63. Johnson, "Along Public Trail, a Church Recounts Its History."
64. Rea, *Devil's Gate*, 8–9.
65. Pioneer Sesquicentennial, Deseret Management Corporation, University of Utah Archives.

Chapter 5

1. M. Russell Ballard, "Faith in Every Footstep" Church of Jesus Christ of Latter-day Saints. www.lds.org/general-conference/1996/10/faith-in-every-footstep/.
2. Susan Arrington Madsen, *The Second Rescue: The Story of the Spiritual Rescue of the Willie and Martin Handcart Pioneers* (Salt Lake City: Deseret Book, 1998), 2–4.
3. Ibid., 14–15.
4. Niels Otto Mortensen Family Records, LDS Church Archives, Salt Lake City.
5. Tom Rea, *Devil's Gate: Owning the Land, Owning the Story* (Norman: University of Oklahoma Press, 2006), 231. See also John D. Giles, "The M.I.A. Preserves History," February 1935, 10231, folder 2, vol. 3. LDS Church Archives.
6. Madsen, *The Second Rescue*, 14.
7. Ibid., 15.
8. LR 10231, folder 2, vol. 3, LDS Church Archives.
9. Second Rescue Mission Files, folder 1, LDS Church Archives. See, for example: memo, Don Smith to the Willie File, February 15, 1990, Riverton state Presidency to Loren C. Dunn, May 20, 1990, Loren C. Dunn to Scott Lorimer, May 31, 1990, all in LR 10231, folder 2, vol. 3, LDS Church Archives.
10. Robert S. Lorimer Oral History Interview, Riverton, Wyoming. September 22, 1992. OH 1232. LDS Church Archives, 2.

11. LR 10231 22, Second Rescue Mission Files, LDS Church Archives.

12. Desiree Lorimer's reminiscence of the Second Rescue, in *Remember: The Willie and Martin Handcart Companies and Their Rescuers—Past and Present*, compiled and written by members of the Riverton Wyoming Stake (Salt Lake City: Publishers Press, 1997), F-14.

13. *Remember,* 146.

14. Elizabeth A. Castelli, *Martyrdom and Memory: Early Christian Culture Making* (New York: Columbia University Press, 2007), 34.

15. Ibid., 34, 173, 197.

16. For a discussion of understandings of martyrdom in early Christianity, see David Chidester, *Christianity: A Global History* (San Francisco: HarperOne, 2001), 75–90.

17. Castelli, *Martyrdom and Memory,* 2.

18. Ibid., 3.

19. Ibid., 3.

20. Ibid., 3.

21. Ibid., 34–36.

22. Ibid., 4.

23. Ibid., 11–17. Maurice Halbwachs, *On Collective Memory* (Chicago, IL: University of Chicago Press, 1992).

24. Kitchen, Riverton Wyoming Stake Meeting, July 21, 1991. In *Remember, 147.*

25. Lorimer Oral History, 13–14.

26. *Remember,* 155.

27. Lorimer Oral History, 14.

28. Ibid., 14.

29. Andrew D. Olsen and Jolene S. Allphin, *Follow Me to Zion: Stories from the Willie Handcart Pioneers* (Salt Lake City: Deseret Book, 2013), 96–97.

30. Ibid., 93–94.

31. See, for example, Bodil Mortensen, Opener to Tremonton South Stake Youth Trek, video, posted July 26, 2009, Youtu.be/i2P248pbgxE, and Bodil (from "Remember the Journey"), video posted April 13, 2009, Youtube/BG1SxFL8xc4, accessed May 5, 2019.

32. Bodil (from "Remember the Journey") video posted April 13, 2009, YouTube/BG1SxFL8xc4, accessed February 23, 2015.

33. Rachel Mecham Goates, "Bodil's Theme," soundtrack from the Mormon Handcart Pageant, posted September 8, 2011, accessed February 23, 2015.

34. Andrew D. Olsen, *The Price We Paid: The Extraordinary Story of the Willie and Martin Handcart Pioneers* (Salt Lake City: Deseret Book, 2006), vii, 211.

35. C. Vinn Roos, *The Martin and Willie Handcart Companies and Their Rescuers* (Provo, UT: BYU Printing Services, 2006), 5.

36. See Castelli, *Martyrdom and Memory,* 190–199, for a discussion of the function of martyr stories in contemporary American evangelicalism.

37. For a discussion of the nineteenth-century rescue, see Chad M. Orton, "The Martin Handcart Company at the Sweetwater: Another Look," *BYU Studies* 45, no. 3 (2006): 4–37. Orton clarifies many common misunderstandings about the initial rescue, providing information about the number of rescuers and discussing how the Martin company members played a role in rescuing one another.

38. Madsen, *The Second Rescue*, 26.
39. Lorimer Oral History, 3.
40. Lorimer Oral History, 9.
41. Madsen, *The Second Rescue*, 25.
42. LR 10231 2, folder 21, LDS Church Archives.
43. Quoted on Madsen, *The Second Rescue*, 34.
44. LR 10231 21, folder 21, LDS Church Archives.
45. LR 10231, folder 2, vol. 3, Church History Archives.
46. *Remember*, 169.
47. Quoted in Madsen, *The Second Rescue*, 5–6.
48. "Alphabetical Listing of Ordinances Performed" LR 10231 22, Second Rescue Mission Files, folder 7, LDS Church Archives.
49. Quoted in Madsen, *The Second Rescue*, 37. Also see Diane McKinnon's reminiscence in *Remember*, F-18.
50. Madsen, *The Second Rescue*, 102.
51. Ibid., 15.
52. Gerald Haycock, "Seek Ye First the Kingdom of God," unpublished manuscript, excerpt, MS 22479. LDS Church Archives.
53. Madsen, *The Second Rescue*, 6.
54. Lorimer Oral History, 11–12.
55. *Remember*, F-10.
56. Haycock, 48.
57. Ibid., 46.
58. Quoted in Pioneer Trails Workshop, 2000, M 273.4 P6624 2001. LDS Church Archives.
59. *Remember*, 144.
60. Madsen, *The Second Rescue*,17.
61. Ibid., x.
62. Lorimer Oral History.
63. Ibid., 18.
64. *Remember*, 172. Kim McKinnon at the Riverton Wyoming Stake Pioneer Day Celebration at Veil Crossing, July 26, 1997. LR 10231 27 LDS Church Archives.
65. Scott Lorimer, at the Riverton Wyoming Stake Pioneer Day Celebration at Veil Crossing, July 26, 1997. In *Remember*, 146.
66. Haycock, "Seek Ye First the Kingdom of God," 51.
67. Quoted in Olsen and Allphin, *Follow Me to Zion*, 93–94.

Chapter 6

1. Sons of Utah Pioneers, Angels Are Near Us Monument Dedication, MS 19168, LDS Church Archives.
2. Eric A. Eliason, "Pioneers and Recapitulation in Mormon Popular Historical Expression," in Tad Tuleja, ed., *Usable Pasts: Traditions and Group Expressions in North America* (Logan: Utah State University Press, 1997), 201.

3. See Eric Alden Eliason, "Celebrating Zion: Pioneers in Mormon Popular Historical Expression" (Ph.D. diss., University of Texas at Austin, 1998), 96–109.

4. Hill and Landon, "The Pioneer Sesquicentennial Celebration," in Susan Easton Black, ed., *Out of Obscurity: The LDS Church in the Twentieth Century* (Salt Lake City: Deseret Book, 2000), 164.

5. Pioneer Sesquicentennial Celebration, BX 8608 A1a 8568. L. Tom Perry Special Collections, Provo, Utah.

6. *Sesquicentennial Star* 1, no. 1, November 1995. University of Utah Archives.

7. Ibid.

8. Sarah Jane Weaver, "Performers Journey 'Barefoot to Zion,'" *Church News* June 14, 1997 www.thechurchnews.com/archive/1997-06-14/performers-journey-barefoot-to-zion-12298, and Ivan M. Lincoln, "'Barefoot to Zion' makes the journey with drama, humor, and lots of characters" *Deseret News* June 21, 1997. www.deseret news. com/article/567694/Barefoot-to-Zion-makes-the-journey-with-drama-humor-and-lots-of-characters.html, accessed May 5, 2019.

9. Promised Valley Productions, *Barefoot to Zion* (script) (Salt Lake City: Church of Jesus Christ of Latter-day Saints, 1997), LDS Church Archives.

10. Ibid.

11. Eric Alden Eliason, "Celebrating Zion," 96–109.

12. Utah Pioneer Sesquicentennial Education Handbook, Utah Pioneer Sesquicentennial Celebration Coordinating Council, 1997, LDS Church Archives.

13. Pioneer Sesquicentennial Celebration: Drama and Musical Presentations, BX 8608 A1a no. 7988. L. Tom Perry Special Collections.

14. Pioneer: Sesquicentennial, Deseret Management Corporation, University of Utah Archives.

15. Pioneer Sesquicentennial Celebration: Drama and Musical Presentations.

16. *Faith in Every Footstep* (video), 1997. VC 258, L. Tom Perry Special Collections.

17. Pioneer Sesquicentennial Celebration: Drama and Musical Presentations.

18. website of Daughters of the Utah Pioneers, http://www.dupinternational.org/, accessed June 13, 2013.

19. Ibid.

20. Daughters of the Utah Pioneers, *The First Twenty-Five Years*, (Salt Lake City: Daughters of Utah Pioneers, [1986?]. LDS Church Archives.

21. D. James Cannon, ed., *Centennial Caravan: Story of the 1947 Centennial Reenactment of the Original Mormon Trek* (Sons of the Utah Pioneers, 1948), n.p.

22. Itinerary for Utah Centennial Pioneer Trek sponsored by the Sons of Utah Pioneers, July 14–22, 1947, < LDS Church Archives.

23. Pamphlet, "Souvenir Program and Guide for the Utah Centennial Trek, following along the Old Mormon Pioneer Trail," Sponsored by The Sons of the Utah Pioneers, n.d. 1847, LDS Church Archives.

24. The Mormon Pioneer Trail: Church Pioneer Sesquicentennial (150th) Celebration, A Highway and Trail Etiquette Guide, n.d. University of Utah Archives.

25. Duane S. Carling Reminiscence (b. 1943–), MS 16320, LDS Church Archives.

26. Wendy Westergard Journal, July 17, 1997, Utah Education Network http://heritage. uen.org, accessed June 15, 2013.

27. Richard O. Cowan, *The Latter-day Saint Century* (Salt Lake City: Bookcraft, 1999), 282–283.

28. Brian and Karen Hill, *Angels among Us*, AC 5027, Stories from the Sesquicentennial Wagon Train, L. Tom Perry Special Collections.

29. Brent C. Moore Journal, May 21, 1997, http://heritage.uen.org, accessed June 15, 2013.

30. Margaret Clark Journals, April 27, 1997 Utah Education Network. http://heritage. uen.org, accessed June 15, 2013.

31. Jeffrey Holland, "What Mean These Stones?," Ogden Pioneer Days Fireside, July 23, 1995, LDS Church Archives.

32. Pioneer Sesquicentennial, Deseret Management Corporation.

33. Church Educational System, *Faith in Every Footstep: Instructor's Guide, 1847–1997* (Salt Lake City: Church of Jesus Christ of Latter-day Saints, 1996), LDS Church Archives.

34. John Lodefink Journal, July 17, 1997, MS 15583, LDS Church Archives.

35. This process, of embracing shared identity as participants in pilgrimage is a common occurrence in religious pilgrimages. For a discussion, see Victor Turner and Edith Turner, *Image and Pilgrimage in Christian Culture* (New York: Columbia University Press, 2011).

36. Brian and Karen Hill, *Angels among Us*.

37. Ibid.

38. Wendy Westergard Journal, May 21, 1997.

39. See, for example, Duane S. Carling Reminiscence (b. 1943), MS 16320, and Sons of Utah Pioneers, Angels Are Near Us Monument Dedication, MS 19168, LDS Church Archives.

40. Brian and Karen Hill, *Angels among Us*. .

41. Ibid.

42. Ibid.

43. Wendy Westergard Journal, May 21, 1997.

44. *The Mormon Pioneer Trail: Church Pioneer Sesquicentennial (150th) Celebration. A Highway and Trail Etiquette Guide,* University of Utah Archives.

45. Brian and Karen Hill, *Angels among Us*.

46. John Lodefink Journal, July 22, 1997.

47. Brian and Karen Hill, *Angels among Us*.

48. AV 2049, Pioneer Rendezvous Footage, Sesquicentennial Celebration at BYU, tape 82, L. Tom Perry Special Collections.

49. Rone Tempest, "A Rocky Path for Pilgrims," *Los Angeles Times*, September 6, 2004.

50. Laura Sietz, "Participants Know Popular Treks Are a Far Cry from the Handcart Pioneers' Sufferings," *Deseret News*, July 23, 2010.

Chapter 7

1. Beginning in 1975, TITP Park began to acquire nineteenth-century buildings and to construct replicas of other buildings in order to create the living history portion of the park. For a timeline of the various acquisitions and replica building projects, see This Is The Place Heritage Park. www.thisistheplace.org/info/parkhistory.html/.

2. Eric A. Eliason writes an important reminder for when one imagines Latter-day Saints around the world participating in trek when he tells the story of a student from Samoa who "remembered donning sunbonnets and lavalavas and pulling model wagons across the beach." Eliason asserts: "this activity may seem silly, and some may call it a mindless surrender to American cultural pressures, but is it any sillier or any more of a cultural acquiescence than the Mesa Arizona Temple pageant where mostly white youth costume themselves as first-century Semitics from Palestine to enact the Easter story." See Eric A. Eliason, "The Cultural Dynamics of Historical Self-Fashioning: Mormon Pioneer Nostalgia, American Culture, and the International Church," *Journal of Mormon History* 28, no. 2 (Fall 2002): 165. See also Anne Barrett, "Modern Mormon Handcart Treks: Issues of Identity and History" Church History Symposium, March 13, 2014, http://youtu.be/XF7NiwVEmQs

3. Michael H. Madsen, "The Sanctification of Mormonism's Historical Geography," *Journal of Mormon History* v. 34, no. 2 (Spring 2008): 228–255. See also Michael H. Madsen, " 'Mormon Meccas': The Spiritual Transformation of Mormon Historical Sites from Points of Interest to Sacred Space" (Ph.D. diss., Syracuse University, 2003), 251.

4. Megan Sanborn Jones discusses the contemporary communal bond in trek reenactments in "(Re)living the Pioneer Past: Mormon Youth Handcart Trek Reenactments," *Theatre Topics* 16, no. 2 (September 2006): 113–130.

5. While trekking was practiced intermittently throughout the second half of the twentieth century, it has been since the 1997 sesquicentennial celebration of trekking that the institutional church has come to focus on trekking as an important ritual for teenagers.

6. James S. Bielo, "Replication as Religious Practice, Temporality as Religious Problem," *History and Anthropology* 28, no. 2 (May 2016): 11.

7. Vanessa Agnew, "Introduction: What Is Reenactment?," *Criticism* 46, no. 3 (2004): 327.

8. Vanessa Agnew, "History's Affective Turn: Historical Reenactment and Its Work in the Present," *Rethinking History* 11, no. 3 (September 2007): 301.

9. Agnew, "Introduction," 331.

10. Ibid., 327–329.

11. Ibid., 329.

12. Hildi Mitchell, "Postcards from the Edge of History: Narrative and the Sacralisation of Mormon Historical Sites," *Journeys: The International Journal of Travel and Travel Writing* 3, no. 1 (2002): 141.

13. E. Marshall Brooks, *Disenchanted Lives: Apostasy and Ex-Mormonism among the Latter-day Saints* (New Brunswick: Rutgers University Press, 2018), 57–62.

14. In the early twentieth century Mormon leaders imagined such pioneer-style activities such as hiking and camping as performing many functions: reducing the problems caused by urbanization, including an imagined loss of masculinity in young boys, spiritual boredom, and bridging the gap between generations of Mormons. They believed that through reclaiming their pioneer heritage, they could teach young men the character traits that were celebrated in the pioneers. See Richard Ian Kimball, *Sports in Zion: Mormon Recreation, 1890–1940* (Urbana: University of Illinois Press, 2003), 125–146.

15. Brooks, *Disenchanted Lives*, 147.

16. D. J. Davies, "Pilgrimage in Mormon Culture," in Makhan Jha, ed., *Social Anthropology of Pilgrimage* (New Delhi: Inter-Indian, 1990), 314.

17. Madsen, "The Sanctification of Mormonism's Historical Geography," 58–60.

18. Davies, "Pilgrimage in Mormon Culture," 310.

19. Paul Elie, *The Life You Save May Be Your Own: An American Pilgrimage* (New York: Farrar, Straus and Giroux, 2003), x.

20. Simon Coleman and John Elsner, *Pilgrimage: Past and Present in the World Religions* (Cambridge, MA: Harvard University Press, 1995), 6.

21. Mitchell, "Postcards from the Edge of History," 134–136.

22. Ibid., 150.

23. Madsen, " 'Mormon Meccas,' " 10.

24. The Church of Jesus Christ of Latter-day Saints. www.lds.org/callings/church-safety-and-health/training-and-video-resoures/trek-safety/, accessed June 15, 2015.

25. Amanda Taylor and Rhett Wilkinson, "Ultimate Guide to Pioneer Trek," 2013. www.ldsliving.com/Ultimate-Guide-to-Pioneer-Trek/s/72517/, accessed June 15, 2015.

26. "Tracy's Trek" The Church of Jesus Christ of Latter-day Saints. www.lds.org/callings/church-safety-and-health/training-and-video-resoures/trek-safety/, accessed June 15, 2015.

27. The Church of Jesus Christ of Latter-day Saints. www.lds.org/youth/activities/bc/pdfs/stake/Handcart-Trek-Guidelines-June-2015.pdf, accessed June 15, 2015.

28. Ibid.

29. The Church of Jesus Christ of Latter-day Saints. www.lds.org/youth/activities/bc/pdfs/stake/Handcart-Trek-Guidelines-June-2015.pdf, accessed June 15, 2015, and Taylor and Wilkinson, "Ultimate Guide to Pioneer Trek."

30. The Church of Jesus Christ of Latter-day Saints. www.lds.org/youth/activities/bc/pdfs/stake/Handcart-Trek-Guidelines-June-2015.pdf, accessed June 15, 2015.

31. Ibid.

32. Ibid.

33. Ibid.

34. Taylor and Wilkinson, "Ultimate Guide to Pioneer Trek."

35. The Church of Jesus Christ of Latter-day Saints. >www.lds.org/youth/activities/bc/pdfs/stake/Handcart-Trek-Guidelines-June-2015.pdf, accessed June 15, 2015.

36. The Church of Jesus Christ of Latter-day Saints. www.lds.org/youth/activities/bc/pdfs/stake/Handcart-Trek-Guidelines-June-2015.pdf, accessed June 15, 2015.

37. Mitchell, "Postcards from the Edge of History," 135.

38. For discussions of international trek participation see Dirk Smillie, "Mormon Trek Now Has a Global Reach," *Christian Science Monitor* 89 (166); Melvin L. Bashore, "Handcart Trekking: From Commemorative Reenactment to Modern Phenomenon," *BYU Studies* 57, no. 1 (2018): 128–158. See also Barrett, Church History Symposium.

39. Survey respondent 2.

40. Survey respondents 7, 58.

41. Survey respondents 38, 44, 49.

42. Survey respondent 2.

43. Survey respondents 12, 39.

44. Survey respondent 65.

45. Survey respondent 20.

46. Survey respondent 76.

47. Survey respondent 23.

48. Survey respondent 29.

49. Survey respondent 51.

50. Survey respondent 58.

51. Agnew, "History's Affective Turn," 302.

52. Survey respondent 9.

53. Survey respondent 49.

54. Survey respondent 43.

55. Philip Deloria, *Playing Indian* (New Haven: Yale University Press, 1998).

56. I'd like to thank Steve Peterson for bringing this incident to my attention. See "Gilbert Ward Connects with Ancestors by Re-enacting Mormon Trek" *East Valley Tribune* November 12, 2005. http://www.eastvalleytribune.com/get_out/gilbert-ward-connects-with-ancestors-by-re-enacting-mormon-trek/article_18f0a27c-2572-5773-8f97-f454a1b762b0.html, accessed June 13, 2019. Trekking led to one woman's death from heatstroke in 2016: Tad Wach, "Mormon Youth Leader Dies on Trek Outing in Oklahoma" *Deseret News* June 21, 2016. https://www.deseretnews.com/article/865656625/Mormon-youth-leader-dies-on-trek-outing-in-Oklahoma.html, accessed June 13, 2019.

57. Elise Boxer, "'This Is the Place!': Disrupting Mormon Settler Colonialism," in Gina Colvin and Joanna Brooks, eds., *Decolonizing Mormonism: Approaching a Postcolonial Zion* (Salt Lake City: University of Utah Press, 2018).

58. Survey respondent 17.

59. Survey respondent 26.

60. Survey respondent 29.

61. Survey respondent 34.

62. Survey respondent 54.

63. Survey respondent 20.

64. Survey respondent 43.

65. Survey respondent 47.

66. Survey respondent 52.

67. Survey respondent 67.

68. Survey respondent 65.
69. Survey respondent 6.
70. Survey respondent 9.
71. Survey respondent 51.
72. Survey respondent 57.
73. Eric A. Eliason, "Pioneers and Recapitulation in Mormon Popular Historical Expression," in Tad Tuleja, ed., *Usable Pasts: Traditions and Group Expressions in North America* (Logan: Utah State University Press, 1997), 316–319.
74. Survey respondent 65.
75. Survey respondent 2.
76. Survey respondent 12.
77. Survey respondent 50.
78. Survey respondent 10.
79. Survey respondent 17.
80. Survey respondent 74.
81. Survey respondent 46.
82. Survey respondent 1.
83. Survey respondent 18.
84. Survey respondent 56.
85. Survey respondent 5.
86. Survey respondent 10.
87. Survey respondent 20.
88. Survey respondent 22.
89. Survey respondent 45.
90. Survey respondent 51.
91. Survey respondent 9.

Chapter 8

1. Melissa Sanford, "Illinois Tells Mormons It Regrets Expulsion," *New York Times* April 8, 2004. Lisa Riley Roche, "Illinois Offers Regrets to LDS," *Deseret Morning News*, April 1, 2004. Elisabeth Liljenquist, "State of Illinois Expresses Regret for Expulsion of Saints, " *Ensign* June 2004. www.lds.org/ensign/2004/06/new-of-the-church/state -of-illinois-expresses-regret-for-expulsion-of-saints, accessed May 26, 2013.
2. Brian A. Weiner, *Sins of the Parents: The Politics of National Apologies in the United States* (Philadelphia: Temple University Press, 2005), 84–87.
3. James S. Bielo, "Replication as Religious Practice, Temporality as Religious Problem," *History and Anthropology* 28 (May 2016): 13.
4. Sanford, "Illinois Tells Mormons It Regrets Expulsion."
5. Alfred L. Brophy, *Reconstructing the Dreamland: The Tulsa Riot of 1921: Race, Reparation, and Reconciliation* (Oxford: Oxford University Press, 2002), 103, and Roy L. Brooks, "The Age of Apology," in Roy L. Brooks, ed., *When Sorry Isn't Enough: The Controversy over Apologies and Reparations for Human Injustice* (New York: New York University Press, 1999), 3.

6. Charles L. Griswold, *Forgiveness: A Philosophical Exploration* (Cambridge: Cambridge University Press, 2007), xv.

7. Griswold, xxii, 7, 38–39.

8. Ibid., 47.

9. Ibid., 104–108.

10. Ibid., xxiv.

11. Ibid., 139–140.

12. Ibid., 140–141.

13. Ibid., 151.

14. Ibid., 190–191.

15. Ibid., 207–209.

16. Elazar Barkan and Alexander Karn, "Group Apology as an Ethical Imperative," in Elazar Barkan and Alexander Karn, eds., *Taking Wrong Seriously: Apologies and Reconciliation* (Stanford: Stanford University Press, 2006), 5, 7; Melissa Nobles, *The Politics of Official Apologies* (Cambridge: Cambridge University Press, 2008; and Jennifer Lind, *Sorry States: Apologies in International Politics* (Ithaca: Cornell University Press, 2008).

17. Weiner, *Sins of the Parents*, 150; 174.

18. Nobles, *The Politics of Official Apologies*, 2; x–xi.

19. Barkan and Karn, "Introduction," *Taking Wrong Seriously*, 17–25.

20. Sanford, "Illinois Tells Mormons It Regrets Expulsion," and James Janega, "160 Years Later, Illinois Ready to Offer Mormons an Apology," *Chicago Tribune* April 7, 2004.

21. Lisa Riley Roche, "Illinois Offers Regrets to LDS," *Deseret News* April 1, 2004.

22. Ibid.

23. T. Ward Frampton, "'Some Savage Tribe': Race, Legal Violence, and the Mormon War of 1838," *Journal of Mormon History* 40 (Winter 2014): 175–207.

24. William G. Hartley, "Missouri's 1838 Extermination Order and the Mormons' Forced Removal to Illinois," May 2013 www.mormonhistoricsites.org, accessed 15. See also Stephen C. LeSueur, *The 1838 Mormon War in Missouri* (Columbia: University of Missouri Press, 1987).

25. Craig C. Campbell, *Images of the New Jerusalem: Latter Day Saint Faction Interpretations of Independence, Missouri* (Knoxville: University of Tennessee Press, 2004), 82.

26. Missouri Extermination Order file, LR 4320 22. LDS Church Archives, Salt Lake City.

27. Quoted in R. Scott Lloyd, "Rescinding an Unjust Directive," *Church News*, September 23, 2006.

28. Ibid.

29. Juanita Brooks, *The Mountain Meadows Massacre* (Norman: University of Oklahoma Press, 1950), vii.

30. Levi Peterson, *Juanita Brooks: Mormon Woman Historian* (Salt Lake City: University of Utah Press, 1988), 141.

31. Will Bagley, *Blood of the Prophets: Brigham Young and the Mountain Meadows Massacre* (Norman: University of Oklahoma Press, 2002), 146–157. Ronald W. Walker, Richard E. Turley Jr., and Glen M. Leonard, *Massacre at Mountain Meadows: An American Tragedy* (New York: Oxford University Press, 2008).

32. Sally Denton, *American Massacre: The Tragedy at Mountain Meadows, September 1857* (New York: Knopf, 2003), 108.

33. For a biography of Pratt, see Terryl L. Givens and Matthew J. Grow, *Parley P. Pratt: The Apostle Paul of Mormonism* (New York: Oxford University Press, 2011).

34. Brooks, *The Mountain Meadows Massacre*, 13–31. Walker et al., *Massacre at Mountain Meadows*, 25.

35. Sara Barringer Gordon and Jan Shipps, "Fatal Convergence in the Kingdom of God: The Mountain Meadows Massacre in American History," *Journal of the Early Republic* 37 (Summer 2017): 309.

36. Bagley, *Blood of the Prophets*, 51. Walker et al., *Massacre at Mountain Meadows*, 25.

37. Brooks, *The Mountain Meadows Massacre*, 219–220. Bagley, *Blood of the Prophets*, 77–89, 98–101. Walker et al., *Massacre at Mountain Meadows*, 89–95.

38. Bagley, *Blood of the Prophets*, xiv. John G. Turner, *Brigham Young: Pioneer Prophet* (Cambridge, MA: Harvard University Press, 2012), 272–279.

39. Quoted in Walker et al., *Massacre at Mountain Meadows*, 184.

40. Ibid., 147; 215–216.

41. Denton, *American Massacre*, 140–142.

42. Bagley, *Blood of the Prophets*, 270–272.

43. Walker et al., *Massacre at Mountain Meadows*, 229–231.

44. Brooks, *The Mountain Meadows Massacre*, 220; Denton, *American Massacre*, 228–229.

45. Bagley, *Blood of the Prophets*, 306–319.

46. Quoted in W. Douglas Seefelt, "Let the Book of the Past Be Closed? Public Memory and the Mountain Meadows Massacre Monument," paper presented at conference of Mormon History Association, Tucson, Arizona, May 16–19, 2002.

47. Turner, *Brigham Young*, 309.

48. Bagley, *Blood of the Prophets*, 350–351.

49. Quoted in Brooks, *The Mountain Meadows Massacre*, 221.

50. Quoted in Bagley, *Blood of the Prophets*, 351.

51. Bagley, *Blood of the Prophets*, 260–261.

52. Brooks, *The Mountain Meadows Massacre*, 223.

53. "LDS Church Expresses 'Regret' for Mountain Meadows Massacre," *Sunstone*, October 2007.

54. Bagley, *Blood of the Prophets*, 362.

55. Ibid., 368–369.

56. *Journal of the Mountain Meadows Association* 1, no. 1 (January 1991), box 1, folder 3, ACCN 1253 University of Utah archives.

57. Quoted in Bagley, *Blood of the Prophets*, 370.

58. Carrie Moore, "Mountain Meadows: Church Asked to turn over site, take names off records," *Deseret News*, September 1, 2007, https://www.deseretnews.com/article/695206187/Mountain-Meadows-Church-asked-to-turn-over-site-take-names-off-records.html, accessed July 5, 2019.

59. Bagley, *Blood of the Prophets*, 371–373.

60. Mountain Meadows Memorial: Memorial Service at the Reinterrment of the Remains of the Victims of the Mountain Meadows Masacre, Video AV311935, (1999) LDS Church Archives.

61. Ibid.
62. Ibid.
63. Ibid.
64. Mountain Meadows Dedication: Dedication Ceremony for the Restoration of the Mountain Meadows Massacre Memorial, AV314067. LDS Church Archives.
65. "President Hinckley Dedicates Mountain Meadows Monument" *Ensign* November 1999. https://www.churchofjesuschrist.org/study/ensign/1999/11/news-of-the-church/president-hinckley-dedicates-mountain-meadows-monument, accessed July 5, 2019.
66. Quoted in Jessica Ravitz, "LDS Church Apologizes for Mountain Meadows Massacre," *Salt Lake Tribune,* September 11, 2007.
67. "LDS Church Expresses 'Regret' for Mountain Meadows Massacre"; Carrie A. Moore, "LDS Church Issues Apology over Mountain Meadows," *Deseret News,* September 12, 2007.
68. Ravitz, "LDS Church Apologizes for Mountain Meadows Massacre."
69. "LDS Church Expresses 'Regret' for Mountain Meadows Massacre."
70. Ravitz, "LDS Church Apologizes for Mountain Meadows Massacre."
71. Peggy Fletcher Stack, "Mountain Meadows Now a National Historic Landmark," *Salt Lake Tribune,* July 5, 2011.
72. "Peace and Violence among Latter-day Saints" Church of Jesus Christ of Latter-day Saints. https://www.churchofjesuschrist.org/study/manual/gospel-topics-essays/peace-and-violence-among-19th-century-latter-day-saints, accessed June 19, 2019.
73. Gordon and Shipps, "Fatal Convergence in the Kingdom of God," 327.

Epilogue

1. James E. Faust, "A Priceless Heritage," *Ensign,* July 2002, 4–6.

Index

For the benefit of digital users, indexed terms that span two pages (e.g., 52–53) may, on occasion, appear on only one of those pages.